Concept Map

TOOLKIT

MOST POWERFUL RESOURCE FOR MASTERING CONCEPTS

Chemistry

A Visual Approach for
Enhanced Learning

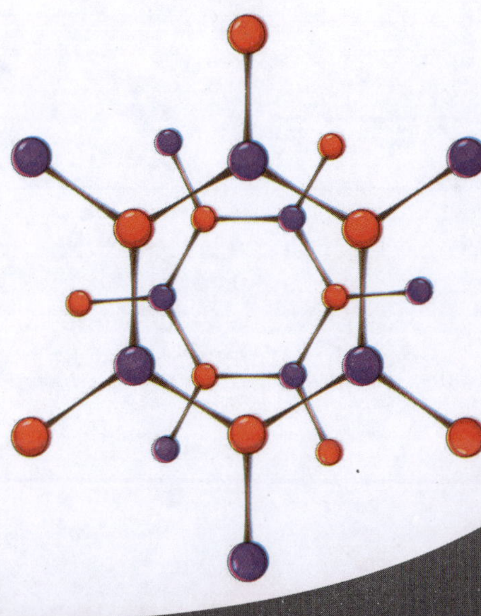

FREE
Online Support
See Inside Cover

Concept Map

TOOLKIT

MOST POWERFUL RESOURCE FOR MASTERING CONCEPTS

Chemistry

A Visual Approach for
Enhanced Learning

Authors
Swati Chauhan *(M.Sc.)*
Mohit Yadav *(M.Sc.)*

arihant
SUCCESS AND NOTHING LESS

ARIHANT PRAKASHAN (Series), MEERUT

Administrative & Production Offices

Regd. Office

'Ramchhaya' 4577/15, Agarwal Road, Darya Ganj, New Delhi -110002
Tele: 011- 47630600, 43518550

Head Office

Kalindi, TP Nagar, Meerut (UP) - 250002
Tel: 0121-7156203, 7156204

Sales & Support Offices

Agra, Ahmedabad, Bengaluru, Bareilly, Chennai, Delhi, Guwahati, Hyderabad, Jaipur, Jhansi, Kolkata, Lucknow, Nagpur & Pune.

PRICE ₹349.00

PO No. : TXT-59-T070201-4-26

Published by Arihant Publications (India) Ltd.

For further information about the books published by Arihant, log on to www.arihantbooks.com or e-mail at info@arihantbooks.com

Follow us on

PRODUCTION TEAM

Project Head	*Coordinator*	*Inner Designer*
Akansha Tomar	Mohd. Akil	Ankit Tyagi
Cover Designer	*Proof Reader*	*Concept Map Designer*
Rakesh Rawat	Nisha Verma	Neelanshu Verma

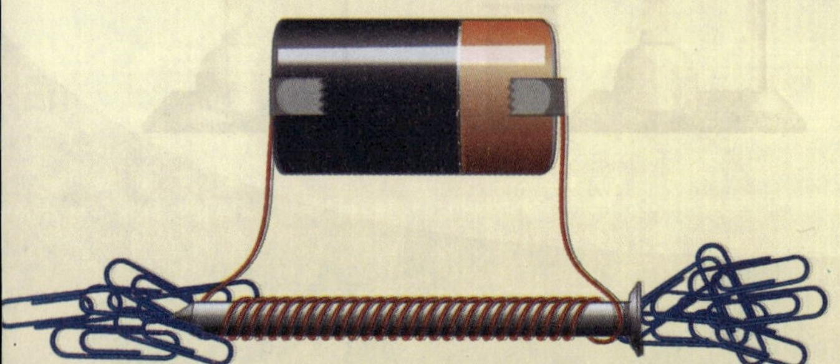

Contents

Class 11th

1. **Some Basic Concepts of Chemistry** **3-5**
   - Classification of Matter, Uncertainty in Measurement and Laws of Chemical Combination 3
   - Atomic and Molecular Masses, Percentage Composition, Empirical and Molecular Formula, Precision and Accuracy 4
   - Mole Concept, Stoichiometry and Concentration Terms 5
2. **Structure of Atom** **6-10**
   - Subatomic Particles, Preliminary Model and Dual Nature of Light 6-7
   - Bohr's Model and Hydrogen Spectrum 8
   - Dual Nature of Matter and Quantum Mechanical Model 9
   - Quantum Number, Electronic Configuration and Rules Related to Filling of Electrons 10
3. **Classification of Elements and Periodicity in Properties** **11-12**
   - Modern Periodic Table and Classification of Element 11
   - Periodic Properties and their Trends (Atomic and Ionic Radius, Ionisation Enthalpy, Electron Gain Enthalpy, Valence, Oxidation State and Chemical Reactivity) 12
4. **Chemical Bonding and Molecular Structure** **13-16**
   - Chemical Bonds, Bond Parameters, Fajans Rule 13
   - Hybridisation, VSEPR and VBT 14-15
   - MOT and Hydrogen Bonding 16
5. **Thermodynamics** **17-19**
   - Fundamentals of Thermodynamics 17
   - First Law of Thermodynamics, Reactions Related to Enthalpies and Hess Law 18
   - Second Law of Thermodynamics and Entropy, Gibbs Free Energy and Spontaneity 19
6. **Equilibrium** **20-23**
   - Physical Equilibrium, Chemical Equilibrium, Law of Mass Action and Equilibrium Constant 20
   - Factors Affecting Equilibrium and Le-Chatelier's Principle 21
   - Ostwald's Dilution Law and Concepts Of Acids and Bases 22
   - Solubility Product, Common Ion Effect, pH, Buffer Solution and Salt Hydrolysis 23
7. **Organic Chemistry : Some Basic Principles and Techniques** **24-31**
   - Fundamentals of Carbon 24
   - Nomenclature and Isomerism 25-27
   - Bond Fission, Electron Displacement in Organic Molecules and Reagent and Reaction Intermediates 28-29
   - Chemical Analysis of Elements, Methods of Purification of Organic Compounds 30-31

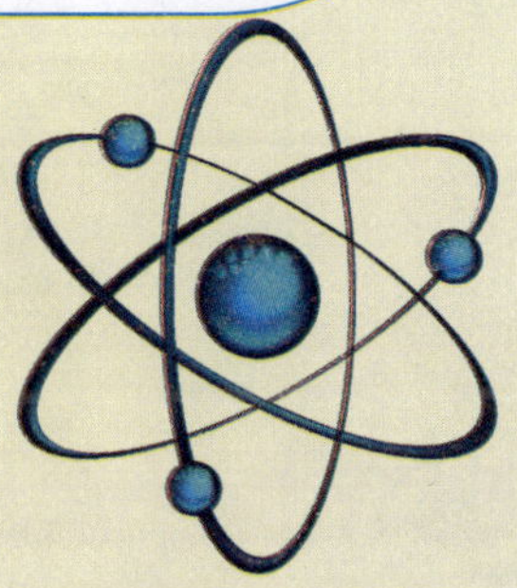

8. Hydrocarbons **32-39**
- Alkanes 32-33
- Alkenes 34-35
- Alkynes 36-37
- Aromatic Hydrocarbons 38-39

Class 12th

1. Solutions **43-45**
- Expression of Concentration of Solution 43
- Vapour Pressure, Henry's Law and Raoult's Law 44
- Colligative Properties, Abnormal Molecular Mass and van't Hoff Factor 45

2. Electrochemistry **46-51**
- Redox Reactions 46-47
- Conductance and Electrolysis 48-49
- Electrochemical Cells and Batteries 50-51

3. Chemical Kinetics **52-55**
- Rate of Chemical Reaction and Rate Expression 52
- Order, Molecularity and Methods of Determination of Order 53
- Arrhenius Theory, Activation Energy, Collision and Related Theories 54-55

4. *d*- and *f*- Block Elements **56-59**
- Properties of Transition Elements & Important Compounds of Transition Elements 56-57
- Inner Transition Elements 58-59

5. Coordination Compounds **60-63**
- Coordination Number and Nomenclature of Coordination Compounds 60-61
- Isomerism of Coordination Compounds, Valence Bond Theory, CFT and Organometallic Compounds 62-63

6. Haloalkanes and Haloarenes **64-65**
- Haloalkanes 64
- Haloarenes and Polyhalogen Compounds 65

7. Alcohols, Phenols and Ethers **66-71**
- Preparation, Properties and Uses of Alcohols 66-67
- Preparation, Properties and Uses of Phenols 68-70
- Preparation, Properties and Uses of Ethers 71

8. Aldehydes, Ketones and Carboxylic Acids **72-77**
- Preparation of Aldehydes and Ketones 72-73
- Properties of Aldehydes and Ketones 74-75
- Preparation, Properties of Carboxylic Acids and their Derivatives 76-77

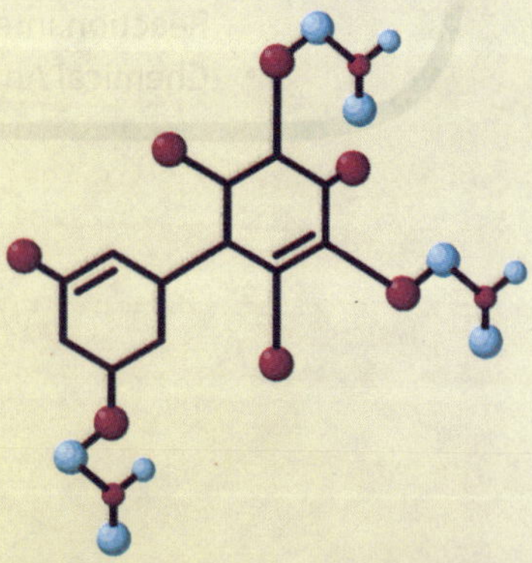

9.	**Amines**	**78-83**
	• Aliphatic Amines	78-79
	• Aromatic Amines	80-81
	• Diazonium Salts and Other Nitrogen Containing Compounds	82-83
10.	**Biomolecules**	**84-89**
	• Carbohydrates	84-85
	• Proteins and Enzymes	86-87
	• Vitamins, Nucleic Acids and Hormones	88-89
11.	**Principles Related to Practical Chemistry**	**90-95**
	• Experiments involving Physical Chemistry	90-91
	• Analysis of Inorganic Compounds	92-93
	• Analysis of Organic Compounds	94-95
12.	***p*- Block Elements**	**96-101**
	• Group 13 Elements	96
	• Group 14 Elements	97
	• Group 15 Elements	98
	• Group 16 Elements	99
	• Group 17 Element and Group 18 Elements	100-101

Concept Map

Class 11th

Ch-1 to 8

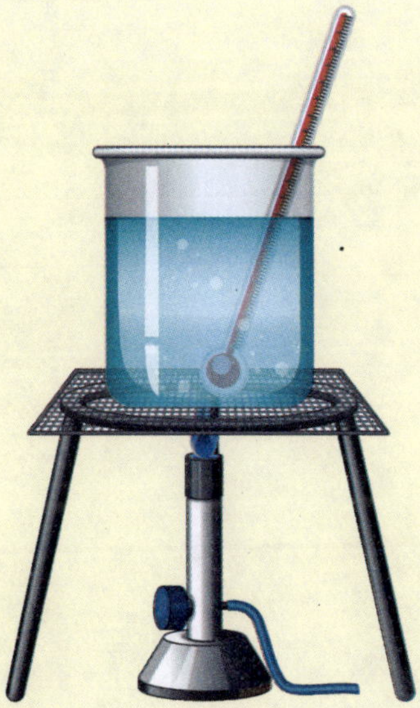

Chapter **01**

Some Basic Concepts of Chemistry

01 MATTER

- Anything that has mass and occupies space.
- The 3 states of matter are along with their interconversion.

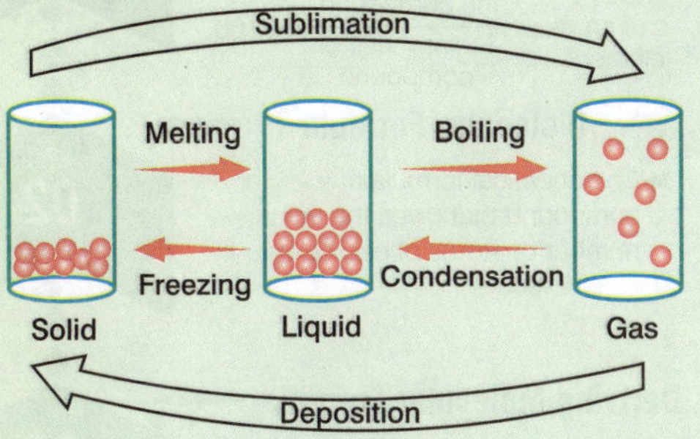

Classification of Matter

Pure substance
- Fixed composition
- **Example** Gold, Silver

Mixture
- Variable composition
- **Example** Water, air

Elements
- Consists of one type of particle either atom or molecule. **Example** Hydrogen, sodium.

Compounds
- Two or more different elements combine with each other. **Example** Water

Homogeneous Mixture
- Particles of component are uniformly distributed. **Example** Sugar solution

Heterogeneous Mixture
- Particles of component are non-uniformly distributed. **Example** Oil and water

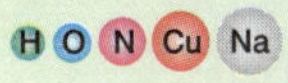

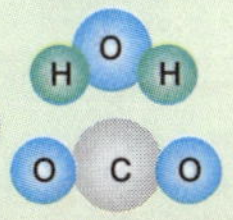

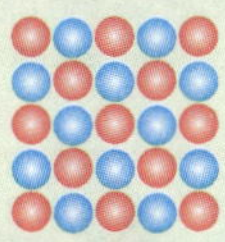

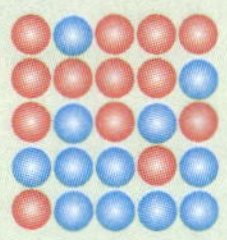

02 LAWS OF CHEMICAL COMBINATION

Law of Definite Proportions

Different samples of a pure chemical substance always contain the same proportions of elements by mass.

Joseph Proust

Law of Conservation of Mass

Mass is neither created nor destroyed in chemical reactions.

Lavoisier

Gay Lussac's Law of Gaseous Volumes

If the gases react or combine at constant T and p, they do so in a simple ratio by volume.

Gay Lussac

Law of Multiple Proportions

If two elements combine in different ways to form different compounds, the mass ratio are in simple whole number multiples of each other.

John Dalton

Avogadro's Law

Equal volume of gases at same temperature and pressure should contain equal number of molecules.

Amedeo Avogadro

Dalton's Atomic Theory

Postulates
- Matter consist of indivisible atoms.
- All the atoms of a given element have identical properties including identical mass.
- Atoms of different elements differ in mass.
- Compounds are formed when atoms of different elements combined in a fixed ratio.
- Atoms can not be created or destroyed in chemical reactions, only rearranged.

Limitations
- Could not explain laws of gaseous volumes.
- Could not provide the reason for combining of atoms.

Significant Figures

Meaningful digits which are known with certainty plus one which is estimated or uncertain.

0.000 4 00 7 4 00

- 0.000 — Leading zeroes (Non-significant)
- 00 (between 4 and 7) — In between zeroes (Significant)
- 00 (at the end) — Trailing zeroes (Significant)
- 4, 7, 4 — Non-zero digits (Significant)

03 UNCERTAINTY IN MEASUREMENT

Measurement

- The quantity or dimension usually in comparison to a specific standard.
- Unit is a fixed quantity chosen as the standard of measurement.

Scientific Notation

- Exponential notation in which number can be represented in the form $N \times 10^n$

Arithmetic Calculations in Scientific Notation

For Multiplication and Division
- $(N_1 \times N_2) \times 10^{(n_1+n_2)}$
- $\frac{N_1}{N_2} \times 10^{(n_1-n_2)}$

For Addition and Subtraction
- $(N_1+N_2) \times 10^n$
- $(N_1-N_2) \times 10^n$

Two notations taken for calculation are (a) $N_1 \times 10^{n_1}$ (b) $N_2 \times 10^{n_2}$

Dimensional Analysis

- Conversion of any particular quantity in terms of fundamental quantity.
- Also called as factor lable method or unit factor method.
- Quantity required = Quantity given × C.F (conversion factor)

RULES FOR ROUNDING OFF THE RESULT

If the right most digit to be removed is more than 5, the preceding number is increased by one and if it less than 5, the preceding number is not changed.

For Addition and Subtraction
Result is rounded off to match the same number of decimal places as the quantity with least number of decimal places.

For Multiplication and Division
Result is rounded off to the same number of significant figures as that of least precise term.

CALCULATION OF EQUIVALENT WEIGHT

Equivalent weight of an ion
$= \dfrac{\text{Formula mass of ion}}{\text{Charge on ion}}$

Equivalent weight of an element
$= \dfrac{\text{Atomic weight}}{\text{Valency of element}}$

Number of gram equivalents
$= \dfrac{\text{Weight of substance}}{\text{Equivalent weight}}$

Equivalent weight of salt
$= \dfrac{\text{Formula mass of salt}}{\text{Total positive or negative charge on cationic or anionic part}}$

Equivalent weight of organic base
$= \dfrac{\text{Molar mass}}{\text{No. of } H^+ \text{ ions accepted}}$

Equivalent weight of an acidic salt
$= \dfrac{\text{Molecular mass of salt}}{\text{No. of replaceable } H^+ \text{ ions}}$

Equivalent weight of an acid
$= \dfrac{\text{Molecular mass of acid}}{\text{No. of replaceable } H^+ \text{ ions}}$

Equivalent weight of base
$= \dfrac{\text{Molecular mass of base}}{\text{No. of replaceable } OH^- \text{ ions}}$

01 Percentage Composition

➤ Relative mass of each of the constituent elements in 100 parts of a compound.

$$\text{Mass\% of an element} = \frac{\text{Mass of element in the compound}}{\text{Molar mass of compound}} \times 100$$

02 Molecular Formula

➤ The chemical formula of a compound that gives the actual number of atoms of each element in a molecule.

03 Deriving Molecular Formula

➤ Divide the molecular mass with empirical formula mass. i.e.

$$n = \frac{\text{Molecular formula mass}}{\text{Empirical formula mass}}$$

04 Empirical Formula

➤ The chemical formula of a compound that shows relative number of atoms in their simplest ratio.

05 Deriving Empirical Formula

Divide mass of all elements by atomic weight. → Divide all the obtained values with lowest obtained value. → Make the obtained number, a whole number, if not. → Write the obtained number below the symbol of the element in subscript.

PRECISION AND ACCURACY

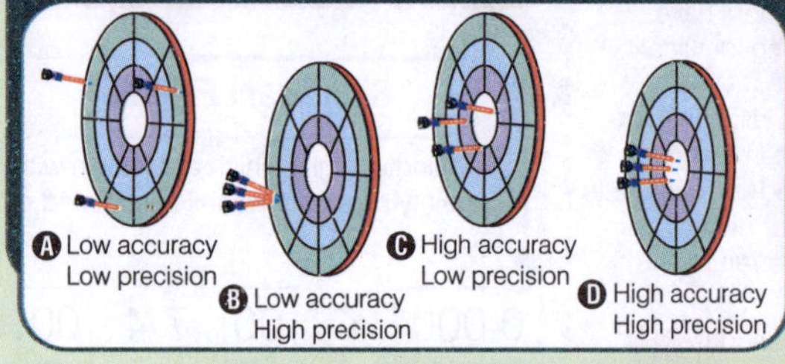

MASSES

01 Formula Mass
➤ The sum of atomic masses of all atoms in the formula unit of compound.
➤ Calculated for ionic compound as they don't have definite molecular structure.

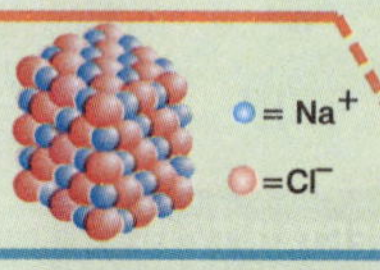

02 Equivalent Mass
➤ Mass which will combine or displace with 1.008 g hydrogen, 35.5 g chlorine, 80 g bromine, 127 g iodine or 12 g carbon.
➤ It depends on the nature of chemical reactions in which it takes part.

03 Gram Molecular Mass
➤ Molecular mass of a substance expressed in gram.
➤ It should not be confused with mass of one molecule of substance in gram.
➤ e.g. Mass of one molecule of oxygen is 5.32×10^{-23} g and gram molecular mass is 32.

04 Molecular Mass
➤ The sum of atomic masses of the elements present in a molecule.
➤ Calculated for covalent compound as they have definite molecular structure.

05 Average Atomic Mass
➤ Average of masses of all naturally occurring isotope of an element.
e.g. $M_{avg} = \dfrac{m_1x + m_2y + m_3z}{x + y + z}$
➤ m_1, m_2, m_3 are masses whereas x, y and z are ratio in which they are present.

06 Atomic Mass
➤ Measured by comparing mass of an atom with mass of a particular atom chosen as standard.
➤ Atomic mass $= \dfrac{\text{Mass of one atom of the element}}{\text{1/12 th part of the mass of one atom of C-12}}$ = Equivalent mass × Valency

STEPS INVOLVED IN CALCULATIONS

- Write balanced chemical equation.
- Find out the substance whose mass or volume is given or to be calculated.
- Write the relative number of moles or relative masses of reactants and products involved below their formula.
- In case of gases write 22.4 L at STP in place of 1 mole.
- Apply unitary method to make required calculations.

LIMITING REAGENT

- Reactant that is consumed first in a chemical reaction.
- It limits the amount of product formed.
- Reactant that is present in amount in a chemical reaction is excess reagent.

STOICHIOMETRY

- Based on the quantitative relationship between the reactants and products.
- No. used to balance a chemical equations are stoichiometric coefficients.

TYPES OF STOICHIOMETRIC RELATIONSHIPS

- MOLE-MOLE RELATIONSHIP
- MASS-MASS RELATIONSHIP
- MASS-MOLE RELATIONSHIP
- MASS-VOLUME RELATIONSHIP
- VOLUME-VOLUME RELATIONSHIP

Moles

Collection of 6.022×10^{23} particles

1. Atomic Substance

1 mole = Gram atomic mass = 1 gram atom = 6.022×10^{23} atoms

2. Molecular Substance

1 mole = Gram molecular mass = 1 gram molecule = 6.022×10^{23} molecules

RELATIONSHIP IN MOLES

- Particles: × By 6.02×10^{23} ÷
- Mass (in Grams): × By Molar Mass ÷
- Volume (in Litres): ÷ By 22.4 ×

CONCENTRATION TERMS

Molality

- Number of moles of solute present in per kilogram of solvent.

$$\text{Molality } (m) = \frac{\text{No. of moles of solute}}{\text{Mass of solvent (in kg)}}$$

Normality

- Number of gram equivalents dissolved in per litre of solution.

$$\text{Normality } (N) = \frac{\text{No. of gram equivalents}}{\text{Volume of solution in litres}}$$

Molarity

- Number of moles of solute present in per litre of solution.

$$\text{Molarity } (M) = \frac{\text{No. of moles of solute}}{\text{Volume of solution in litre}}$$

Concentration in ppm, ppb and ppt

- $\text{Concentration (in ppm)} = \frac{\text{mass of solute}}{\text{mass of solution}} \times 10^6 \text{ ppm}$
- $\text{Concentration (in ppb)} = \frac{\text{mass of solute}}{\text{mass of solution}} \times 10^9 \text{ ppb}$
- $\text{Concentration (in ppt)} = \frac{\text{mass of solute}}{\text{mass of solution}} \times 10^{12} \text{ ppt}$

Normality (N) = Molarity $(M) \times Vf$
Vf = Valence factor

Mole Fraction

- Fraction of substance in a mixture expressed in terms of mole.
- In a mixture of A and B, the mole fraction of A and B respectively are

$$\chi_A = \frac{n_A}{n_A + n_B}, \quad \chi_B = \frac{n_B}{n_A + n_B}$$

n_A = no. of moles of A,
n_B = no. of moles of B

Chapter 02 Structure of Atom

DISCOVERY OF SUBATOMIC PARTICLES

1 DISCOVERY OF ELECTRON

- Discovered by J.J Thomson.
- Used **cathode rays discharge tube experiment**.
- The electron was the first identification of a sub-atomic particles

2 DISCOVERY OF PROTON

- Discovered by E. Goldstein.
- Used modified cathode ray tube experiment.
- The rays associated were called **anode rays**.

3 DISCOVERY OF NEUTRON

- Discovered by James Chadwick.
- By bombarding a thin sheet of beryllium by α-particles.
- Neutrons are electrically neutral particles having mass slightly greater than proton.

Cathode Ray Discharge Tube Experiment

Results of Experiment

- Cathode rays (negatively charged particles) starts from cathode and move towards the anode.
- They themselves are not visible but their behaviour can be observed with the help of fluorescent material.
- In absence of electrical or magnetic field, they travel in straight line.
- In presence of electric or magnetic field, behaviour of cathode rays is similar to electrons.

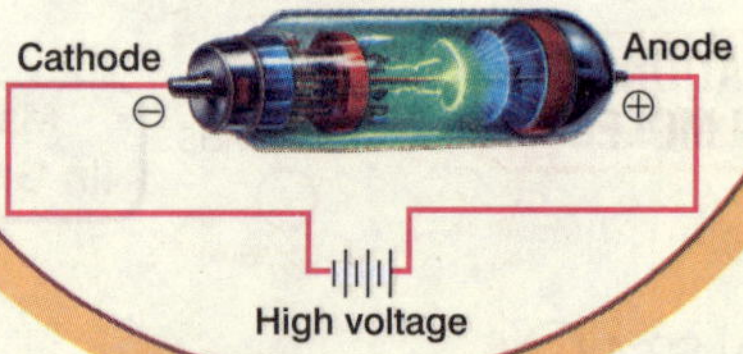

CHARACTERISTICS OF ELEMENTARY PARTICLES

- They depends upon the nature of gas present in the cathode ray discharge tube.
- Behaviour of positively charged particles in electrical or magnetic field is opposite to that observed for cathode rays.

CHARGE

- Charge on electron → -1.6×10^{-19} C.
- Charge on proton → $+1.6 \times 10^{-19}$ C.
- Charge on neutron = 0

MASS

- Mass of electron = 9.109×10^{-31}kg
- Mass of proton = 1.672×10^{-27}kg
- Mass of neutron = 1.674×10^{-27}kg

RATIO OF CHARGE/MASS

- Charge/mass ratio was determined by J.J. Thomson.
- $e/m_e = 1.758820 \times 10^{11}$C/kg

ATOMIC NUMBER & MASS NUMBER

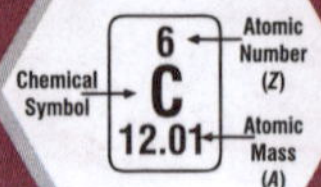

01 Atomic Number (Z): Number of protons in the nucleus of an atom = Number of electrons in a neutral atom

02 Mass Number (A): Number of protons (P) + Number of neutrons (N)

ATOMIC SPECIES

ISOTOPES

- The atoms that have same atomic number (Z) but different mass number (A).
- **Example** $_1H^1$, $_1H^2$, $_1H^3$ are three isotopes of hydrogen.

ISOBARS

- The atoms of different elements that have same mass number (A) but different atomic number.
- **Example** $_{18}Ar^{40}$, $_{19}K^{40}$

ISOTONES

- The atoms that have same number of neutron (N).
- **Example** $_{15}P^{31}$, $_{16}S^{32}$

ISODIAPHERS

- A set of nuclides with the same difference in the number of protons and neutrons in their nucleus.
- **Example** $_{92}U^{238}$, $_{90}Th^{234}$

PRELIMINARY MODELS

Thomson's Atomic Model

- Also called as plum pudding model.
- Mass of the atom is assumed to be uniformly distributed over the atom.
- Explained the overall neutrality of atom.

Limitations

- Could not satisfactorily explained the result of scattering experiment carried out by Rutherford.

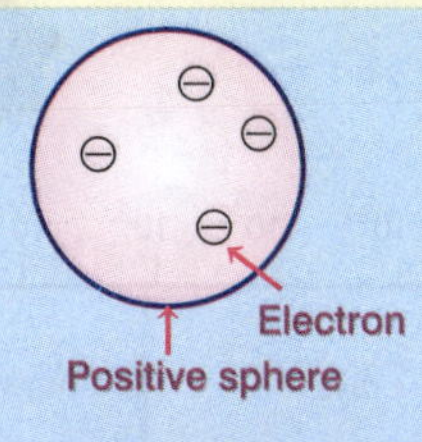

Rutherford's Atomic Model

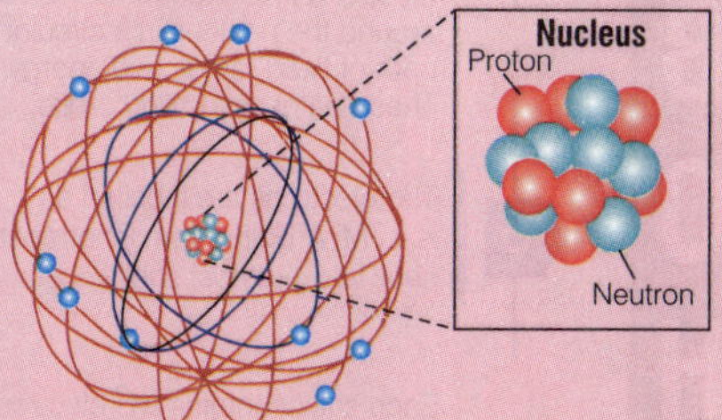

Postulates

- Most part of the atom is empty.
- Atom possess a highly dense, positively charged center called nucleus.
- Entire mass of the atom is concentrated inside the nucleus.
- Electrons revolve around the nucleus in circular orbits.
- Electrons and the nucleus are held together by strong electrostatic forces of attraction.

Limitations

- Gives no idea about how electrons are distributed around nucleus and what are the energies of these electrons.
- Maxwell suggested that, an electron in an orbit should emit radiations, lose energy with every turn and move closer to nucleus following a spiral path, but this did not happen. Thus, could not explain stability of atom.

ELECTROMAGNETIC WAVES

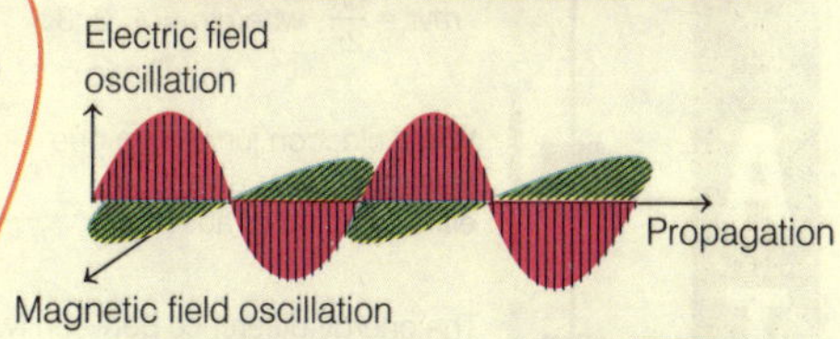

CHARACTERISTICS OF ELECTROMAGNETIC WAVE

01 Frequency (ν)

- Number of waves that pass through a given point in one second.
- SI unit is Hertz or s^{-1}. $\nu = c/\lambda$

02 Amplitude (a)

- Height of the crest or depth of the trough.
- Expressed in unit of length.

03 Wave number ($\bar{\nu}$)

- Number of waves in unit wavelength.
- It's unit is m^{-1}.
- $\bar{\nu} = \frac{1}{\lambda}$

04 Velocity (v)

- Linear distance travelled by a wave in one second.
- In vacuum all types of electromagnetic waves travel with same speed.

05 Wavelength (λ)

- Distance between two consecutive crests or troughs.
- SI unit is metre.

WAVE PARTICLE DUALITY OF LIGHT

BLACK BODY RADIATION

- An ideal body which is a perfect absorber and perfect emitter of radiations of all frequencies uniformly is a black body.
- The radiation emitted by such a body is **black body radiation**.

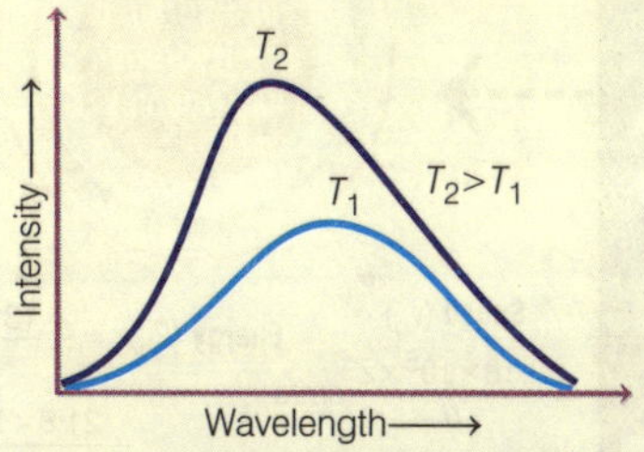

PLANCK'S QUANTUM THEORY

- Atoms or molecules body can emit or absorb energy discontinuously in the form of small packets of energy called **quanta**.
- A quantum of light is called **photon**.
- Energy of each quantum is directly proportional to frequency $E \propto \nu$ where $E = h\nu$ where, h is planck's constant.

PHOTOELECTRIC EFFECT

- $K.E = h(\nu - \nu_0)$ $= hc\left(\frac{1}{\lambda} - \frac{1}{\lambda_0}\right)$
- No of electrons ejected $\propto$ intensity of incident radiation.
- K.E of electrons $\propto$ frequency of incident radiation.
- Each photon having energy equal to or greater than threshold energy can eject only one electron.

DIFFERENT TYPES OF SPECTRA

- Atomic spectra
- Molecular spectra
- Absorption spectra
- Continuous spectra
- Emission spectra
- Discontinuous spectra
- Band spectra
- Line spectra

BOHR'S ATOMIC MODEL

POSTULATES

- Electrons in the atom can move around the nucleus in a circular path of fixed radius and energy. These paths are called orbits.
- The electrons are labelled as *K, L, M, N* going from innermost shell to outermost shell.
- Each shell contains $2n^2$ electrons.
- Each shell contains one or more subshell. Each subshell contains one or more atomic orbitals.
- The electrons revolve only in those orbit whose angular momentum is an integral multiple of $\frac{h}{2\pi}$ i.e. $mvr = \frac{nh}{2\pi}$ where $n = 1, 2, 3$
- When electron jump from one level to another energy is either emitted or absorbed.
- The energy difference between two states is given by $\Delta E = E_2 - E_1$
  $E_2 - E_1 > E_3 - E_2 > E_4 - E_3 > ...$

ELECTROMAGNETIC SPECTRUM

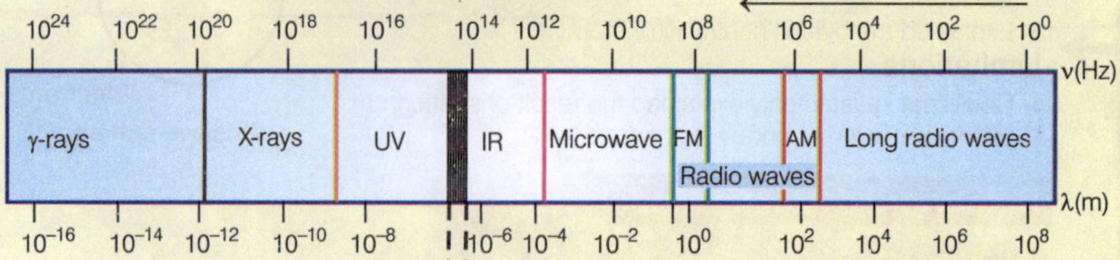

(a) The spectrum of electromagnetic radiation.

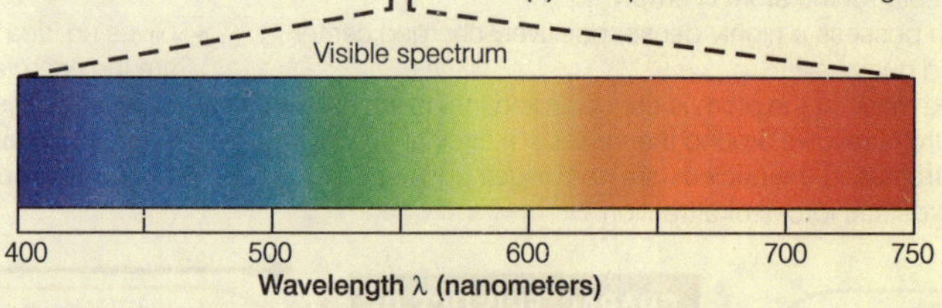

(b) Visible spectrum. The visible region is only a small part of the entire spectrum.

SPECTRAL LINE OF HYDROGEN ATOM

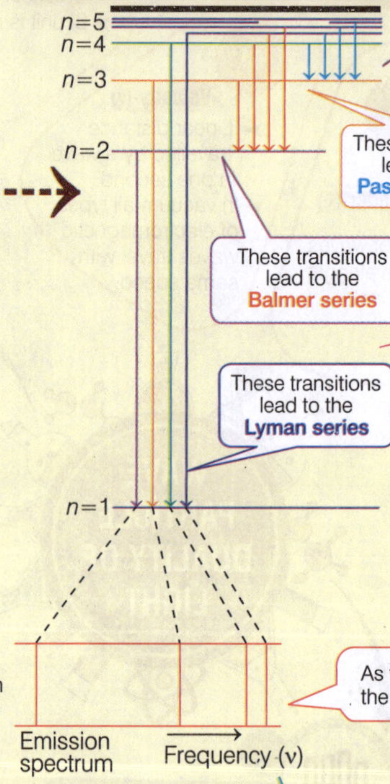

As the energy changes of the transitions becomes greater, the lines in the spectrum appear at higher frequencies

SPECTRAL INTERPRETATION OF HYDROGEN ATOM

- It represents the radiation of energy absorbed or emitted by an atom.
- It is the pictorial representation of arrangement of radiations in increasing order of wavelength or decreasing order of frequency.

Series	n_1	n_2	Spectral Region
Lyman	1	2, 3...	Ultraviolet
Balmer	2	3, 4, ...	Visible
Paschen	3	4, 5, ...	Infrared
Brackett	4	5, 6, ...	Infrared
Pfund	5	6, 7, ...	Infrared

IMPORTANT FORMULA

For Hydrogen and Hydrogen like Species

Radius (r_n) $= \frac{0.529 \times n^2}{Z}$ Å

Angular momentum $mvr = \frac{nh}{2\pi}$

Speed (v_n) $= \frac{2.18 \times 10^8 \times Z}{n}$ cm/s

Energy (E_n) $= -\frac{1312 \times Z^2}{n^2}$ kg/mol

$= -\frac{21.8 \times 10^{-19} \times Z^2}{n^2}$ J/atom

$= -\frac{13.6 \times Z^2}{n^2}$ eV/atom

Rydberg Formula

$$\Delta E = R_H\left(\frac{1}{n_1^2} - \frac{1}{n_2^2}\right) = 2.18 \times 10^{-18}\left(\frac{1}{n_1^2} - \frac{1}{n_2^2}\right)$$

for hydrogen and hydrogen like species

$$\frac{1}{\lambda} = \bar{\nu} = R_H Z^2\left(\frac{1}{n_1^2} - \frac{1}{n_2^2}\right)$$

- In absorption spectrum, $n_2 > n_1$, ΔE = positive, energy is absorbed.
- In emission spectrum, $n_1 > n_2$, ΔE = negative, energy is released.

LIMITATIONS

- Cannot explain distribution of electron in orbits.
- Cannot explain Zeeman and Stark effect.
- Could not explain formation of molecules.
- Ion consistent with de-Broglie and Heisenberg uncertainty principle.
- Fails to explain electronic repulsion in multielectronic atom.

QUANTUM MECHANICAL MODEL

DE-BROGLIE PRINCIPLE (DUAL BEHAVIOUR OF MATTER)

- Suggested the dual nature of electron.
- Gave the relationship between wavelength and velocity of electron.
- $E = mc^2 = h\nu = \frac{hc}{\lambda}$
- $\lambda = \frac{h}{p} = \frac{h}{mv} = \frac{h}{\sqrt{2m\,KE}}$

HEISENBERG'S UNCERTAINTY PRINCIPLE

- It is impossible to know simultaneously the position and velocity of a microscopic moving particle.
- $\Delta x . \Delta p \geq \frac{h}{4\pi}$ or $\Delta x . \Delta(mv) \geq \frac{h}{4\pi}$

  or $\Delta x . \Delta v \geq \frac{h}{4\pi m}$

  where,

  Δx = uncertainty in position

  ΔV = uncertainty in velocity.
- Significant only for motion of microscopic objects.

ATOMIC ORBITALS

- Three-dimensional space around the nucleus.
- Probability of finding an electron of given energy is maximum here.

SCHRODINGER WAVE EQUATION

- Behaviour of electron in an atom is given by schrodinger wave equation.

$$\frac{\partial^2\psi}{\partial x^2} + \frac{\partial^2\psi}{\partial y^2} + \frac{\partial^2\psi}{\partial z^2} + \frac{8\pi^2 m}{h^2}(E - V)\psi = 0$$

E is total energy and V is potential energy of electron,

- If energy does not change, then

$$\hat{H}\psi = E\psi$$

Hamiltonian operator ($\hat{H}$); Energy Eigen value (E)

Difference between ψ and ψ^2

ψ:
- Describes the wave characteristics of a particle.
- Can have negative amplitude.

ψ^2:
- Measure the probability density at a point in an atom.
- Can never have negative amplitude.

ATOMIC ORBITAL AND RADIAL WAVE FUNCTION

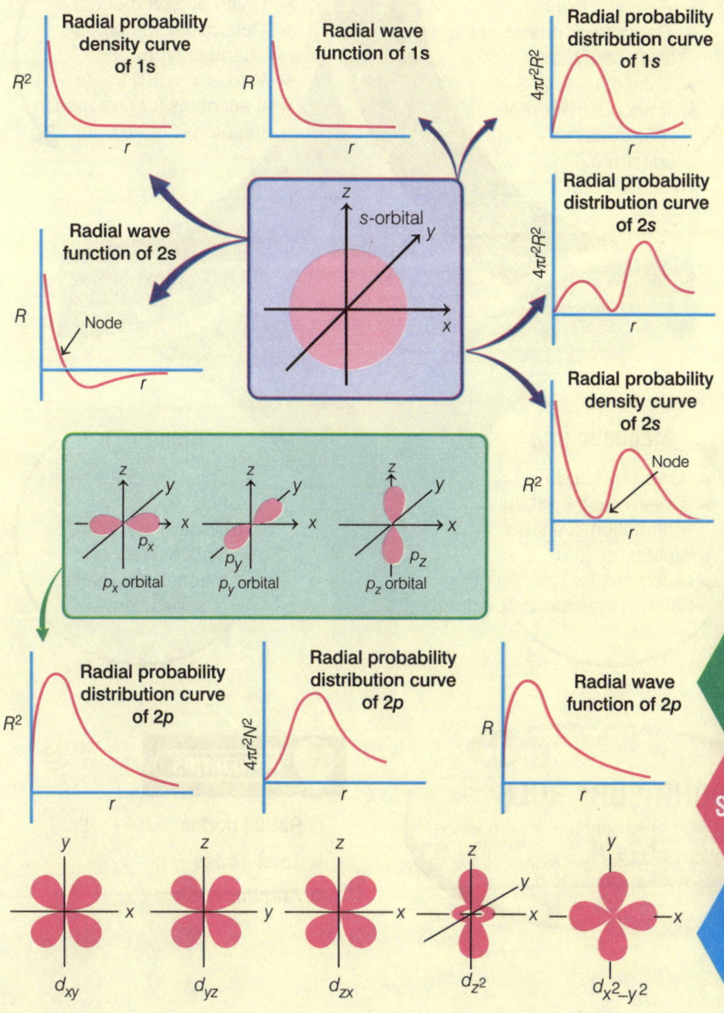

Orbital	3-D region in which probability of finding an electron is maximum. It can accommodate maximum of two electrons with exactly equal energy.
Subshell	Aggregation of group of exactly similar orbitals. Subshells are named as *s*, *p*, *d* and *f*.
Orbit	An imaginary 2-D circular path around the nucleus in which probability of finding electrons is maximum. Maximum number of electrons is $2n^2$.

Electronic Configuration

- Distribution of electrons into orbitals of an atom.

Representation

$s^a p^b d^c$ ...notation | Orbital diagram

Principle quantum number → nS^a ← No. of electrons

Subshell

Orbital of the subshell

Electron with positive spin

Electron with negative spin

Stability of Completely Filled and Half-filled Orbital

- Symmetrical distribution of electrons
- Exchange energy

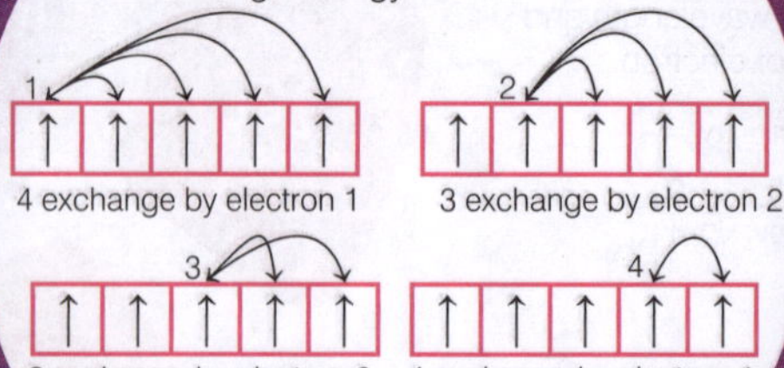

Possible exchange for a d^5 configuration.

RULES RELATED TO FILLING OF ELECTRONS IN ORBITALS

01 Pauli's Exclusion Principle

No two electrons in an atom can be represented by same values of all quantum numbers.

02 Hund's Rule

Pairing of electrons in the orbitals of particular subshell, does not take place until all the orbitals of a subshell are singly occupied.

03 Aufbau Principle

- Orbitals are filled according to increase in energy.
- Order of increasing energy is calculated by $(n+l)$ rule.

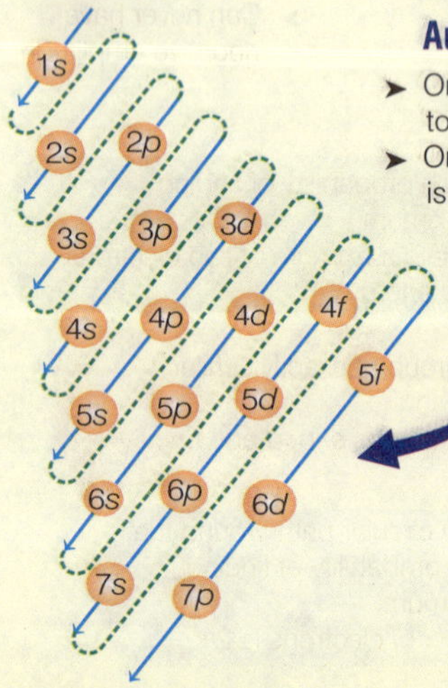

Energy sequence of orbitals

Quantum Numbers

Set of four numbers that gives complete information about an electron in an atom.

Principle (n)

- Given by Bohr.
- Determines orbital size and energy.
- Values $n = 1, 2, 3, ...\infty$
- It accounts for main lines in atomic spectrum.

Azimuthal (l)

- Given by Sommerfeld.
- Determines the orbitals shape or type.
- Values, $l = 0, 1, 2..., (n-1)$
- It accounts for fine lines in the atomic spectrum.

Magnetic (m_l)

- Given by Lande.
- Determine the orbital orientation in shape.
- Values $-l$ .... 0 .... $+l$
- Accounts for splitting of lines in the atomic spectrum.

Spin (m_s)

- Given by Uhlenbeck and Goudsmit
- Value + 1/2 or −1/2
- It accounts for magnetic properties of substance.

BOHR-BURY RULE

- Energy of subshell $\propto (n+l)$ value
- If value of $n+l$ is same then, energy of subshell $\propto n$.

POWER TIPS

- Radial nodes $= n - l - 1$
- Total nodes $= n - 1$
- Angular node $= l$

Chapter 03 Classification of Elements and Periodicity in Properties

GENESIS OF PERIODIC CLASSIFICATION

Dobereiner's Triad

- A group of three elements having similar chemical and physical properties.
- The atomic weight of the middle element was the arithmetic mean of atomic weight of other two.

TRIADS

Elements	Atomic wt.	Elements	Atomic wt.
Li	7	Ca	40
Na	23	Sr	88
K	39	Ba	137

Arithmetic mean of 40 and 137

Newland's Law of Octaves

- Elements follow musical notes.
- Every eighth element show properties similar to element at first position.

Sa	re	ga	ma	pa	dha	ni	sa
Li	Be	B	C	N	O	F	Na

Similar Properties

IUPAC Nomenclature

For elements with atomic number > 100.
(Numerical root for 0 to 9+ium)

Digit	Root	Digit	Root
0	nil	5	pent
1	un	6	hex
2	bi	7	sept
3	tri	8	oct
4	quad	9	enn

Mendeleev's Periodic Law

- Properties of the elements are periodic function of their atomic weight.
- The table consist of vertical column called **groups**.
- Horizontal rows called **period**.

Modern Periodic Table

- Long form of Periodic Table
- Based on Modern Periodic Law
- Follows Bohr Scheme of arrangement

Groups

- Consists eighteen vertical columns.
- Elements in the same group share similar chemical properties.

Modern Periodic Law

- Given by **Henry Moseley**.
- Physical and Chemical Properties of elements are periodic function of their atomic number.

Periods

- Denotes the highest principal quantum number (n)
- No. of elements in each period is twice of the atomic orbitals available in the energy level that are filled.

Blocks and Arrangement of Elements

- *s*-block elements + *p*-block elements = Representative elements
- Actinoids +lanthanoids = inner transition element (*f*-block) placed at bottom of periodic table
- *d*-block elements (Transition elements) flanked between *s* and *p*-block elements.

CLASSIFICATION OF ELEMENTS

On the basis of electronic configuration

s-Block Elements

- **Group** 1-2
- **E.C.** ns^{1-2}
- Group 1 elements form M^+ ions.
- Group 2 elements form M^{2+} ions.

p-Block Elements

- **Group** 13-18
- **E.C.** $ns^2\, np^{1-6}$ (except Helium)
- Elements show variable oxidation state except fluorine and noble gases.

d-Block Elements

- **Group** 3 to 12
- **E.C.** $(n-1)\, d^{1-10}\, ns^{1-2}$
- Show variable valencies and oxidation state.

f-Block Elements

- 4*f* series are called **lanthanoids**.
- 5*f* series are called **actinoids**. **E.C.** $(n-2)\, f^{1-14}(n-1)d^{0-1}ns^2$
- Show variable oxidation states.

Classification as metal, non-metal and metalloids

Metals

- >78% of all known element.
- Appear on left hand side of periodic table.
- Generally solids at room temp. except mercury.
- Have high M.P. and B.P. except Ga, Cs.

Non-Metals

- Lie on top right hand side of periodic table.
- Usually solid or gases at room temperature.
- Poor conductor of heat and electricity.

Metalloids or Semi-metals

- Show characteristics of both metals and non-metals.
- **Example** Si Ge As

PERIODIC PROPERTIES

Electron Gain Enthalpy

- When an electron is added to a neutral gaseous atom (X) to convert it into a negative ion, the enthalpy change accompanying this process is electron gain enthalpy.
- It provides measure of ease with which an atom adds an electron to form anion.
- Equation
  $X(g) + e^- \longrightarrow X^-(g)$

Ionisation Enthalpy

- Quantitative measure of the tendency of an element to lose electron.
- Represents the energy required to remove an electron from isolated gaseous atom (X) in its ground state.

Equation

$X(g) \longrightarrow X^+(g) + e^-$ (1st I.E.)

$X^+(g) \longrightarrow X^{2+}(g) + e^-$ (IInd I.E.)

Electronegativity

- Qualitative measure of the ability of an atom in a chemical compound to attract shared pair of electrons to itself.
- It is not a measurable quantity.

Anomalous Properties of Second Period Elements

- Li and Be form covalent compounds.
- Li, Be shows a diagonal relationship with Mg and Al.

POWER TIPS

Lother Meyer Curve

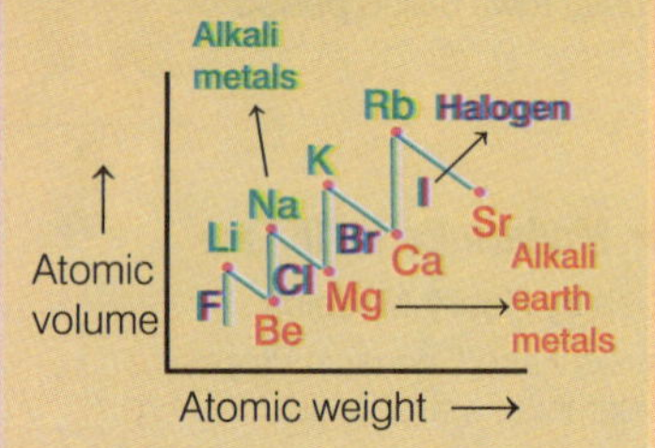

CHEMICAL PROPERTIES

01 Valence

- The combining capacity of an element.
- Never be zero.
- Only a number and is not assigned a positive or negative sign.
- In a group it remains same.

02 Oxidation States

- The hypothetical charge left on an atom if all of its bonds to other atoms were fully ionic.
- Its value can be positive, negative or fractional.

03 Chemical Reactivity

- Highest at the two extremes of a period and is lowest at the centre.
- Highly reactive elements are always found in combined state.

VARIATIONS IN PERIODIC PROPERTIES

ACROSS THE PERIOD

Property	Trend
Size	↓
Ionisation Enthalpy	↑
Electron Gain Enthalpy	↑
Electronegativity	↑

DOWN THE GROUP

Property	Trend
Size	↑
Ionisation Enthalpy	↓
Electron Gain Enthalpy	↓
Electronegativity	↓

PERIODIC TABLE

- *s*-BLOCK ELEMENTS
- *p*-BLOCK ELEMENTS
- *d*-BLOCK ELEMENTS (TRANSITION ELEMENTS)
- *f*-BLOCK ELEMENTS (INNER-TRANSITION ELEMENTS)

NATURE OF OXIDE

Basic Oxide
Oxide formed by the element on extreme left is basic oxide.
e.g. Na_2O.

Amphoteric/Neutral Oxide
Oxides of the elements in the centre are amphoteric or neutral.
e.g. CO, ZnO.

Acidic Oxide
Oxides formed by the element on extreme right are acidic oxides.
e.g. Cl_2O_7.

ATOMIC RADIUS

Distance from the center of the nucleus to the outermost shell of electrons.

Covalent radius

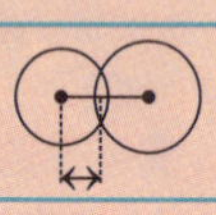

van der Waal's radius

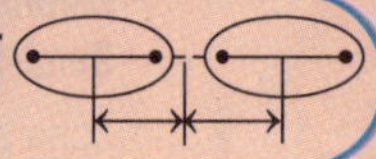

Crystal radius

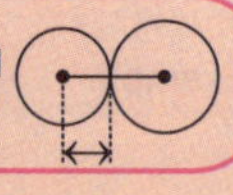

IONIC RADIUS

- The distance between the centre of nucleus and its outermost shell.
- Radius of cation < Radius of anion

ATOMIC RADIUS ORDER

van der Waal's radius > Crystal radius > Covalent radius

Chapter 04

Chemical Bonding and Molecular Structure

CHEMICAL BOND
Attractive force that holds the constituents (atoms, ions etc) together in different chemical species.

METALLIC BOND
- Chemical bond in metals.
- Atoms share a "sea of electrons" that are free to move through-out the entire structure.

IONIC BOND
- Bonds formed due to electrostatic attraction between positive and negative ions.
- High melting and boiling points.
- Conducts electricity when molten or dissolved in water.

Example NaCl, MgO

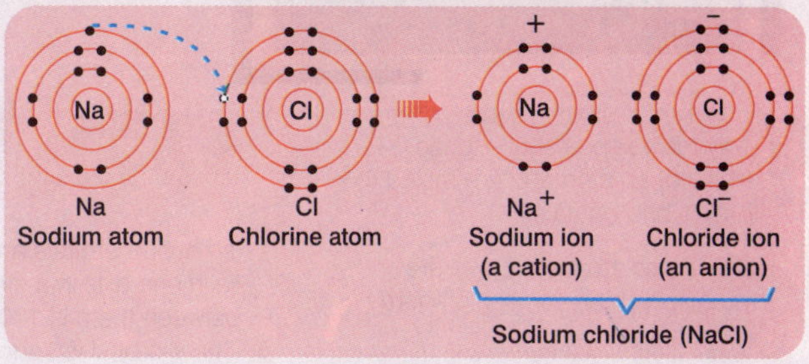

COVALENT BOND
- Bonds formed by the mutual sharing of electrons.
- Low melting and boiling points.
- Poor electrical conductivity.

Example CCl_4, N_2, CO_2

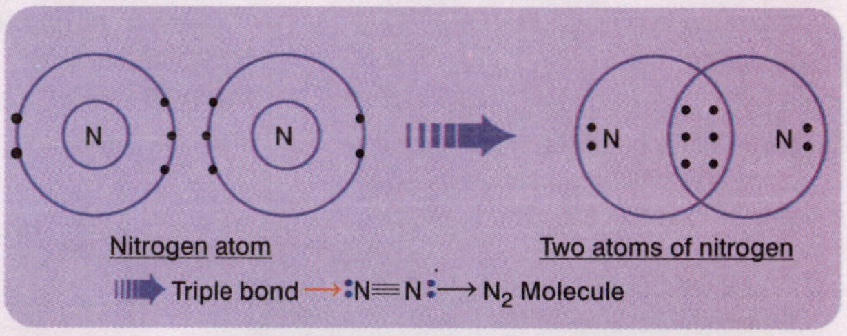

POLARITY OF BONDS
The distribution of electrical charge over the atoms joined by the covalent bond.

Polar Covalent Molecules
- Molecules in which the electrons are shared unequally due to difference in the electronegativity of bonded atoms.
- Generally posses permanent dipole moments (μ).

e.g. HF, H_2O

The dipole moment $\mu NF_3 < \mu NH_3$

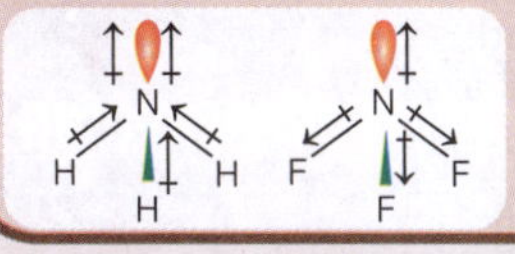

Non-polar Covalent Molecules
- Molecules in which electrons are shared equally between atoms (usually homonuclear) resulting in no partial charges.
- Non-polar molecules are symmetrical to cancel out.

e.g. BeF_2, BF_3

Dipole moment

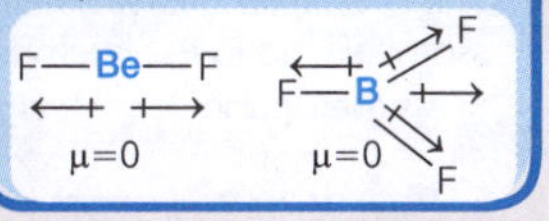

Coordinate Bond
A covalent bond (a shared pair of electron) in which both electrons comes from the same atom.

LEWIS SYMBOLS
- Outer shell electrons (valence electrons) take part in a chemical reaction.

  Li Be B C

- Dots = number of valence electrons
- Group valence is equal to number of dots (*n*) or (8–*n*).

OCTET RULE
The tendency of atoms to prefer to have eight electrons in the valence shells.

LIMITATIONS OF OCTET RULE
- Incomplete octet

  Li : Cl   H : Be : H
- Odd electron molecules

  N = O   O = N – O
- Expanded octet

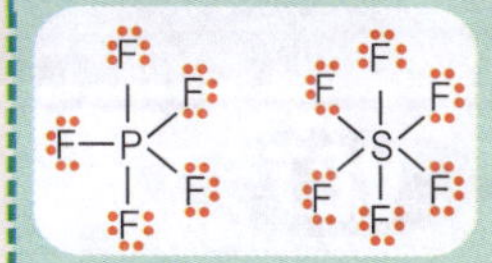

- Does not predict the shape or relative stability of molecules.

Some noble gases form compounds, contradicting the inert nature assumed by the octet rule.

e.g.

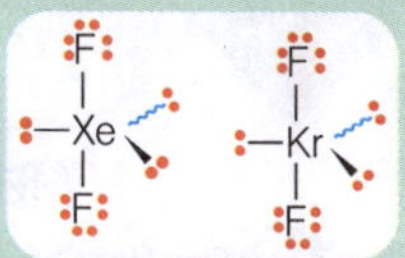

FAJANS' RULE
- Small, highly charged cations will exert a greater effect in polarising anions than large and/or singly charged cations.
- High charge and large size of anion are more prone to polarisation and covalent character, cations are not particularly polarizable.

BOND PARAMETERS

01 BOND ANGLE
- Angle between the orbitals containing bonding electrons around the central atom in a molecule/complex ion.

02 BOND ENTHALPY
- Amount of energy required to break one mole of bonds of a particular type between two atoms in a gaseous state.

03 BOND LENGTH
- Equilibrium distance between the nuclei of two bonded atoms.

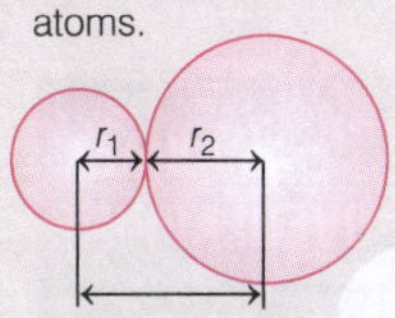

Total bond length $= r_1 + r_2$

04 BOND ORDER
- The number of bonds between the two atoms in a molecule.
- Isoelectronic molecules and ions have identical bond order.

Bond order ∝ Bond enthalpy $\propto \frac{1}{\text{bond length}}$

Formal Charge
Formal charge on an atom in a Lewis structure = [Total number of valence electrons in the free atom] – [Total number of non-bonding (lone pair) electrons] – $\left(\frac{1}{2}\right)$ [Total number of bonding (shared) electrons]

Resonance
The hypothetical phenomenon showing different structural forms each of which can explain some of the properties of the molecule but none can explain all the properties.

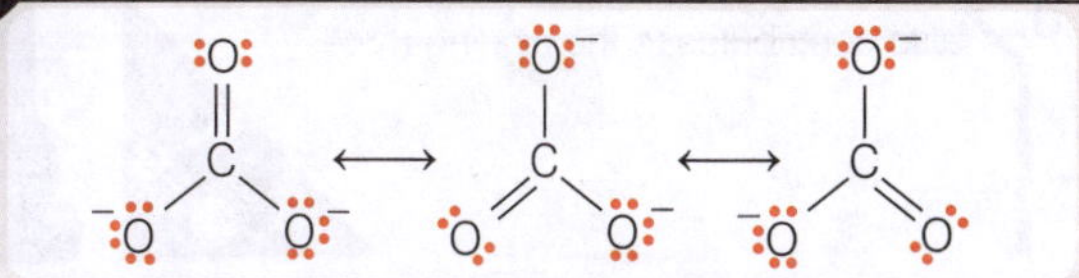

HYBRIDISATION

- Only the valence shell atomic orbital of an atom/ion are mixed to form hybrid orbitals.
- Only those atomic orbitals are mixed which are similar in energy and symmetry.
- The atomic orbitals involved in the formation of π-bonds remain excluded from hybridisation process.
- If the central atom or ion has one or more lone pair of electrons, then completely filled atomic orbitals are also involved in the hybridisation.
- Empty atomic orbitals may also be involved in hybridisation. e.g. B_2H_6.
- The hybrid orbitals are degenerate.
- The type of hybridisation indicates the geometry of molecules.

TYPES OF HYBRIDISATION

1 *sp* HYBRIDISATION

- *sp* hybrid orbitals are collinear i.e. they lie in one axis in a straight line. So, angle between them is 180°.
- The *s*-orbital is spherical and *p*-orbital is dumb-bell shaped but *sp*-orbital has linear geometry.
- The *sp*-orbital has 50% *s*-character and 50% *p*-character.

Example $BeCl_2$

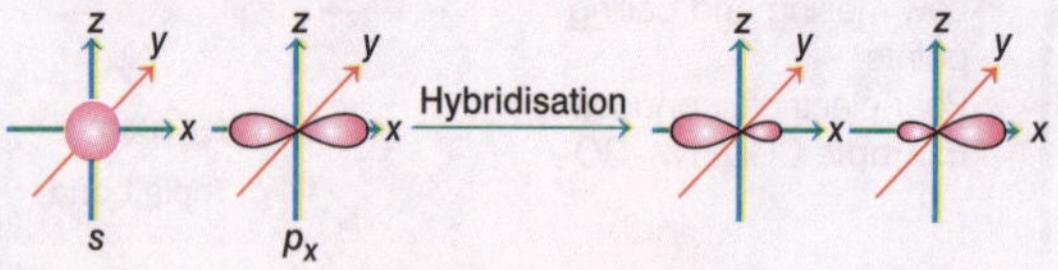

2 sp^2 HYBRIDISATION

- sp^2 orbitals lie in one plane directed towards corners of an equilateral triangle.
- The spatial arrangement of sp^2 orbitals is trigonal.
- The sp^2 orbital has 33% *s*-character and 67% *p*-character.

Example BCl_3

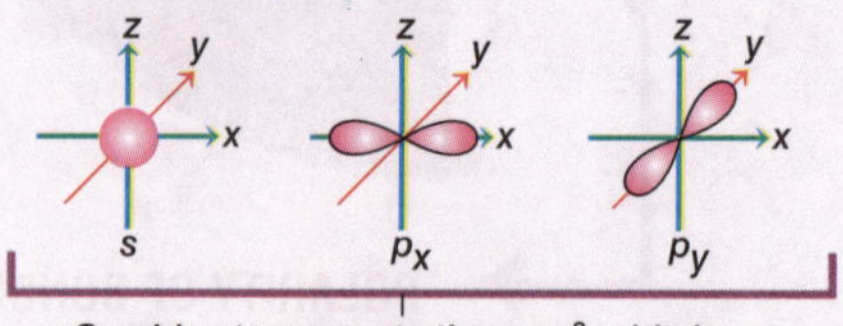

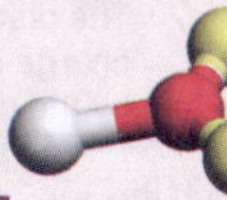

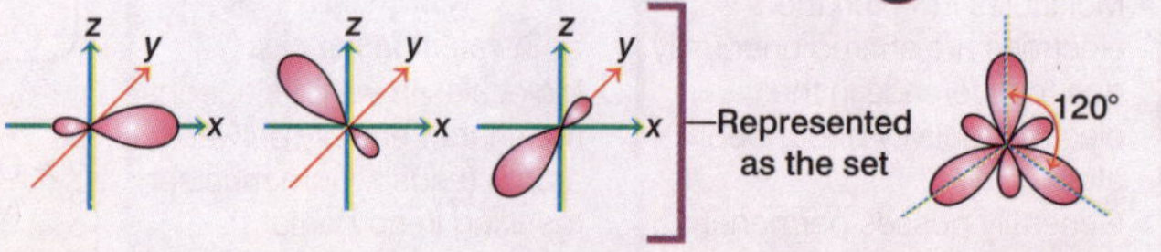

VBT

(HEITLER AND LONDON)

1. Covalent bond is formed due to the overlap of orbitals.
2. The atomic orbitals overlap to form a localised bonding orbital between the two atoms.
3. The two electrons occupying the bond orbitals must obey Pauli's exclusion principle.
4. Each electron may be considered to belong to both the nuclei.
5. Due to overlapping, the maximum electron density is between the two atoms.
6. The neutralisation of spin magnetic moments also contributes to the binding force.

OVERLAPPING OF ORBITALS

01 *s-s* OVERLAPPING

The overlapping of two half-filled *s*-orbitals along the internuclear axes.

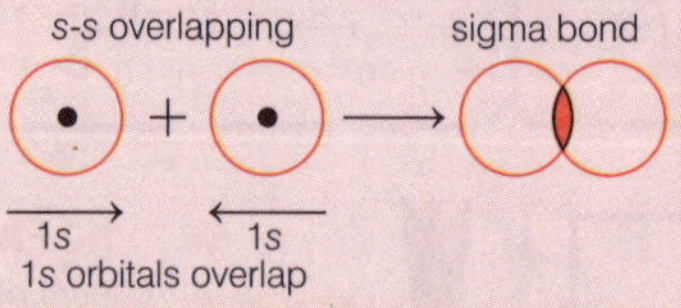

02 *s-p* OVERLAPPING

The overlapping of half-filled *s*-orbitals and half-filled *p*-orbitals of another atom.

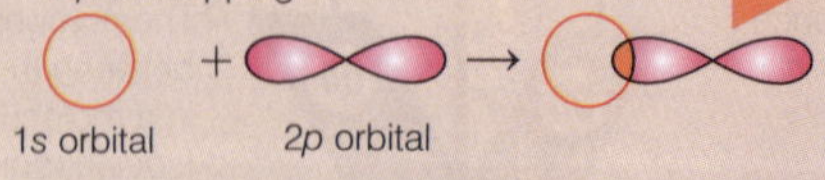

03 *p-p* AXIAL OVERLAPPING

The overlapping of half-filled *p*-orbitals between two approaching atoms.

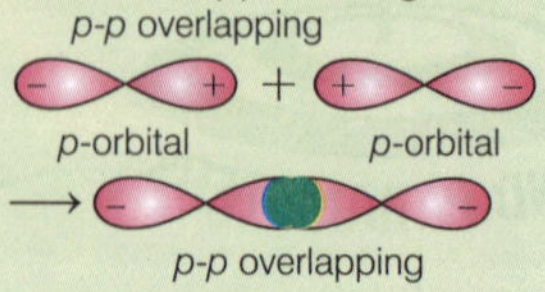

3 sp^3 HYBRIDISATION

- sp^3 hybrid orbitals are directed towards four corners of a regular tetrahedron. The angle between each of them is 109° 28′ .
- Each of the four sp^3-hybrid orbitals, has 25% s-character and 75% p-character. sp^3 hybrid orbitals are more spread and shorter in length than pure p-orbital.

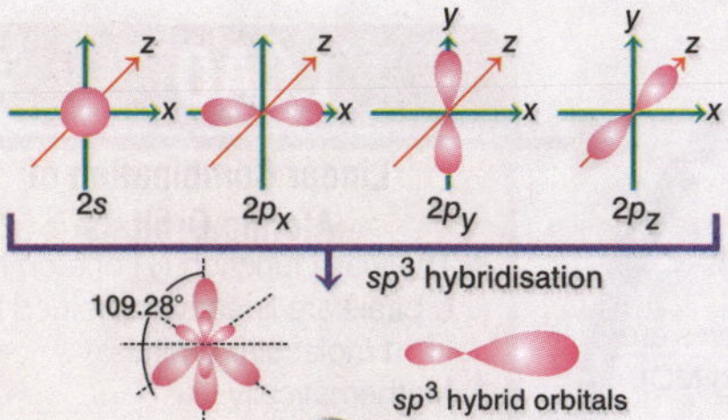

POWER TIPS

- sp^3d-hybridisation involved orbitals $= s, p_x, p_y, p_z, d_{z^2}$
- sp^3d^2-hybridisation involved orbitals $= s, p_x, p_y, p_z, d_{x^2-y^2}, d_{z^2}$

VSEPR (NYHOLM AND GILLESPIE)

- The shape of a molecule depends upon the number of valence shell electron pairs.
- Electron pairs arrange themselves to minimise repulsion achieving a stable geometry. Theory can be applied to resonance structures of a molecule.
- The repulsive interaction of electron pair decreases in the order: lone pair-lone pair > lone pair-bond pair > bond pair-bond pair

Bond Pair	Lone Pair	Shape	Hybridisation	Example
2	0	Linear	sp	:Ö = C = Ö:
1	1	Linear	sp	[:C ≡ N:]⁻
3	0	Trigonal Planar	sp^2	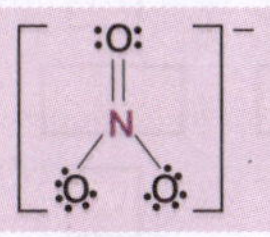
2	1	Bent	sp^2	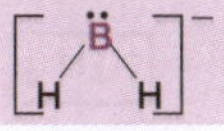
1	2	Linear	sp^2	:Ö = Ö:
4	0	Tetrahedral	sp^3	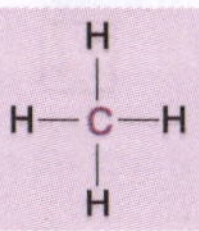
3	1	Trigonal Pyramidal	sp^3	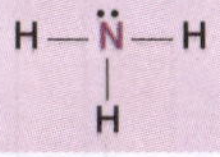
2	2	Bent	sp^3	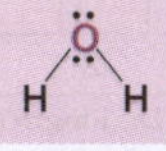
1	3	Linear	sp^3	[:Ö — H]⁻
5	0	Trigonal bipyramidal	sp^3d	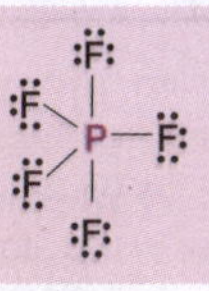

Bond Pair	Lone Pair	Shape	Hybridisation	Example
3	2	T-shaped	sp^3d	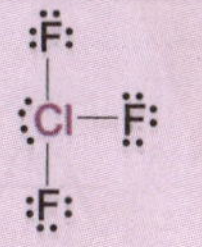
2	3	Linear	sp^3d	[:I̤—I̤—I̤:]⁻
6	0	Octahedral	sp^3d^2	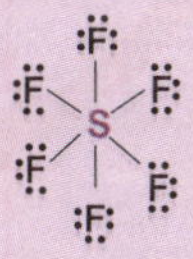
5	1	Square pyramidal	sp^3d^2	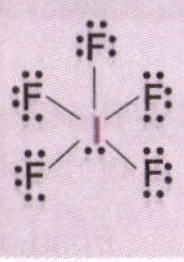
4	2	Square planar	sp^3d^2	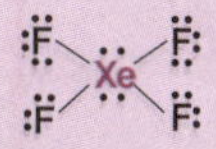
4	1	See-Saw	sp^3d	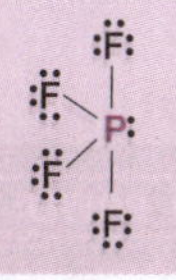

1 σ-Bonding

- Covalent bond formed by end to end (head on) overlap of bonding orbitals along the internuclear axis.

2 π-Bonding

- Covalent bond formed by the sidewise overlapping of atomic orbitals.
- The axis of atomic orbitals remain parallel to each other and perpendicular to the internuclear axis.

p-p Sidewise Overlapping

Two saucer shaped charge clouds, above and below the plane of participating atoms are formed.

⊕ represents the nucleus

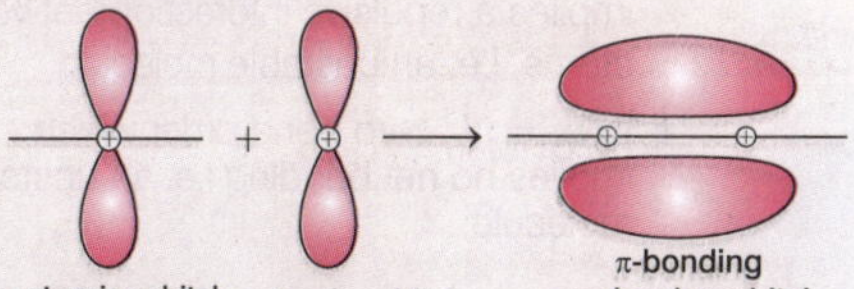

p atomic orbital p atomic orbital π-bonding molecular orbital

Constructive Interference

- In phase combination of atomic wave function.
- The amplitude of wave when two waves are in phase. $\psi_{MO} = \psi_A + \psi_B$ (Bonding MO)

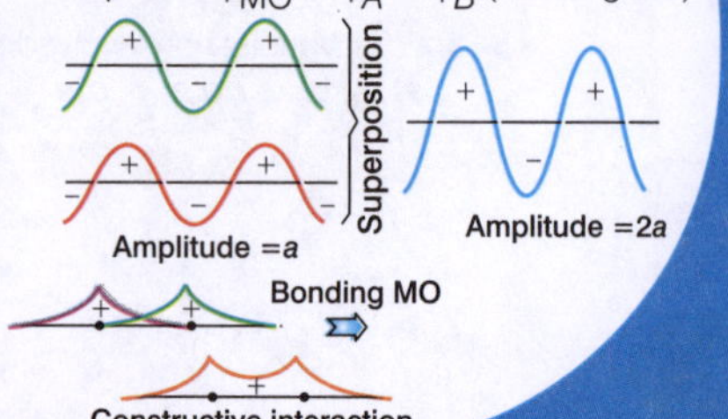

LCAO

Linear Combination of Atomic Orbitals

- The wave function (χ) of atomic orbitals are linearly combined to form molecular orbitals.
- Mathematically, it is given by $\psi_{MO} = \psi_A \pm \psi_B$

Salient Features of MOT

- M.O. are formed by the combination of atomic orbitals of comparable energy and proper symmetry.
- The number of molecular orbitals is equal to the numbers of combining atomic orbitals.
- Two atomic orbitals combine to give a bonding molecular orbital and an antibonding molecular orbital.
- Bonding molecular orbital has lower energy and greater stability than antibonding molecular orbital.

CONDITIONS FOR LINEAR COMBINATION OF ATOMIC ORBITALS

- In Homonuclear diatomic molecules (H_2, O_2 etc.) only orbitals of similar energy combines to form bonding and antibonding molecular orbitals.
- In Heteronuclear molecules (HF, HCl, etc.) the difference in electronegativity shifts the atomic orbitals to allow bonding of 1s and 2s orbitals.

Destructive Interference

- Out of phase combination of atomic wave functions.
- The amplitude of wave when two waves are out of phase. $\psi_{MO} = \psi_A - \psi_B$ (Antibonding MO)

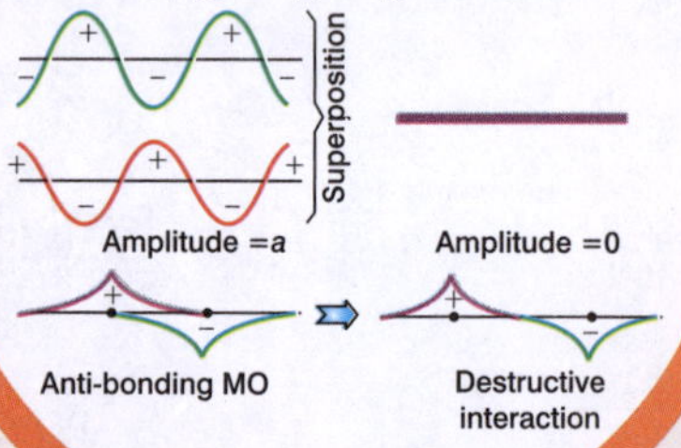

MOLECULAR ORBITAL THEORY (MOT)

Bond Energy ↑

	With 2p-sp mixing			Without 2p-sp mixing			
	B_2	C_2	N_2	O_2	F_2	Ne_2	
σ^*_{2p}	□	□	□	□	□	↑↓	σ^*_{2p}
π^*_{2p}	□□	□□	□□	↑ ↑	↑↓ ↑↓	↑↓ ↑↓	π^*_{2p}
σ_{2p_z}	□	□	↑↓	↑↓ ↑↓	↑↓ ↑↓	↑↓ ↑↓	π_{2p}
π_{2p}	↑ ↑	↑↓ ↑↓	↑↓ ↑↓	↑↓	↑↓	↑↓	σ_{2p_z}
σ^*_{2s}	↑↓	↑↓	↑↓	↑↓	↑↓	↑↓	σ^*_{2s}
σ_{2s}	↑↓	↑↓	↑↓	↑↓	↑↓	↑↓	σ_{2s}

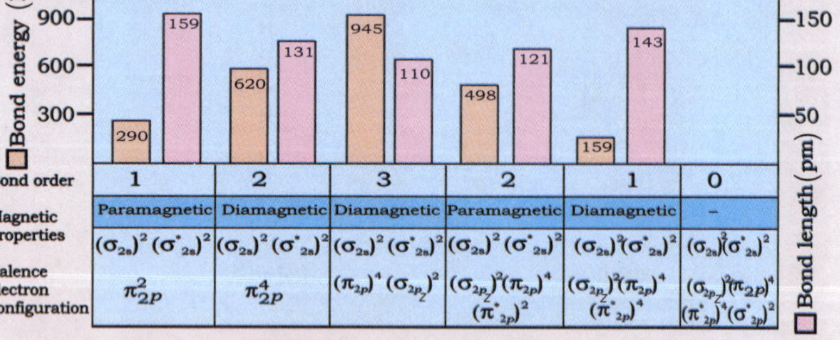

	B_2	C_2	N_2	O_2	F_2	Ne_2
Bond order	1	2	3	2	1	0
Magnetic properties	Paramagnetic	Diamagnetic	Diamagnetic	Paramagnetic	Diamagnetic	–
Valence electron configuration	$(\sigma_{2s})^2(\sigma^*_{2s})^2 \pi^2_{2p}$	$(\sigma_{2s})^2(\sigma^*_{2s})^2 \pi^4_{2p}$	$(\sigma_{2s})^2(\sigma^*_{2s})^2(\pi_{2p})^4(\sigma_{2p_z})^2$	$(\sigma_{2s})^2(\sigma^*_{2s})^2(\sigma_{2p_z})^2(\pi_{2p})^4(\pi^*_{2p})^2$	$(\sigma_{2s})^2(\sigma^*_{2s})^2(\sigma_{2p_z})^2(\pi_{2p})^4(\pi^*_{2p})^4$	$(\sigma_{2s})^2(\sigma^*_{2s})^2(\sigma_{2p_z})^2(\pi_{2p})^4(\pi^*_{2p})^4(\sigma^*_{2p})^2$

BOND ORDER

- The strength and stability of chemical bond between atoms.

Bond order $= \dfrac{N_b - N_a}{2}$

- where, N_b = number of electrons in bonding molecular orbitals.
  N_a = number of electrons in anti-bonding molecular orbitals.

POWER TIPS

- If $N_b > N_a$ positive bond order which implies a stable molecule
- If $N_b < N_a$ negative bond order which implies a repulsive interaction between atoms, i.e. an unstable molecule.
- If $N_b = N_a$ zero bond order which implies no net bonding i.e. an unstable molecule.

HYDROGEN BONDING

The attractive electrostatic force between a hydrogen atom covalently bonded to highly electronegative atom (i.e. F, O and N).

INTRAMOLECULAR HYDROGEN BONDING

- When a H-bond is formed between two atoms within the same molecules.
- Low boiling point and melting point.

e.g.

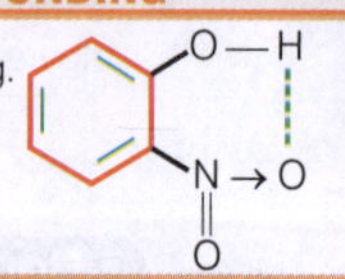

INTERMOLECULAR HYDROGEN BONDING

- Interaction between two or more molecules that have hydrogen bond donor or acceptor sites.
- High boiling point and melting point. e.g. H_2O.

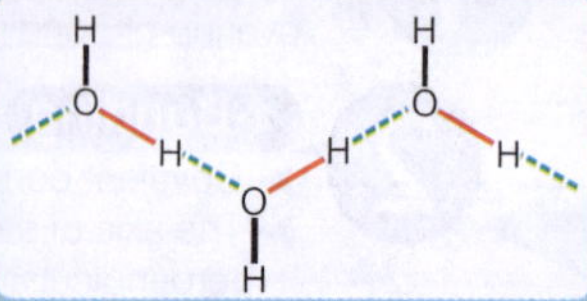

Chapter 05

Thermodynamics

FUNDAMENTAL'S OF THERMODYNAMICS

System

Specific part of universe which is under thermodynamic observation.

Types of System

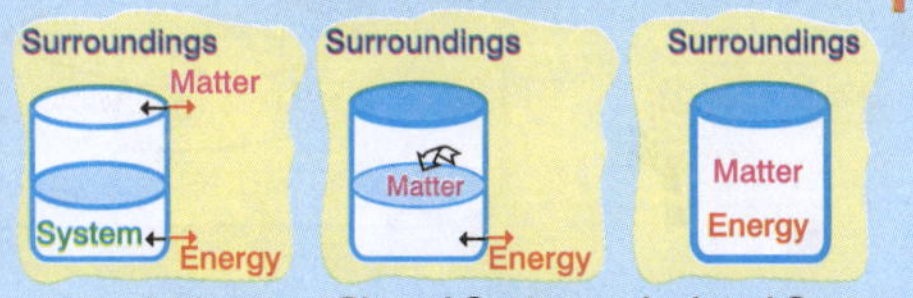

Open System | Closed System | Isolated System

Boundary

- ✓ Separates system from surrounding.
- ✓ Real or imaginary surface.

Surrounding

- ✓ It include everything other than the system.
- ✓ The system and surroundings make up the universe.

Reversible Process

- Ideal process that takes infinite time for completion.
- Work obtained is maximum.

Irreversible Process

- It takes finite time for completion.
- Work obtained is not maximum.

MODES OF EXCHANGE OF ENERGY

HEAT

Mode of energy transfer between system and surroundings due to temperature difference between them.

WORK

Mode of energy transfer from or to the system associated with change in volume against external pressure.

1. **Isothermal Irreversible**

   $W = -p_{ext} dV$

   $W_{expansion}$ = negative

   $W_{contraction}$ = positive

2. **Isothermal Reversible**

   $W = -2.303\, nRT \log \frac{V_2}{V_1}$

   Reversible work of expansion = maximum

   Reversible work of compression = minimum

3. **Adiabatic Reversible**

   $W = nC_v \Delta T = nC_v (T_2 - T_1)$

   $= \frac{nR}{\gamma - 1}(T_2 - T_1)$

4. **Adiabatic Irreversible**

   ❖ **In free expansion**

   $\Delta U = W = 0$

   ❖ **In Intermediate expansion**

   $W = -Rp_{ext}\left(\frac{T_2 p_1 - T_1 p_2}{p_1 p_2}\right)$

Thermodynamic Process

1. **Adiabatic Process**
   Completely insulated
   $dq = 0$
2. **Isothermal Process**
   Process carried out at constant temperature $\Delta T = 0$
3. **Isobaric Process**
   Process carried out at constant pressure. $\Delta P = 0$
4. **Isochoric Process**
   Process carried out at constant volume $\Delta V = 0$.
5. **Cyclic Process**
   Process in which system returns to its original step, after number of steps.
   $\Delta U = 0$ and $\Delta H = 0$

Macroscopic Properties

- **Intensive Properties**: Independent of the quantity or size of the matter. e.g. Temperature, pressure, etc.
- **Extensive Properties**: Depends upon the quantity or size of matter. e.g. Internal energy, volume, enthalpy etc.
- **State Function**: Depends only on the initial and final state of a system. e.g. Pressure, volume, enthalpy.
- **Path Function**: Depend upon the path followed by system to attain that state. e.g. Work, heat.
- **Thermo-dynamic Equilibrium**: System in which the macroscopic properties do not undergo any change with time.

Sign Convention

Work

$\xrightarrow{W}$ System $\xrightarrow{W}$

+ve (compresion) work done on the gas

−ve (expansion) work done by the gas

Heat

+ve Q ↓ System ↓ Q −ve

POWER TIPS

Expansion

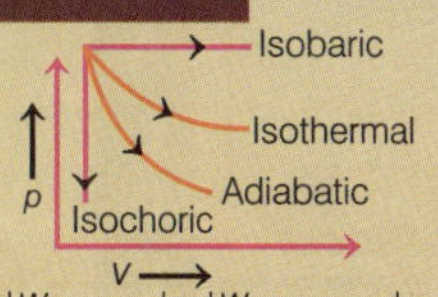

$|W_{Isobaric}| > |W_{Isothermal}| > |W_{Adiabatic}| > |W_{Isochoric}|$

Compression

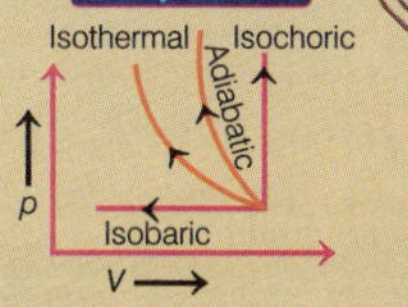

$|W_{Adiabatic}| > |W_{Isothermal}| > |W_{Isobaric}| > |W_{Isochoric}|$

Relationship in between p, V, T and γ

pV^{γ} = cont., $TV^{\gamma-1}$ = cont., $p^{1-\gamma}T^{\gamma}$ = cont.

ENTHALPY

Total heat content of the system at constant pressure.

Sign Convention

- For exothermic reaction $\Delta H < 0$, i.e. negative.
- For endothermic reaction $\Delta H > 0$, i.e. positive.

Hess Law of Constant Heat Summation

Heat change accompanying a reaction is always same, whether it takes place in one step or multi steps.

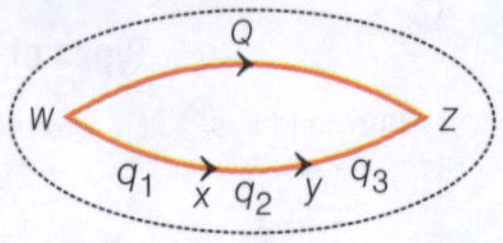

$Q = q_1 + q_2 + q_3$

ZEROTH LAW OF THERMODYNAMICS

If two systems is in thermal equilibrium with a third object then they are also in thermal equilibrium with each other.

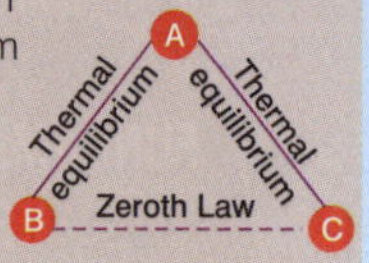

FIRST LAW OF THERMODYNAMICS

Energy can neither be created nor be destroyed although it can be changed from one form to another.

$\Delta U = q + w$

ΔU – Change in internal energy; q – Heat; w – Work

Relationship between ΔH and ΔU

$\Delta H = \Delta U + p\Delta V$

or

$\Delta H = \Delta U + \Delta n_g RT$

- When $\Delta n_g = 0$ then $\Delta H = \Delta U$
- When $\Delta n_g > 0$ then, $\Delta H > \Delta U$
- When $\Delta n_g < 0$ then, $\Delta H < \Delta U$

Internal Energy

Every substance is associated with a definite amount of energy that depends upon its chemical nature as well as upon its temperature, volume and pressure. This energy is internal energy.

Enthalpy of a Reaction

- Change in enthalpy that accompanies a chemical reaction, represented by a balanced chemical equation.

  $\Sigma\Delta_r H = \Sigma H_P - \Sigma H_R$

  ΣH_P = Sum of enthalpy of product.

  ΣH_R = Sum of enthalpy of reactant.
- Enthalpy of reaction expressed at the standard state condition is **standard enthalpy of reaction**, $\Delta H°$.

Lattice Enthalpy

The amount of heat liberated when the requisite amount of ions in gaseous state combine to form 1 mole of crystal lattice.

Born-Haber Cycle

$Na(s) + \frac{1}{2}Cl_2(g) \longrightarrow NaCl(s)$

- Step 1 (Enthalpy of sublimation): $Na(s) \rightarrow Na(g)$
- Step 2 (Dissociation energy): $\frac{1}{2}Cl_2(g) \rightarrow Cl(g)$
- Step 3 (Ionisation energy): $Na(g) \rightarrow Na^+(g)$
- Step 4 (Electron gain enthalpy): $Cl(g) \rightarrow Cl^-(g)$
- Step 5 (Lattice enthalpy): $Na^+(g) + Cl^-(g) \rightarrow NaCl(s)$

$\Delta_f H\,(NaCl) = \Delta H_1 + 1/2\,\Delta H_2 + \Delta H_3 + \Delta H_4 + \Delta H_5$

Heat Capacity of a System

The quantity of heat required to raise the temperature of the system by 1°C.

$C = \frac{q}{\Delta T}$

Specific Heat Capacity or Specific Heat (C)

The amount of heat required to raise the temperature of 1 gram of the substance through 1°C.

$q = mC\Delta T$

Molar Heat Capacity (C_m)

The amount of heat required to raise the temperature of 1 mol of the substance through 1°C.

$C_m = \frac{C}{n}$

Relationship between C_p and C_V

- $C_p = \frac{\Delta H}{\Delta T}$
- $C_V = \frac{\Delta U}{\Delta T}$
- $C_p - C_V = R$
- $\frac{C_p}{C_V} = \gamma$

TYPES OF ENTHALPIES

Enthalpy of Formation ($\Delta_f H$)

The enthalpy change when one mole of a compound is formed from its elements in most stable state.

e.g. $C(s) + 2H_2(g) \rightarrow CH_4(g)$; $\Delta_f H = -74.8$ kJ/mol

Enthalpy of Combustion ($\Delta_c H$)

Change in enthalpy when one mole of a substance is completely burnt in oxygen.

e.g. $C(s) + O_2(g) \rightarrow CO_2(g)$; $\Delta_c H = -393.5$ kJ/mol)

Enthalpy of Solution ($\Delta_{sol} H$)

Change in enthalpy when one mole of a solute is dissolved completely in excess of solvent.

Enthalpy of Dilution ($\Delta_{dil} H$)

Enthalpy change when the solution containing one mole of a substance is diluted from one concentration to another.

$\Delta_{dil} H = \Delta_{sol\,2} H - \Delta_{sol\,1} H$ (at infinite dilution)

Enthalpy of Neutralisation ($\Delta_n H$)

The enthalpy change when one equivalent of an acid is neutralised by one equivalent of a base in fairly dilute solution.

e.g. $HCl(aq) + NaOH(aq) \rightarrow NaCl(aq) + H_2O(l)$; $\Delta_n H = -57.1$ kJ/mol

Enthalpy of Fusion ($\Delta_{fus} H$)

Change in enthalpy when one mole of a solid is completely converted into liquid state at its melting point.

e.g. $H_2O(s) \rightarrow H_2O(l)$ at 0°C or 273 K

$\Delta_{fus} H = +6.0$ kJ/mol

Enthalpy of Vaporisation

Change in enthalpy when one mole of a liquid is completely converted into vapours at its boiling point.

e.g. $H_2O(l) \longrightarrow H_2O(g)$ at 100°C or 373 K

$\Delta H_{vap} = +40.6$ kJ/mol

Enthalpy of Sublimation

Change in enthlapy when one mole of a solid is directly converted into vapours.

$\Delta_{sub} H = \Delta_{fus} H + \Delta_{vap} H$

Enthalpy of Atomisation

Enthalpy change on breaking one mole of bonds completely to obtain atoms in the gaseous phase.

e.g. $CH_4(g) \rightarrow C(g) + 4H(g)$; $\Delta_a H = 1665$ kJ/mol

Bond Enthalpy

Change in enthalpy associated with breaking and making of chemical bonds.

e.g. $Cl_2(g) \longrightarrow 2Cl(g)$; $\Delta_{bond} H = 242$ kJ/mol

Entropy (S)

- Property of a system that measures the degree of randomness in a system.
- It is state function.
- Unit is Joule per Kelvin per mole.

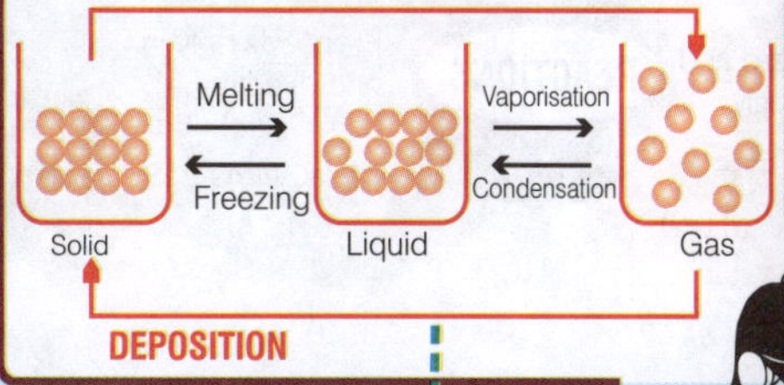

Characteristics

- Change in entropy for a cyclic process is always zero.
- The total entropy change of universe (ΔS).

$$\Delta S = \Delta S_{sys} + \Delta S_{surr}$$

- In a reversible process $\Delta_{rev}S = 0$.
- In irreversible process $\Delta_{irrev}S > 0$.
- If ΔS_{total} or $\Delta S_{universe}$ is positive, process is spontaneous.
- If ΔS_{total} or $\Delta S_{universe}$ is negative, process is non-spontaneous.
- If ΔS_{total} or $\Delta S_{universe}$ is zero, process is in equilibrium.

Standard and Molar Entropy Change

- If entropy is defined per unit of substance, then it is called molar entropy (S_m).
- If entropy change is measured under standard conditions, it is called standard entropy change.
- $\Delta S° = \Sigma \Delta S°_{Products} - \Sigma \Delta S°_{Reactants}$

Entropy Change for Ideal Gas

- For isothermal process, $\Delta S = nR \ln\frac{V_2}{V_1} = nR \ln\frac{p_1}{p_2}$ $(\because \Delta T = 0)$
- For isobaric process, $\Delta S = nC_p \ln\frac{T_2}{T_1}$ $(\therefore p_1 = p_2)$
- For isochoric process, $\Delta S = nC_v \ln\frac{T_2}{T_1}$ $(\therefore V_1 = V_2)$

Entropy Change Formula

Entropy changes	Formula
Entropy during reversible change,	$\Delta S = R \ln\frac{V_2}{V_1}$ $= R \ln\frac{p_1}{p_2}$
Entropy during adiabatic reversible change,	$\Delta S = 0$
When p = constant,	$\Delta S_p = C_p \ln\frac{T_2}{T_1}$
When V = constant,	$\Delta S_V = C_V \ln\frac{T_2}{T_1}$

1 Entropy Change in Reversible Process

Isothermal

- Increase in entropy of system $\Delta S_{sys} = \frac{+q}{T}$
- Decrease in entropy of surrounding $\Delta S_{surr} = -\frac{q}{T}$
- $\Delta S_{total} = 0$

Adiabatic

- $\Delta S_{sys} = 0$
- $\Delta S_{surr} = 0$
- $\Delta S_{total} = 0$

2 Entropy Change in Irreversible Process

- $\Delta S_{process} = \Delta S_{sys} + \Delta S_{surr}$ $= q\left[\frac{T_1 - T_2}{T_1 T_2}\right]$
- Entropy is increased.

3 Entropy and Spontaneity

- Positive values of ΔS shows the process is **spontaneous.**
- Negative values of ΔS shows the process is **non - spontaneous.**
- When an isolated system is in equilibium the entropy is maximum.

4 Entropy Change during Phase Transition

$\Delta S_{melting} = \frac{\Delta H_{fusion}}{T_m}$; $\Delta S_{vap} = \frac{\Delta H_{vap.}}{T_b}$

Solid — Liquid — Gas

$\Delta S_{sublimation} = \frac{\Delta H_{sublimation}}{T_{sub}}$

Gibbs Free Energy and Equilibrium Constant

$\Delta G = \Delta G° + RT \ln Q$

$\Delta G° = -RT \ln K$

$\Delta G°$	$\log K$	K	Comment
$\Delta G° = 0$	$\log K = 0$	1	The equilibrium mixture contains comparable amounts of reactants and products.
$\Delta G° < 0$	$\log K > 0$	$K > 1$	The equilibrium mixture is mainly products.
$\Delta G° > 0$	$\log K < 0$	$K < 1$	The equilibrium mixture is mainly reactants

Second Law of Thermodynamics

Whenever a spontaneous process takes place, it is accompanied by an increase in total entropy of universe.

Device that converts heat into work

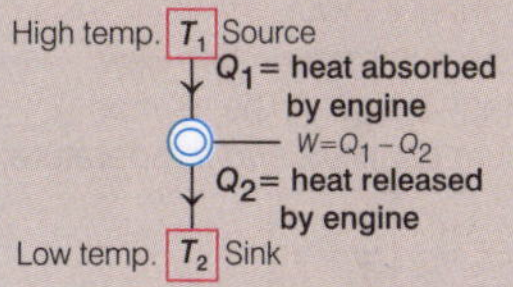

Gibbs Free Energy

The maximum amount of energy that is available to a system, during a process, that can be converted into useful work.

$$\Delta G = \Delta H - T\Delta S$$

ΔG:
- If negative, spontaneous process.
- If positive, non-spontaneous process.
- If zero, equilibrium state.

Standard Free Energy Change

- The free energy change for a process at 298 K and 1 atm pressure in which the reactants in their standard state are converted into products in their standard state ($\Delta G°$).
- Free energy change when 1 mole of the compound is made from its elements in their standard states is called **standard molar free energy of formation of a compound**.

Relation between Gibbs Free Energy & Emf of Cell

$$\Delta G = -nFE_{cell}$$

- ΔG: Gibbs free energy change
- n: No. of electrons
- F: Faraday's constant
- E_{cell}: Emf of cell

CRITERIA FOR SPONTANEITY

ΔS	ΔH	ΔG	Spontaneous/ Non-Spontaneous process
+	−	−ve at all temperatures	Spontaneous at all temperature
−	−	−ve at low temperature but +ve at high temperature	Spontaneous at low temperature but non-spontaneous at high temperature
+	+	+ve at low temperature and −ve at high temperature	Spontaneous at high temperature
−	+	+ve at all temperatures	Non-spontaneous at all temperature

Chapter 06 Equilibrium

REACTIONS

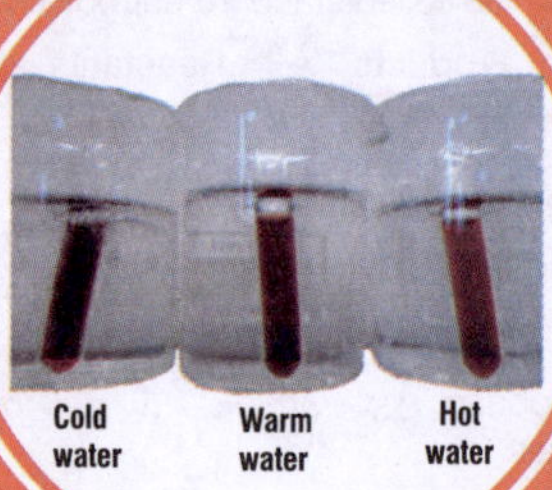

REVERSIBLE REACTION

Proceeds in both the directions, i.e. forward and reverse simultaneously.

$Fe^{3+}(aq) + SCN^{-}(aq) \rightleftharpoons FeSCN^{2+}(aq)$

IRREVERSIBLE REACTION

Proceeds only in one direction.

$Na_2SO_4(aq) + BaCl_2(aq) \longrightarrow 2NaCl(aq) + BaSO_4(aq)$

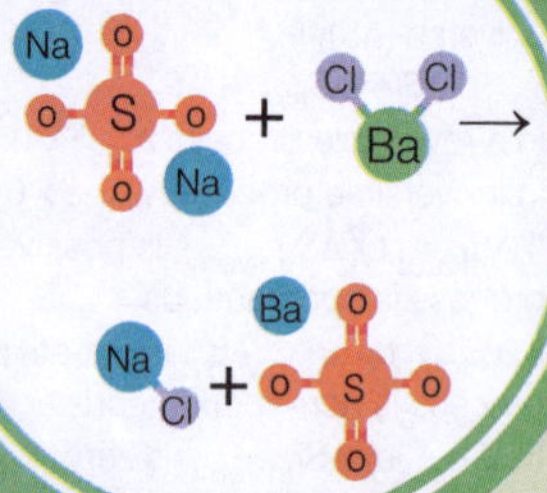

CHEMICAL EQUILIBRIUM

It is the process that involves changes in chemical composition and properties.

Homogeneous Equilibrium

All reactants and products are in the same phase.

$2SO_2(g) + O_2(g) \rightleftharpoons 2SO_3(g)$ (at equilibrium)

formation / decomposition

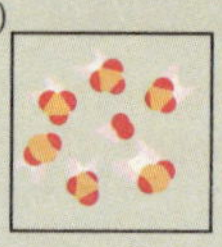

$SO_2(g)$ and $O_2(g)$ (not at equilibrium)

At equilibrium, all three types of molecules are present.

Heterogeneous Equilibrium

- Equilibrium in a system have more than one phase.
- The equilibrium between calcium carbonate and carbon dioxide $CaCO_3(s) \rightleftharpoons CaO(s) + CO_2(g)$
- The equilibrium between a solid and saturated solution. $Ca(OH)_2(s) + H_2O(l) \rightleftharpoons Ca^{2+}(aq) + 2OH^{-}(aq)$

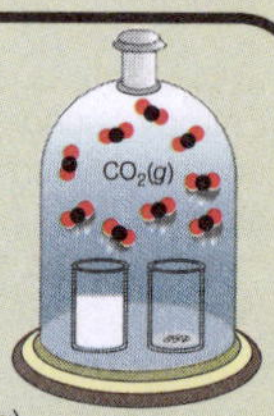

$CaO(s)$ $CaCO_3(s)$

PHYSICAL EQUILIBRIUM

The process that involves physical changes only.

Solid-Liquid Equilibrium

- Solid $\rightleftharpoons$ Liquid

  Example Ice $\rightleftharpoons$ water at 0°C
- Melting point becomes constant at constant pressure

Liquid-Vapour Equilibrium

- Liquid $\rightleftharpoons$ Vapour

  Example water $\rightleftharpoons$ water vapour at 100°C (vapour)
- Vapour pressure becomes constant at constant temperature

Solid-Vapour Equilibrium

- Solid $\rightleftharpoons$ Vapour

  Example $I_2(s) \rightleftharpoons I_2$(vapour)
- The rate of vaporisation is equal to the speed of condention of the vapour

LAW OF MASS ACTION

- *The rate at which a chemical reaction proceeds is proportional to the product of active masses of reacting substance with each conc. term raised to the power of stoichiometric coefficient of that species in the chemical equation.*
- *Active mass is the molar concentration (mol/L).*

Expression of Equilibrium constant

For a homogeneous reversible reaction

$aA + bB \rightleftharpoons cC + dD$

- Equilibrium constant expressed in terms of concentration $K_c = \frac{[C]^c [D]^d}{[A]^a [B]^b}$
- Equilibrium constant expressed in terms of mole fraction $K_x = \frac{[x_C]^c [x_D]^d}{[x_A]^a [x_B]^b}$
- Equilibrium constant expressed in terms of partial pressures $K_p = \frac{p_C^c \cdot p_D^d}{p_A^a \cdot p_B^b}$

Characteristics of Equilibrium Constant

- Independent of initial concentration of reactants, the presence of catalyst and the direction from which equilibrium is attained.
- If the equation is divided by n, then new equilibrium constant is $(K)^{1/n}$. If the equation is reversed, then new equilibrium constant is $1/K$.
- If two equations are added, then new equilibrium constant is $K_1 \times K_2$.
- If two equations are subtracted, then new equilibrium constant is K_1/K_2. The relation between equilibrium constant and temperature.

$$\log \frac{K_2}{K_1} = \frac{\Delta H}{2.303R}\left[\frac{1}{T_1} - \frac{1}{T_2}\right]$$

Units of K_C and K_p

no. of moles of reactant = no. of moles of product	$\Delta n_g > 0$	$\Delta n_g < 0$
$\Delta n_g = 0$	$K_p = (\text{atm})^{\Delta n_g}$	$K_p = (\text{atm}^{-1})^{\Delta n_g}$
K_p and K_C have no unit	$K_C = (\text{mol/L})^{\Delta n_g}$	$K_C = (\text{mol}^{-1}\text{L})^{\Delta n_g}$

Significance of K_C and K_p

- Greater value of equilibrium constant, favours forward direction.
- Greater is the stability of the products
- $K > 10^3$ -Product predominates
- $K < 10^{-3}$ -Reactant predominates
- $10^{-3} \le K \le 10^3$-Both reactants and products are present.

Relationship Between K_p, K_C and K_x

For a gaseous phase reaction

$n_1A + n_2B + \ldots \rightleftharpoons m_1C + m_2D + \ldots$

- $K_p = K_C(RT)^{\Delta n_g}$
- $K_p = K_x(p)^{\Delta n_g}$
- $K_p = K_x\left(\frac{RT}{V}\right)^{\Delta n_g}$

$\Delta n_g = (m_1 + m_2 + \ldots) - (n_1 + n_2 + \ldots)$

= moles of gaseous product – moles of gaseous reactant

When a change is brought about on a system at equilibrium, the system tends to adjust itself to reduce the effect of change.

S.No.	Changes done at equilibrium	Direction of equilibrium shift
1.	Increase in concentration of reactant	Forward direction
2.	Increase in concentration of product	Backward direction
3.	Increase in temperature	Towards endothermic reaction
4.	Decrease in temperature	Towards exothermic reaction
5.	Increase of pressure	Towards lesser no. of gaseous moles
6.	Decrease of pressure	Towards larger no. of gaseous moles

LE-CHATELIER'S PRINCIPLE

APPLICATIONS

01 Boiling of Water

- Water $\rightleftharpoons$ Steam $-x$ kcal
  (Low volume) (Higher volume)
- Factors favouring the formation of steam:
  - High temperature (as the forward reaction is endothermic)
  - Low pressure (as the forward reaction shows increase in volume)

02 Melting of Ice

- Ice $\rightleftharpoons$ water $-x$ kcal
  1.09 mL 1.01 mL
- Factors favouring the melting of ice:
  - High temperature (as the forward reaction is endothermic)
  - High pressure (as the forward reaction shows decrease in volume)

03 Manufacture of Nitrogen Oxide

- $N_2(g) + O_2(g) \rightleftharpoons 2NO(g)$; $\Delta H = +43.2$kcal
- Factors favouring the formation of NO
  - Increase in concentration of N_2 and O_2
  - Unaffected by pressure change ($\Delta n_g = 0$)
  - Increase in temperature (as the forward reaction is endothermic)

04 Haber's Process

$N_2(g) + 3H_2(g) \rightleftharpoons 2NH_3(g)$; $\Delta H = -22.4$kcal

- Favourable conditions for formation of NH_3
  - High concentration of N_2 and H_2
  - High pressure (as $\Delta n_g = -2$)
  - Low temperature (as the forward reaction is exothermic)
- An optimum temperature of 500°C and a pressure of 200 atm is used.

05 Solubility of Salts

- Dissolution accompanied by absorption of heat
  $NaCl(s) + H_2O \rightleftharpoons NaCl(aq)$; $\Delta H > 0$
  - Favoured by high temperature.
- Dissolution accompanied by evolution of heat.
  $KOH(s) + H_2O \rightleftharpoons KOH(aq)$; $\Delta H < 0$
  - Favoured by decrease in temperature.

FACTORS AFFECTING EQUILIBRIUM CONCENTRATION

CHANGE IN CONCENTRATION

Concentration		Equilibrium
(i) Reactant↑	=	Forward direction
(ii) Product↑	=	Backward direction

The Effect of Concentration Changes on Equilibrium

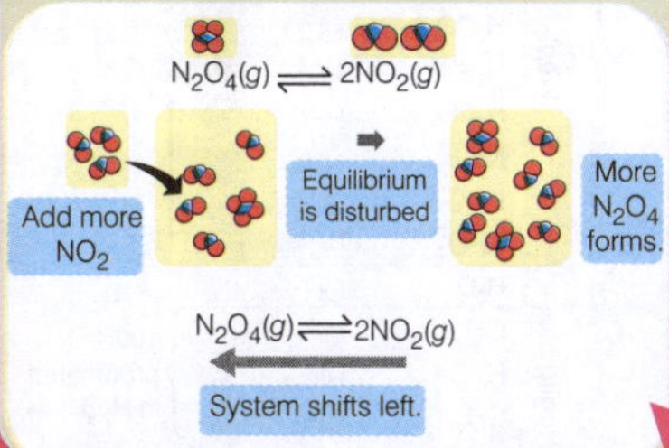

CHANGE IN PRESSURE

- $\Delta n_g = 0$; No effect on equilibrium.
- $\Delta n_g > 0$; Pressure increase ⇒ Backward reaction
- $\Delta n_g < 0$; Pressure increase ⇒ Forward reaction

Change of Pressure $2A(g) \rightleftharpoons B(g)$

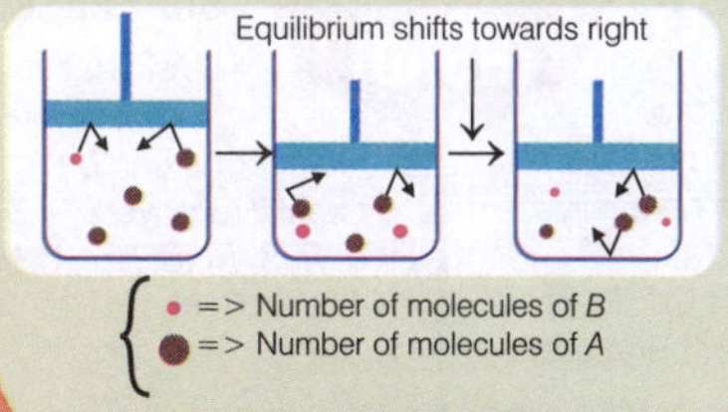

ADDITION OF INERT GAS

Volume = Constant
No effect on equilibrium position.
Addition of inert gas at constant volume
$X(g) \rightleftharpoons 2Y(g)$
Helium is added at constant volume.

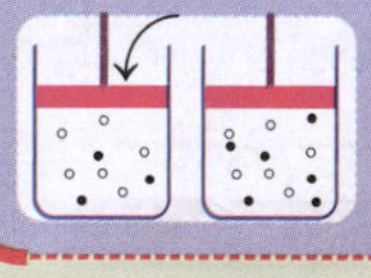

Pressure = Constant
Equilibrium will shift in direction of increase in the number of moles of gases.
Addition of inert gas at constant pressure
$X(g) \rightleftharpoons 2Y(g)$
Helium is added at constant pressure.

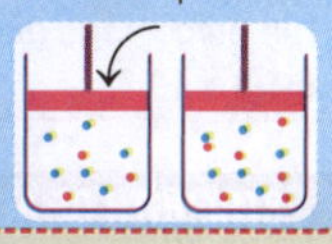

CHANGE IN TEMPERATURE

- **Exothermic reaction ⇒**
  Temp. increase = Backward reaction
- **Endothermic reaction ⇒**
  Temp. increase = Forward reaction.

$N_2O_4 \rightleftharpoons NO_2$

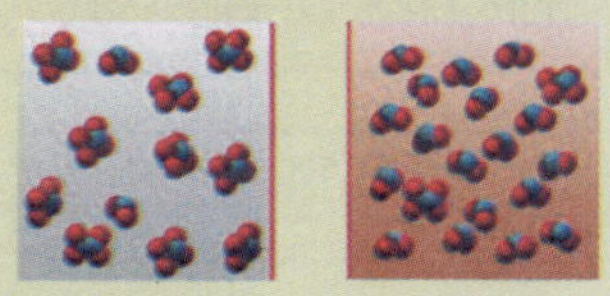

Lower temperature: N_2O_4 favored | Higher temperature: NO_2 favored

EFFECT OF CATALYST

- Catalyst does not affect the equilibrium constant and equilibrium position.

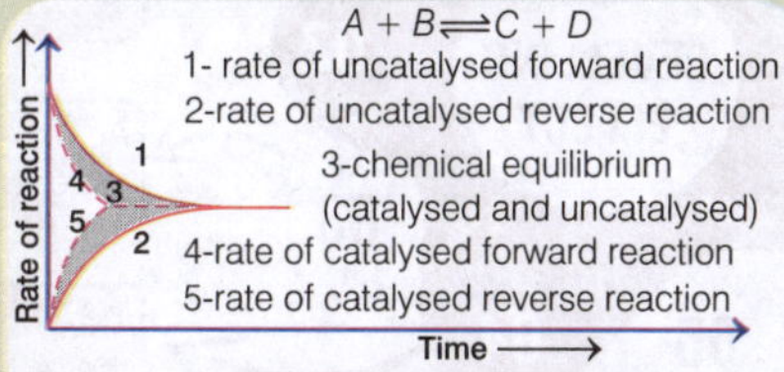

Effect of catalyst on Equilibrium

ELECTROLYTES

- The solutes which dissociate into ions when dissolved in water and conduct electricity.
- Extent of ionisation of electrolytes in solution differ.

Strong Electrolytes

- These are largely or completely dissociated in solution.
- The solution becomes very good conductor of electricity.
  e.g. HCl, H_2SO_4, HNO_3, NaOH, KOH, NaCl, KCl etc.

Weak Electrolytes

- Under ordinary conditions, they dissociate only to a small extent.
- The solution becomes a poor conductor of electricity.
  e.g. CH_3COOH, H_3PO_4, H_3BO_3, NH_4OH, HCN, etc.

Non-electrolytes

- A substance which does not produce ions when dissolved in water.
- The solution is a bad conductor of electricity.
  e.g. Urea, glucose, lactose, kerosene etc.

CONCEPT OF ACIDS AND BASES

OSTWALD DILUTION LAW

- The degree of dissociation of a weak electrolyte is inversely proportional to the square root of molar concentration.
- For a binary electrolyte AB:
  $AB \rightleftharpoons A^+ + B^-$
- Dissociation constant,
  $K = \frac{C\alpha^2}{(1-\alpha)}$
- For weak electrolyte:
  $K = C\alpha^2$ or $\alpha = \sqrt{\frac{K}{C}}$ $(\alpha < 5\%)$
  or $\alpha \propto \frac{1}{\sqrt{C}} \propto \sqrt{v}$

APPLICATIONS

To calculate the degree of dissociation (K) by determining degree of dissociation (α) from conductance measurement $\left(\frac{\lambda v}{\lambda \infty}\right)_C$

LIMITATIONS

This law holds good only in case of weak electrolytes.

01 ARRHENIUS THEORY

- Substances which give H^+ ions in aqueous solutions are acids.
- Substances which furnish OH^- ions in aqueous solutions are bases.
- Basicity is the number of H^+ ions delivered by an acid in its aqueous solution.

LIMITATIONS

- Free H^+ and OH^- ions do not exist in water.
- The concept of acids and base is limited to aqueous solutions only.

02 BRONSTED-LOWRY CONCEPT

- An acid is a substance that can donate a proton.
- An base is a substance that can accept a proton from an acid.

$HA + B \rightleftharpoons A^- + HB^+$

Acid, Base (Reactants); Conjugate base, Conjugate acid (Products)

Bronsted-Lowry Acid-Base Reaction

LIMITATIONS

- Cannot be used to explain the reactions in non-protonic solvents. BF_3, $AlCl_3$ etc., which do not have any hydrogen but are known to behave as acids.

03 LEWIS CONCEPT

- A base is a substance which can donate a pair of electrons or act as a nucleophile.
- An acid is a substance which can accept an electron pair.

Filled orbital, Vacant orbital

B (Lewis base) + A (Lewis acid) $\longrightarrow B—A$

LIMITATIONS

- It cannot explain the strength of acids and bases.
- Catalytic activity of Lewis acid cannot be explained.

IONISATION OF WATER

Pure water is a weak electrolyte:

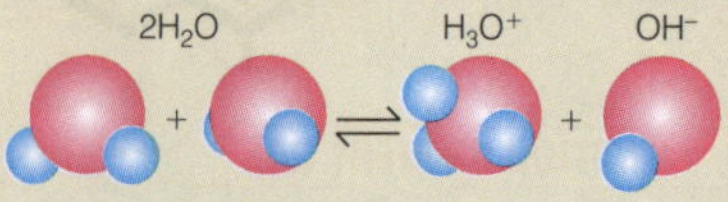

$2H_2O \rightleftharpoons H_3O^+ + OH^-$

- Equilibrium constant,
  $K = [H_3O^+][OH^-]/[H_2O]^2$
  $K_W = [H_3O^+][OH^-]$
  (as concentration of H_2O is high)
- For pure water at 298K,
  $[H_3O^+] = [OH^-] = 10^{-7}M$
- The ionic product of water at 298 K, $K_W = 10^{-14}$ mol^{2}L^{-2}
- The percentage dissociation of water is 1.8×10^{-7}.

Hard, Soft Acids And Bases (HSAB)

HARD ACIDS

- The acceptor atom has small size and high charge with no electron which are easily removed.
- e.g. H^+, Na^+, Be^{2+}, Cr^{3+}, Co^{3+}, Fe^{3+}, Ce^{3+}, As^{3+} BF_3, SO_3 etc.

HARD BASES

- Lewis bases that hold electrons strongly.
- e.g. H_2O, NH_3, OH^-, F^-, Cl^-, R_2O, RNH_2, etc.

SOFT ACIDS

- The acceptor atom has low charge with electrons which can be easily distorted.
- e.g. Pb^{2+}, Cd^{2+}, Pt^{3+}, Hg^{2+}, Cu^+, Br_2, metal atoms etc.

SOFT BASES

- Lewis bases from which electrons can be easily removed.
- e.g. R_2S, RHS, RS^-, I^-, R_3P, CO, C_2H_4, H^-, R^- etc.

Conjugate Acid Base Pair

- The acid-base pair which differ by a proton.
- The compounds which can mutually accept and donate hydrogen ions.

$CH_3COOH + H_2O \rightleftharpoons H_3O^+ + CH_3COO^-$

Acid, Base, Conjugate Acid, Conjugate base

		ACID	BASE		
100% ionised in H_2O	Strong	HCl	Cl^-	Negligible	
		H_2SO_4	HSO_4^-		
		HNO_3	NO_3^-		
		$H_3O^+(aq)$	H_2O		
Acid strength increases ↑	Weak	HSO_4^-	SO_4^{2-}	Weak	Base strength increases ↓
		H_3PO_4	$H_2PO_4^-$		
		HF	F^-		
		$HC_2H_3O_2$	$C_2H_3O_2^-$		
		H_2CO_3	HCO_3^-		
		H_2S	HS^-		
		$H_2PO_4^-$	HPO_4^{2-}		
		NH_4^+	NH_3		
		HCO_3^-	CO_3^{2-}		
		HPO_4^{2-}	PO_4^{3-}		
		H_2O	OH^-		
	Negligible	OH^-	O^{2-}	Strong	100% protonated in H_2O
		H_2	H^-		
		CH_4	CH_3^-		

STRENGTH OF ACIDS AND BASES

- Depends on their tendency to donate/accept the proton.
- Strong base has a weak conjugate acid and a weak base has a strong conjugate acid.

LEVELLING EFFECT

01. All strong acids or bases appear equally strong in water.
02. Strength of an acid depends upon the nature of solvent. $HClO_4$, H_2SO_4, HCl, HNO_3 – same strength in water. $HClO_4 > H_2SO_4 > HCl > HNO_3$ – in acetic acid
03. Acidic strength of hydracids in the same period increases across a period. $CH_4 < NH_3 < H_3O < HF$
04. The hydracids show a regular increase in strength down the group: $NH_3 < PH_3 < AsH_3 < SbH_3 < BiH_3$
05. The acidic character of oxyacids of same element increases with increase in number of oxygen atoms. $HClO < HClO_2 < HClO_3 < HClO_4$
06. The oxyacids of phosphorus. $H_3PO_2 < H_3PO_3 < H_3PO_4$
07. The acidic character of oxyacids of different elements which are in same oxidation state decreases with increase in atomic number. $HClO_4 > HBrO_4 > HIO_4$

pH SCALE

Negative logarithm of the concentration (in mol.L^{-1}) of hydrogen ions. pH = $-\log[H^+]$

$[H^+] = 1 \times 10^{-pH}$

Environmental effects	pH value	Examples
ACIDIC	pH = 0	Battery acid
	pH = 1	Sulphuric acid
	pH = 2	Lemon juice, Vinegar
	pH = 3	Orange juice, Soda
	pH = 4	Acid rain (4.2-4.4)
	pH = 5	Acidic lake (4.5) Bananas (5.0-5.3) Clean rain (5.6)
NEUTRAL	pH = 6	Healthy lake (6.5) Milk (6.5-6.8)
	pH = 7	Pure water
	pH = 8	Sea water, Eggs
	pH = 9	Baking soda
	pH = 10	Milk of Magnesia
	pH = 11	Ammonia
	pH = 12	Soapy water
	pH = 13	Bleach
BASIC	pH = 14	Liquid drain cleaner

pOH VALUE

- Negative logarithm of the concentration (in mol L^{-1}) of hydroxyl ions

$$[pOH] = -\log[OH^-];$$
$$[OH^-] = 1 \times 10^{-pOH}$$

RELATION BETWEEN pH AND pOH

- At 298K in aqueous solution:

$$[H^+][OH^-] = K_w = 1 \times 10^{-14};$$
$$pH + pOH = 14$$
$$pK_a + pK_b = pK_w = 14$$

- In case of pure water:

$$[H^+] = [OH^-] = 1 \times 10^{-7}$$
$$pH = pOH = 7$$

- In case of acidic solution:

  $[H^+] > [OH^-]$; pH < 7 and pOH > 7

  In case of alkaline solution:

  $[H^+] < [OH^-]$; pH > 7 and pOH < 7

LIMITATIONS OF pH SCALE

- Do not give immediate idea of the relative strengths of the solutions.
- Applicable to aqueous solutions only.

POWER TIPS

- pH of blood = 7.4
- pH of blood is maintained by buffer of carbonic acid H_2CO_3 and $NaHCO_3$. Range of buffer pH: pH = $pK_a \pm 1$
-

COMMON ION EFFECT

- The degree of dissociation of an electrolyte is suppressed by the addition of another electrolyte containing a common ion.
- Effect of common ion on solubility.

$$AgCl(s) \rightleftharpoons Ag^+(aq) + Cl^-(aq)$$
$$NaCl(s) \longrightarrow Na^+(aq) + Cl^-(aq)$$

Common ion

The concentration of Cl^- increase - equilibrium shifts towards left.

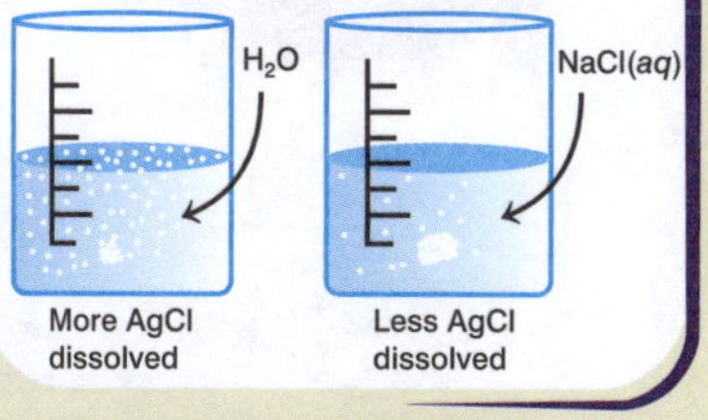

SOLUBILITY AND SOLUBILITY PRODUCT

Solubility (*S*)

- The concentration of substance in a saturated solution
- Depends on the solvent and temperature.

Solubility Product (K_{sp})

- For a general electrolyte A_xB_y:

$$A_xB_y \rightleftharpoons xA^{y+} + yB^{x-}$$
$$K_{sp} = [A^{y+}]^x[B^{x-}]^y = x^x y^y S^{x+y}$$

- It varies with temperature.

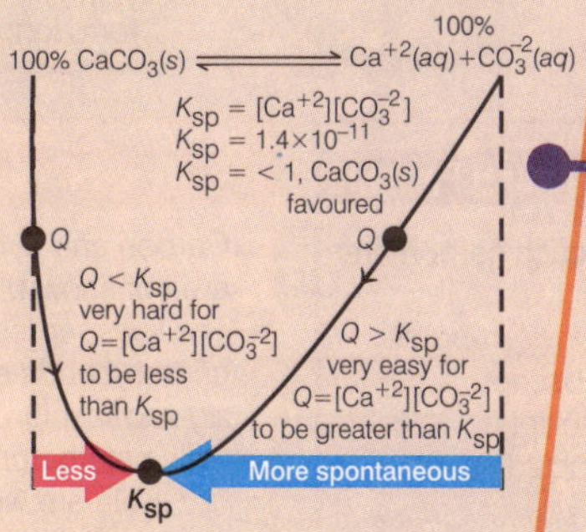

PREDICTING PRECIPITATE FORMATION FROM K_{sp}

- Ionic product (*Q*) is the product of concentration of ions.
- If $Q > K_{sp}$: precipitation occurs
- If $Q < K_{sp}$: no precipitation occurs
- If $Q = K_{sp}$: reaction is at equilibrium

SALT OF STRONG ACID AND WEAK BASES

- Halides, sulphates and nitrates of metals other than sodium and potassium.

$$BA \longrightarrow B^+ + A^-$$
$$B^+ + A^- + H_2O \rightleftharpoons BOH + H^+ + A^-$$

- Degree of hydrolysis, $h = \sqrt{\frac{K_w}{K_b \cdot C}}$
- $pH = 7 - \frac{1}{2}(pK_b + \log C)$ at 25°C
- pH <7, i.e. solution is acidic.

SALT OF STRONG ACID AND STRONG BASES

- Halides, sulphates, nitrates of sodium and potassium.

$$B^+ + A^- + H_2O \rightleftharpoons AB + H_2O$$

- No hydrolysis occurs.
- Solution remains neutral.
- The salt is stable in water and does not react with it to form the original acid or base.

SALT HYDROLYSIS

- Salt *BA* gets dissociated in aqueous solution:

$$\underset{\text{Salt}}{BA} + H_2O \rightleftharpoons \underset{\text{Acid}}{HA} + \underset{\text{Base}}{BOH}$$

- Hydrolysis constant:

$$K_h = \frac{[\text{Acid}]\,[\text{Base}]}{[\text{Salt}]}$$

SALT OF WEAK ACIDS AND WEAK BASES

- The salts other than halides, sulphates, nitrates of metals (other than sodium, potassium)

$$B^+ + A^- + H_2O \rightleftharpoons BOH + HA$$

- Degree of hydrolysis, $h = \sqrt{\frac{K_w}{K_a \cdot K_b}}$
- pH of solution, $7 + \frac{1}{2}(pK_a - pK_b)$ at 25°C

If $pK_a = pK_b$: pH = 7 (neutral); $pK_a > pK_b$: pH > 7 (basic)

$pK_a < pK_b$: pH < 7 (acidic)

SALT OF WEAK ACIDS AND STRONG BASES

- Salts of sodium and potassium other than halides, sulphates and nitrates.

$$B^+ + A^- + H_2O \rightleftharpoons HA + OH^- + B^+$$

- Degree of hydrolysis, $h = \sqrt{\frac{K_w}{K_a \cdot C}}$
- pH of solution, $= 7 + \frac{1}{2}(pK_a + \log C)$ at 25°C
- pH > 7, i.e. solution is basic.

ACIDIC BUFFER

- A weak acid with its salt of strong base.

  e.g. $CH_3COOH + CH_3COONa$

- Henderson-Hesselbalch equation:

$$pH = pK_a + \log\frac{[\text{salt}]}{[\text{acid}]}$$

BUFFER SOLUTION

It maintains its pH constant even upon addition of small amounts of acid or base.

BASIC BUFFER

- A weak base with its salt of strong acid.

  e.g. $NH_4OH + NH_4Cl$

- Henderson - Hesselbalch equation:

$$pOH = pK_b + \log\frac{[\text{salt}]}{[\text{base}]}$$
$$pH = 14 - pOH$$

Chapter 07

Organic Chemistry : Some Basic Principles and Techniques

FUNDAMENTALS OF CARBON

TETRAVALENCY

- Carbon has four valence electrons.
- It allows carbon to form four covalent bonds with other atoms such as hydrogen, oxygen, nitrogen etc.
- The ability to form four stable, directional bonds makes carbon versatile.

CATENATION

- Ability of carbon atoms to bond with each other.
- It results in the formation of long chains, branched chains or rings.
- The catenation tendency of C, Si and Ge is in the order Ge < Si < C.

SHAPES OF CARBON COMPOUNDS

- Hybridisation influences the shapes of molecules besides the bond length and bond enthalpy.
- *sp* hybrid orbitals contain more *s*-character and forms shorter bonds.
- sp^3 hybrid orbitals contain more *p*-character and form longer bonds.

STRUCTURAL REPRESENTATION OF ORGANIC COMPOUND

Complete Structural Formula

- Every bond formed between every atoms in the compound are explicitly shown.

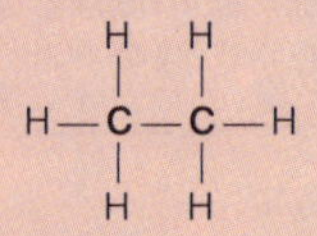
(Ethane)

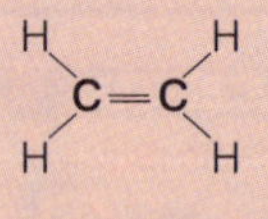
(Ethene)

$H-C\equiv C-H$ **(Ethyne)**

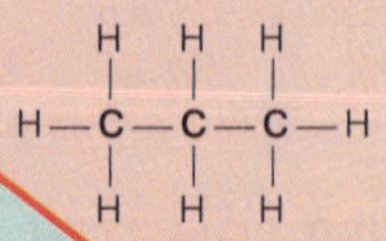
(Propane)

Condensed Structural Formula

- The bonds to each carbon are omitted.
- Each distinct unit (group) is written with subscript designating multiple substituents, including hydrogens.

CH_3CH_3 **(Ethane)**

$CH_2=CH_2$ **(Ethene)**

$HC\equiv CH$ **(Ethyne)**

Bond Line Formula

- Carbon and hydrogen atoms are not shown.
- The lines representing carbon-carbon bonds are shown in *zig-zag* fashion.
- Only heteroatoms such as O, Cl, Na are written.

(Butane)

(But-2-ene)

(But-1-yne)

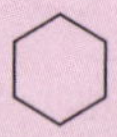
(Cyclohexane)

(Furan)

3D Representation of Organic Compound

- It can be represented on paper (2-dimensional) by using wedge (▬) and dash (┅) in the formula.

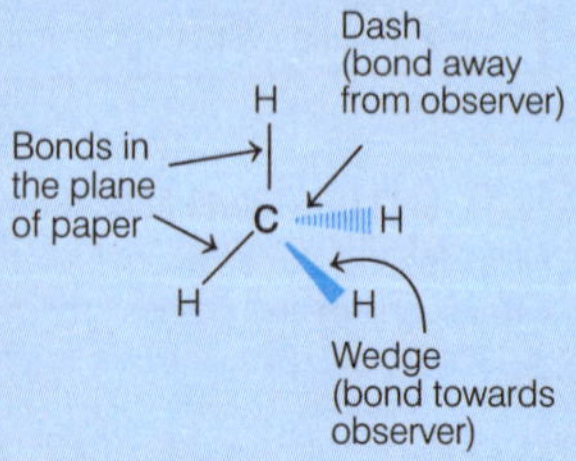

SYSTEMS OF NOMENCLATURE OF ORGANIC COMPOUNDS

Trivial System

These names are based on source or some important property.
e.g. Citric acid (derived from citrus).

IUPAC System

The name of an organic compound consists of following components :
Primary prefix + Secondary prefix + Root word + Primary suffix + Secondary suffix

Steps for writing IUPAC names

- Choose the longest possible chain with as many as possible secondary functional groups along with multiple bond.
- Select the word root corresponding to the length of longest possible chain.
- Number the longest possible chain in accordance to lowest set of locants and the order of priority of various functional groups.
- Add suitable prefixes and suffixes to indicate the number and position of each side chain, substituent or functional group.

Note:- Suffix-2 will used when carbon of functional group is not present in main chain.

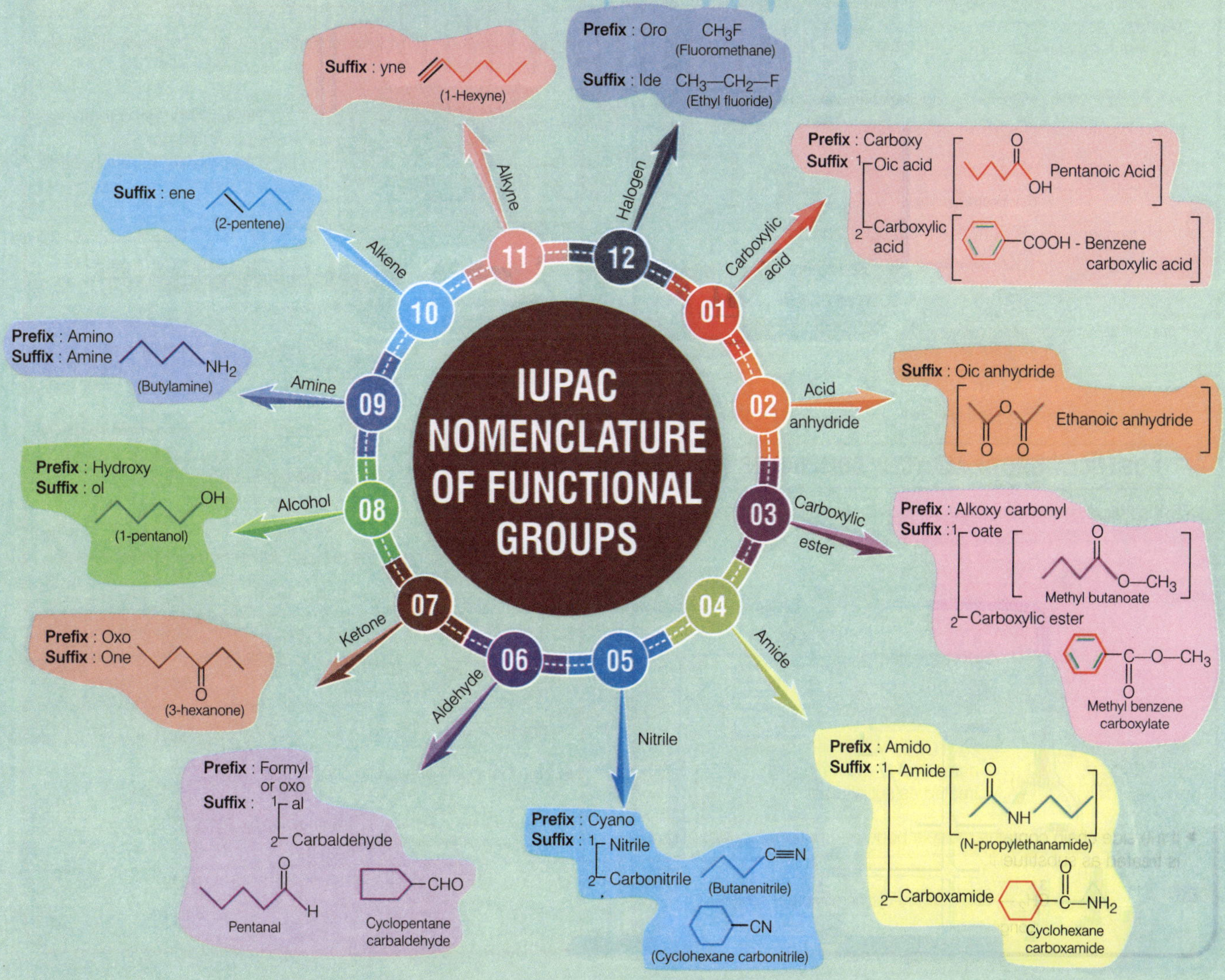

Nomenclature of Complex Locant

Complex locant is defined as which consist of substituent in substituent.

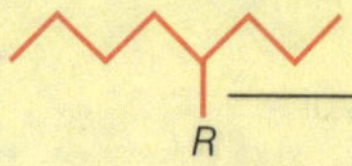

S.No.	Complex Locant	Common Name	IUPAC Name
1.	$-CH(CH_3)-CH_3$	*iso*-propyl	1-methyl ethyl
2.	$-CH(CH_3)-CH_2-CH_3$	*sec*-butyl	1-methyl propyl
3.	$CH_3-CH(CH_3)-CH_3$	*iso*-butyl	2-methyl propyl
4.	$CH_3-C(CH_3)_2-$	*tert*-butyl	1, 1-dimethyl ethyl
5.	$CH_3-C(CH_3)_2-CH_2-$	*neo*-pentyl	2, 2-dimethyl propyl

NOMENCLATURE OF CYCLIC COMPOUNDS

Nomenclature of Aromatic Compounds

- The use of *ortho* (o–), *meta* (m–) or *para* (p–) is avoided in IUPAC names.
- If two different alkyl group are attached to the benzene ring :

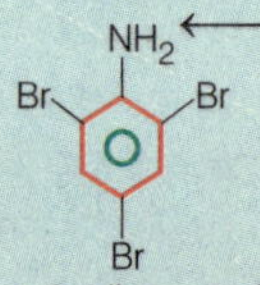

2, 4, 6- tribromoaniline

- If the benzene ring is attached to an open chain :

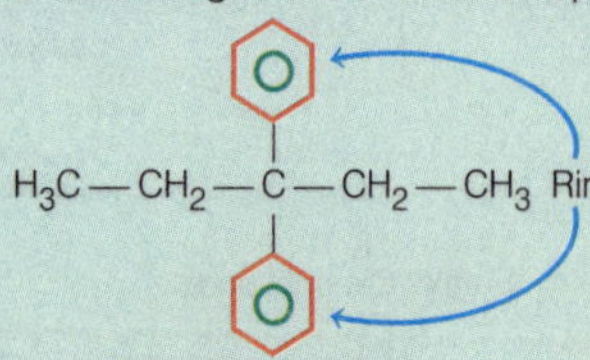

3, 3-biphenyl pentane

NOMENCLATURE OF ALICYCLIC COMPOUNDS

- Substituted cycloalkanes are named as alkyl cycloalkanes.

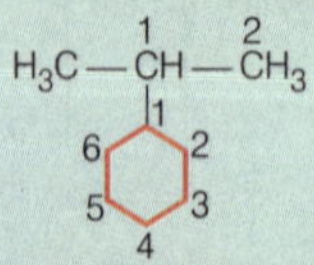

1-(1-methyl)-ethyl cyclohexane

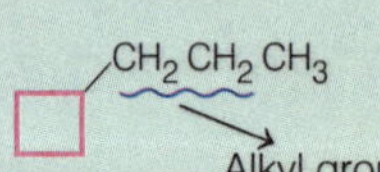

(Propyl cyclobutane)

Alkyl group with lesser or equal number of C-atoms in ring treated as substituent

- If the side chain contains multiple bond or functional group, ring is treated as substituent.

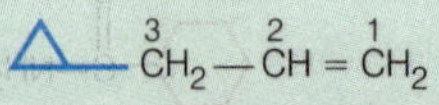

3-cyclopropylprop-1-ene

Longest chain

NOMENCLATURE OF BI AND POLYCYCLIC COMPOUNDS

- Unbranched assemblies consisting of two or more identical ring systems:

1, 1′ 3′, 1″ tercyclobutane

Prefix — bi, ter, quater, quiniques etc. Used before parent hydride.

- Unbranched assemblies containing unidentical ring:

Cyclopropyl cyclopentane

Smaller ring is treated as a substituent.

- Spiro union is a linkage between two rings consisting of single atom common to both.
- Numbering of spiro compounds :

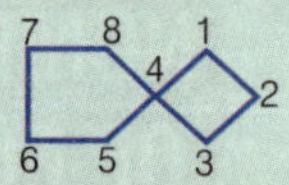

Spiro [3, 4] octane

Starts from ring atom next to the spiro atom in the smaller ring into the larger ring.

- Saturated homogeneous bicyclic systems having two or more atoms in common :

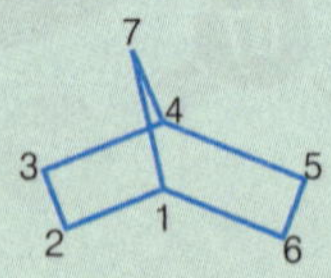

Bicyclo [2, 2,1] heptane

Prefix — bi, tri, cyclo is used to the name of parent acyclic hydride.

- Numbering in polycyclic ring system:

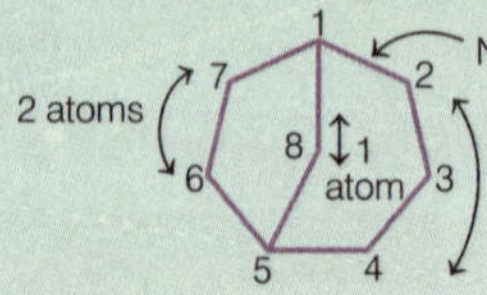

ISOMERISM

- The phenomenon of compounds having same molecular formula but difference in properties.
- The difference in properties is due to difference in structural formula and spatial arrangement of atoms.

1 STRUCTURAL ISOMERISM

CHAIN ISOMERISM

- Due to difference in the order in which carbon atoms are bonded to each other.
- e.g. $CH_3-CH_2-CH_2-CH_2-CH_3$ (*n*-pentane) and $CH_3-C(CH_3)_2-CH_3$ (2, 2-dimethyl propane)

POSITION ISOMERISM

- Due to difference in the position of substitutent or functional group or atom in the same chain.
- e.g. $CH_3CH_2CH=CH_2$ (But-1-ene) and $CH_3CH=CH-CH_3$ (But-2-ene)

FUNCTIONAL ISOMERISM

- Due to difference in functional group.
- e.g. CH_3CH_2OH (Ethyl alcohol) and CH_3OCH_3 (Dimethyl ether)

METAMERISM

- Due to difference in the nature of some alkyl group attached to the polyvalent functional group.
- e.g. $CH_3CH_2-C(=O)-CH_2CH_3$ (Pentan-3 one) and $CH_3-C(=O)-CH_2-CH_2CH_3$ (Pentan-2 one)

TAUTOMERISM

- Due to wandering nature of hydrogen atom in between two polyvalent atoms.
- Tautomers always exist in dynamic equilibrium.

e.g. $NH_2-C(=O)-NH_2 \underset{OH^-}{\overset{H^+}{\rightleftharpoons}} NH=C(OH)-NH_2$

Keto — Enol

RING CHAIN ISOMERISM

- Due to open chain structure of one isomer and cyclic structure of the other isomers.
- e.g. $CH_3-CH=CH_2$ (Propene) and CH_2-CH_2 / CH_2 (Cyclopropane)

ISOTOPIC ISOMERISM

- Due to the presence of different isotopes of an element.
- e.g. $^{12}CH_4$ and $^{14}CH_4$

2 STEREOISOMERISM

Stereoisomerism occurs due to difference in three dimensional arrangement of atoms or configuration.

GEOMETRICAL ISOMERISM

- Due to restriction of free rotation around π bond in alkene $(>C=C<)$, oximes $(>C=N)$, azo compounds $(-N=N-)$
- The restriction in rotation is also frozen about carbon-carbon single bond in cycloalkanes (△).
- They are of two types, i.e. *cis* and *trans*.

e.g.

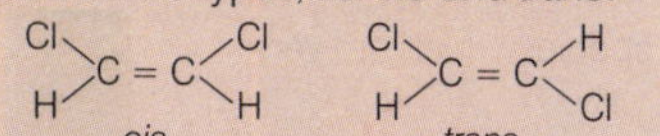

cis — *trans*

- *E*, *Z* notation is used for different substituents

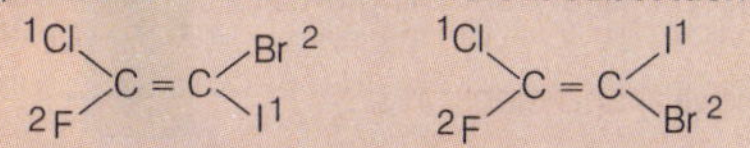

E (same priority groups onopposite side) — *Z* (same priority group on same side)

OPTICAL ISOMERISM

- Occurs in substances with same molecular and structural formula but differ in behaviour towards plane polarised light.
- Enantiomers are non-superimposable mirror images of a compound.

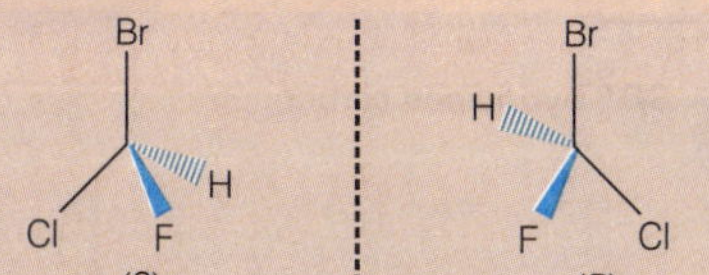

(*S*) — (*R*)

- Diastereoisomers are compounds with at least two chiral centers having different configuration in at least one of those centers.

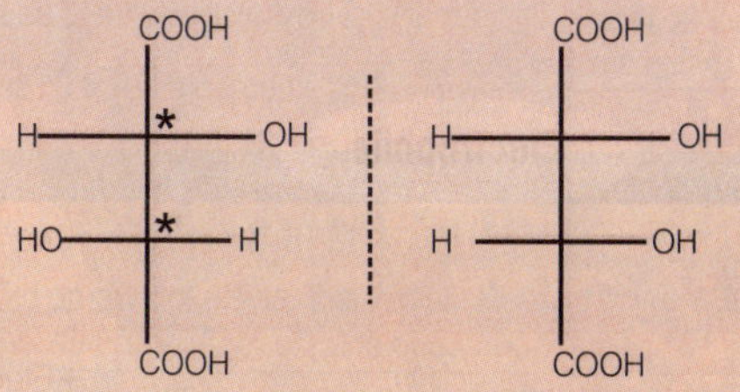

- *Meso* compounds have a plane of symmetry and are optically inactive.

Number of Stereoisomers

In unsymmetrical molecule

- Number of enantiomer $= 2^n$
- *Meso* form = 0
- Total optical isomer $= 2^n$

In symmetrical molecule

Meso form $= 2^{\frac{(n-1)}{2}}$

when *n* is even

No. of enantiomer $= 2^{(n-1)}$

Meso form $= 2^{\frac{(n-1)}{2}}$

when *n* is odd

No. of enantiomer $= 2^{(n-1)} - 2^{(n/2-1/2)}$

CLEAVAGE OF COVALENT BOND

Homolytic Fission

- Each atom takes away one electron of the shared pair.

$$A - B \xrightarrow{\text{Homolysis}} \dot{A} + \dot{B}$$

Free radicals

- It takes place in gaseous phase or in the presence of non-polar solvents (CCl_4, CS_2).
- Presence of peroxides, UV light, heat (≥ 500°C) also favour homolysis.

Heterolytic Fission

- Both the electrons of shared pair are taken by one of the bonded atoms

$$X - Y \xrightarrow{\text{Heterolysis}} X^+ + Y^-$$

(X is less electronegative than Y)

- It is observed in compounds with polar covalent bonds.
- It is favoured by polar solvents.

POWER TIPS

Other Intermediates

- Carbene – 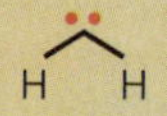
- Nitrene – $R—\ddot{N}:$
- Benzyne – 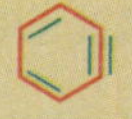

REACTION INTERMEDIATE

01 Carbocation

- Chemical species bearing positive charge on carbon and carry six electrons in its valence shell.
- Planar species (sp^2 hybridised) with an empty p-orbital.
- Electrophilic and lewis acids.
- The stability of carbocation : 3° > 2° > 1°.

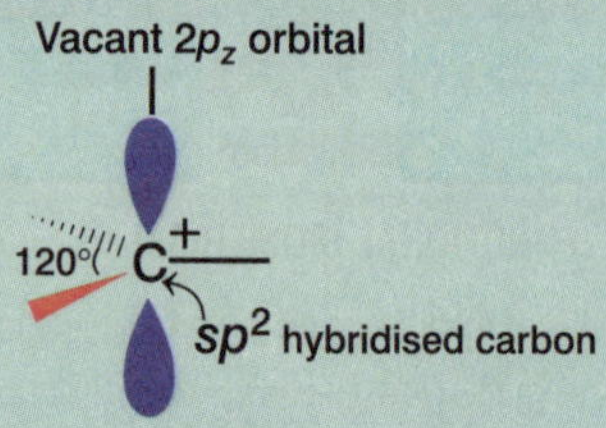

02 Carbanion

- Chemical species bearing negative charge on carbon and carry eight electrons in its valence shell.
- Pyramidal species (sp^3 hybridised).
- Nucleophilic and lewis base.
- The stability of carbanion : 1° > 2° > 3°.

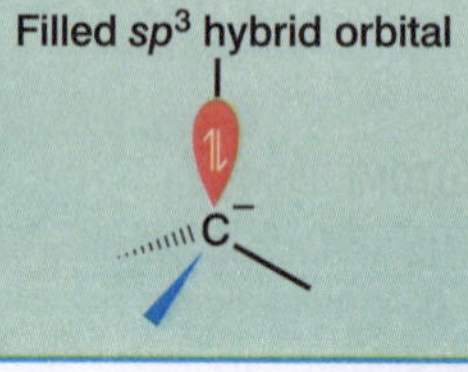

03 Free Radical

- Odd electron species which are very reactive.
- Planar species (sp^2 hybridised) with an unhybridised orbital containing an odd electron.
- Electrically neutral and electron deficient.
- The order of stability :

$Ph_3C^\bullet > Ph_2\dot{C}H > Ph\dot{C}H_2 > 3° > 2° > 1° > \dot{C}H_3$

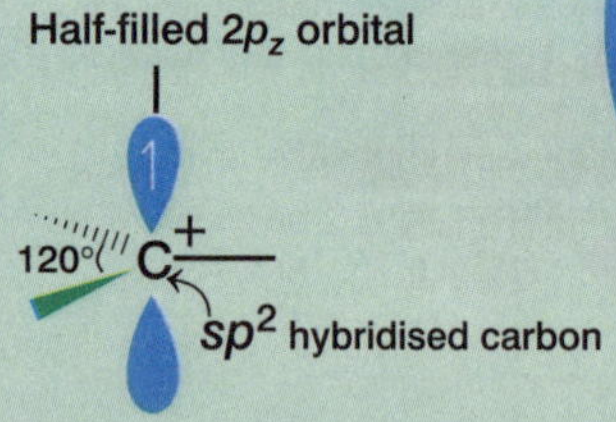

REAGENT OR ATTACKING SPECIES

01 Electrophile

- Electron deficient species.
- Behaves as Lewis acids.
- It can be both positively charged and neutral.
- Positively charged electrophiles H^+, Cl^+, Br^+, I^+, NO_2^+ etc.
- Neutral electrophiles CR_2, NR, $AlCl_3$, BF_3 etc.

02 Nucleophile

- Electron rich species.
- Behaves as Lewis bases.
- It can be negatively charged or neutral.
- Negatively charged nucleophiles H^-, OH^-, X^-, CN^-, N_3^-,
- RO^-, R^-, RS^-, SH^-, NO_2^-, NH_2^-, $HC \equiv C^-$, $RCOO^-$
- Neutral nucleophiles NH_3, H_2O, ROH, RSH, $RMgX$, Ph_3P, RLi, $LiAlH_4$ etc.

03 Ambiphile

- Behaves both as electrophile and nucleophiles.
- They contain a multiple bond as well as a more electronegative atom.

e.g.

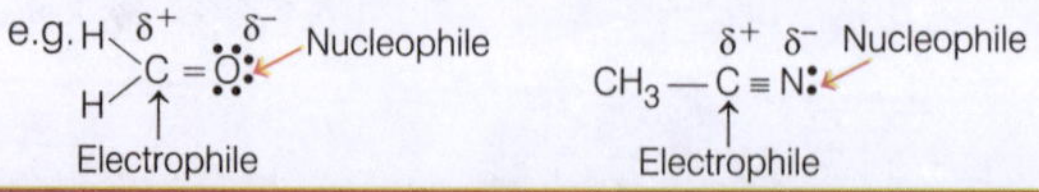

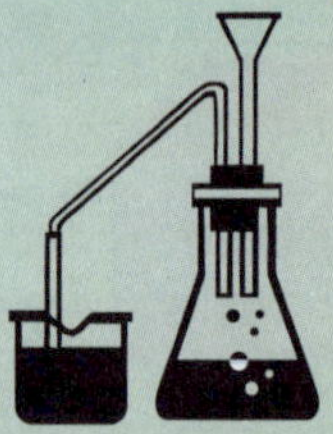

ELECTRON DISPLACEMENT EFFECT

Inductive Effect

- Polarity produced in a molecule due to the presence of a polar bond.
- Order of decreasing strength of –*I* effect due to EWG :

$-NO_2 > -CN > -COOH > -F > -Cl > -Br > -I$

- Order of decreasing strength of +*I* effect due to EDG :
$(CH_3)_3C- > (CH_3)_2CH- > CH_3CH_2- > CH_3- > H$

Electromeric Effect

- The transfer of two π electrons to any one of the bonded atoms, when π bond is exposed to a reagent.
  - **+ *E* effect** $CH_3-CH=CH_2 + H^+ \longrightarrow CH_3-\overset{\oplus}{C}H-CH_3$
  - **– *E* effect** $>C=O + \overset{\ominus}{C}N \longrightarrow >C(CN)-O^-$

Hyperconjugation

Stabilising interaction from the delocalisation of σ bond (usually C—H or C—C) with an adjacent empty or partially filled *p*-orbital or a π orbital.

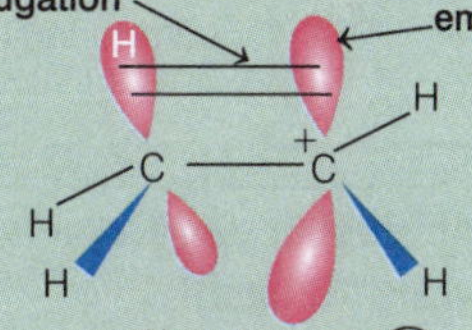

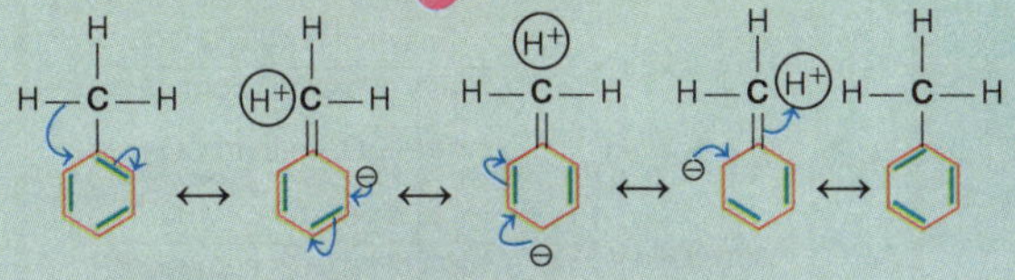

Resonance or Mesomeric Effect

- Polarity produced in a molecule due to conjugation of two π bonds or between a π bond and a lone pair.
  - **+ *R* or + *M* effect groups**
    —OH, —O*R*, —OCO*R*, —SH, —S*R*, —NH_2, —NH*R*
  - **– *R* or – *M* effect groups**
    —COOH, —CO, —CHO, —COO*R*, —CN, —NO_2

TYPES OF ORGANIC REACTIONS

Addition Reaction

- Reactions involving the combination of reacting molecules to given single product.
  - **Free radical (in presence of peroxides)**
    $R-CH=CH_2 + HBr \xrightarrow{ROOR} RCH_2CH_2Br$ (Anti-Markovnikov)
  - **Ionic**
    - **Nucleophilic addition:**
      $H_2\overset{\delta+}{C}=\overset{\delta-}{O} + \overset{\ominus}{C}N \longrightarrow H_2C(CN)-O^{\ominus} + H^+ \longrightarrow H_2C(CN)-OH$
    - **Electrophilic addition:**
      $CH_3-CH=CH_2 + H-Br \rightarrow CH_3-\overset{\oplus}{C}H-CH_3 + Br^{\ominus} \rightarrow CH_3-CH(Br)-CH_3$ (Markovnikov)

Elimination Reaction

- α-**elimination** Loss of two atoms or groups from the same atom of the substrate.
  e.g. $HO^{\ominus} + HCCl_2Cl \longrightarrow :CCl_2 + H_2O + Cl^-$
  $:CCl_2$ is an intermediate in carbylamine and Reimer-Tiemann reaction.
- β-**elimination** Loss of two atoms or groups from the adjacent atoms of the substrate.
  e.g. $H-CH_2-CH_2-OH \xrightarrow[\Delta]{Conc.H_2SO_4} CH_2=CH_2 + H_2O$

Rearrangment Reaction

Involves migration of an atom or a group within the same molecule

$CH_3-CH_2-CH_2-CH_2-Br \xrightarrow{Anhy.\ AlCl_3} CH_3CH_2-CH(Br)-CH_3$

Substitution Reaction

- Replacement of an atom or group of atom by another atom or group of atoms.
- Based on intermediate species:
  - **Free radical substitution:**
    $2R-Br \xrightarrow{Na} R-R$ (Wurtz reaction)
  - **Ionic**
    - **Electrophilic substitution:**

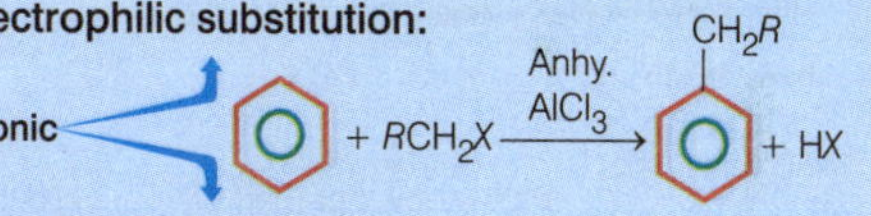

- **Nucleophilic substitution:**

S_N1

- First order, unimolecular, two step reaction

(i) $CH_3-C(CH_3)_2-X \overset{Slow}{\rightleftharpoons} CH_3-\overset{\oplus}{C}(CH_3)_2 + X^{\ominus}$

(ii) $CH_3-\overset{\oplus}{C}(CH_3)_2 + Nu^{\ominus} \xrightarrow{Fast} CH_3-C(CH_3)_2-Nu$

The order of reactivity of *RX*:
Benzyl > allyl > 3° > 2° > 1° > Me

S_N2

- Second order, bimolecular, one step reaction

$H-CH_2-X + Nu^{\ominus} \longrightarrow Nu-CH_2-H$

- The order of reactivity of *RX*: Me > 1° > 2° > 3°

CHEMICAL ANALYSIS OF ELEMENTS

QUALITATIVE ANALYSIS

Detection of Carbon and Hydrogen

- $C + 2CuO \longrightarrow CO_2 + 2Cu$
- $2H + CuO \xrightarrow{\Delta} Cu + H_2O$
- $\underset{\text{White}}{CuSO_4} + 5H_2O \longrightarrow \underset{\text{Hydrated copper sulphate (blue)}}{CuSO_4.5H_2O}$
- $Ca(OH)_2 + CO_2 \longrightarrow \underset{\text{Milky}}{CaCO_3 \downarrow} + H_2O$

Detection of Nitrogen

- **Sodalime test**

$CH_3CONH_2 + \underset{\text{Sodalime}}{NaOH + CaO} \longrightarrow CH_3COO^- Na^+ + NH_3\uparrow$

- **Using Lassaigne's test**

Lassaigne extract: $Na + C + N \xrightarrow{\Delta} \overset{+}{Na}\overset{-}{C} \equiv N$

(i) $2NaCN + FeSO_4 \longrightarrow Na_2SO_4 + Fe(CN)_2$

(ii) $Fe(CN)_2 + 4\,NaCN \longrightarrow Na_4\,[Fe(CN)_6]$

(iii) $3Na_4\,[Fe(CN)_6] + 4\,FeCl_3 \longrightarrow \underset{\text{Ferric ferrocyanide (Prussian blue)}}{Fe_4\,[Fe(CN)_6]_3.xH_2O} + 12\,NaCl$

Detection of Sulphur

- $Na_2S + (CH_3COO)_2\,Pb \xrightarrow{H^+} \underset{\text{Black ppt.}}{PbS \downarrow} + 2CH_3COO^-Na^+$
- $Na_2S + \underset{\text{Sodium nitroprusside sol.}}{Na_2\,[Fe(CN)_5\,NO]} \longrightarrow \underset{\text{Purple colours}}{Na_4\,[Fe(CN)_5\,NOS]}$
- Purple colour confirms the presence of S.

Detection of Halogens

$Na + X \longrightarrow NaX$ (soda extract) [X=Cl,Br,I]

$NaCl + AgNO_3$	$NaBr + AgNO_3$	$AgNO_3 + NaI$
↓	↓	↓
$AgCl\downarrow + NaNO_3$	$AgBr\downarrow + NaNO_3$	$AgI\downarrow + NaNO_3$
White ppt.(soluble in NH_4OH)	Pale yellow ppt.(Partially soluble in NH_4OH)	yellow ppt. (Insoluble in NH_4OH)

Detection of Phosphorus

- Compound is fused with sodium peroxide.

$5Na_2O_2 + 2P \longrightarrow 2Na_3\,PO_4 + 2Na_2O$

(i) $Na_3PO_4 + 3HNO_3 \longrightarrow H_3PO_4 + 3\,NaNO_3$

(ii) $H_3PO_4 + 12\,(NH_4)_2\,MoO_4 + 21\,HNO_3 \longrightarrow \underset{\text{Yellow ppt.}}{(NH_4)_3\,PO_4.12\,MoO_3 \downarrow} + 21\,NH_4NO_3 + 12\,H_2O$

QUANTITATIVE ANALYSIS

Estimation of Carbon and Hydrogen (Liebig Method)

- $\% \text{ of carbon} = \dfrac{12 \times \text{mass of } CO_2 \times 100}{44 \times \text{mass of organic compound}}$
- $\% \text{ of hydrogen} = \dfrac{2 \times \text{mass of } H_2O \times 100}{18 \times \text{mass of organic compound}}$

Estimation of Halogen (Carius Method)

- Organic compound is heated in a sealed tube with fuming HNO_3 in the presence of $AgNO_3$.
- $\% \text{ of chlorine} = \dfrac{35.5}{143.5} \times \dfrac{\text{mass of AgCl}}{\text{mass of compound}} \times 100$

Estimation of Sulphur and Oxygen (Carius Method)

- $\% \text{ of sulphur} = \dfrac{32}{233} \times \dfrac{\text{mass of } BaSO_4 \times 100}{\text{mass of organic compound}}$
- CO is passed through warm I_2O_5 to form CO_2.
- $\% \text{ of oxygen} = \dfrac{32}{44} \times \dfrac{\text{mass of } CO_2 \times 100}{\text{mass of organic compound}}$

Estimation of Phosphorus

- Organic compound $\xrightarrow[HNO_3]{\Delta} \xrightarrow[MgCl_2,\ NH_4Cl/NH_4OH]{\Delta}$ $MgNH_4PO_4 \xrightarrow{\text{Dry } \Delta} Mg_2P_2O_7$
- $\% \text{ of P} = \dfrac{62}{222} \times \dfrac{\text{mass of } Mg_2P_2O_7 \times 100}{\text{mass of organic compound}}$

TEST FOR NITROGEN

KJELDAHL'S METHOD

Nitrogeneous compound is heated with conc. H_2SO_4 in the presence of potassium sulphate and $CuSO_4$.

$\% \text{ of N} = \dfrac{1.4 \times N \times V}{m}$

N = Normality of acid
V = Volume of acid
m = Mass of organic compound

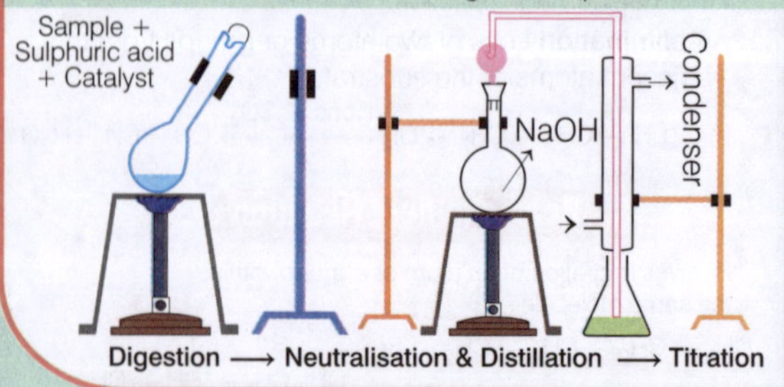

DUMA'S METHOD

- Organic compound is heated with dry copper oxide in a combustion tube in presence of CO_2.
- The volume of N_2 evolved is recorded with Schiff's nitrometer tube.

Oxides of $N + Cu \longrightarrow N_2 + CuO$

$\% \text{ of N} = \dfrac{28V \times 100}{22400 \times m}$

V = volume of N_2 at STP
m = mass of organic compound

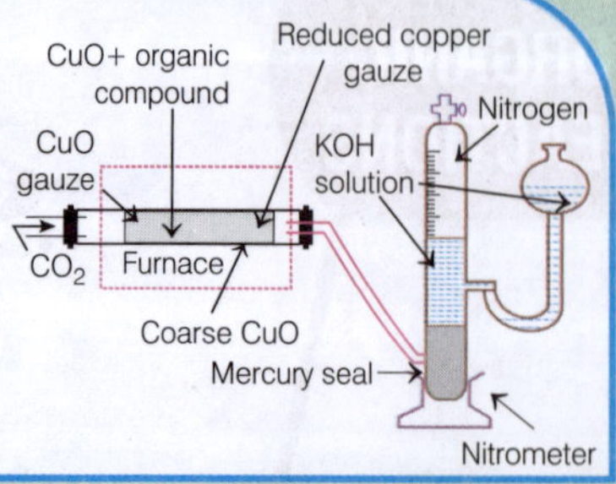

METHODS OF PURIFICATION

DISTILLATION

- Based upon the difference in the boiling points of two liquids.
- Generally used to separate volatile liquids from non-volatile in purities.

Fractional Distillation

- Used for the separation of two liquids having nearly equal boiling points (within the limit of 10 to15 K).
- Acetone (b.p. ~ 329 K) and methyl alcohol (b.p. ~ 338 K) are separated through this method.

Steam Distillation

- Used to purify the substance which are volatile in steam but are immiscible with water (contain non-volatile impurities).
- *Ortho* and *para* nitrophenol are purified or obtained by this process.

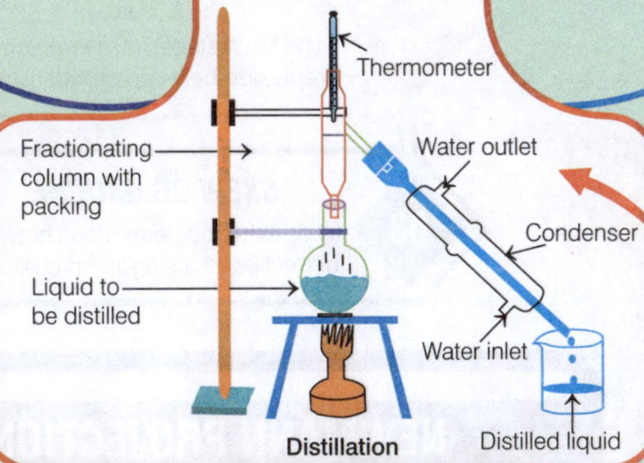

Distillation

SUBLIMATION

- Process employed for those solids which convert directly into vapour on heating.

$$\text{Solid} \underset{\text{Cool}}{\overset{\text{Heat}}{\rightleftharpoons}} \text{Vapour}$$

- e.g. Impure samples of naphthalene, anthracene, camphor, benzoic acid, NH_4Cl, $HgCl_2$ etc.provided the impurities are non-volatile.

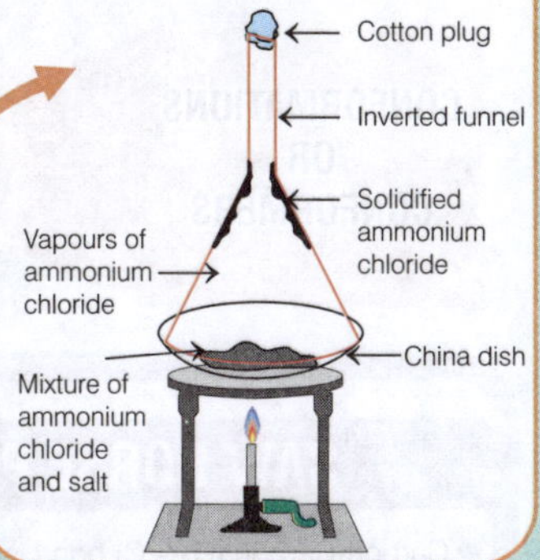

POWER TIPS

Distillation Under Reduced Pressure

- Used to purify liquids having very high boiling points.
- Such liquids decompose at or below their boiling points.
- At 12 mm of Hg pressure, glycerol boils at 453 K without decomposition.

CHROMATOGRAPHY

Based on the principle of differential affinities of components of a mixture for a stationary and a mobile phase.

1 Adsorption Chromatography

- **Separates compounds based on their tendency to adhere to a solid stationary phase.**
- Silica gel or alumina are commonly used adsorbents.

2 Column Chromatography

- Separate compounds by passing a mixture through a column filled with a solid adsorbent.
- e.g. Mixture of naphthalene and benzophenone.

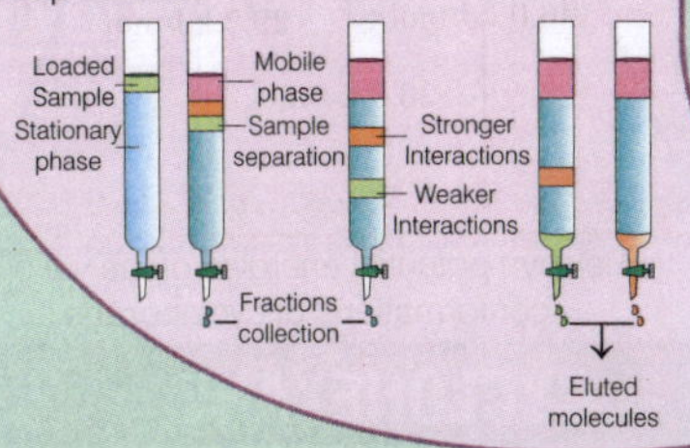

3 Partition Chromatography

- Separate compounds based on their distribution between two liquid phases- one stationary and one mobile.

4 Paper Chromatography

- Separates compounds by moving solvent (mobile phase) through paper (stationary phase). Different components travel at different speeds, resulting in separation.
- e.g. Sugar is separated from amino acid.

$$R_f = \frac{\text{Distance moved by the component of mixture from base line}}{\text{Distance moved by mobile phase}}$$

5 Thin Layer Chromatography (TLC)

- Separating compounds by applying a mixture to a thin layer of adsorbent on a flat plate.
- Amino acids are detected using ninhydrin solution using TLC.

CRYSTALLISATION

- Based on the difference in the solubilities of the compound and impurities in a suitable solvent.
- Sugar having common salt (impurity) can be crystallised through hot ethanol.

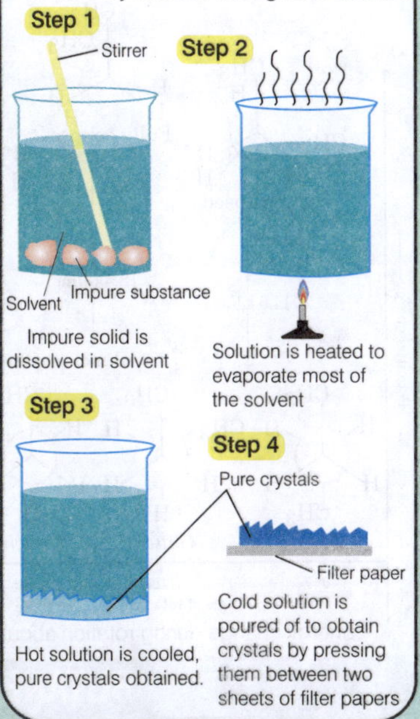

Chapter **08**

Hydrocarbons

ALKANES

- Homologous series made of saturated hydrocarbons, containing carbon and hydrogen atoms joined by sigma bonds.
- They are also known as **Paraffins** due to low reactivity. General formula: C_nH_{2n+2}
- Each carbon is sp^3 hybridised with bond angle 109°28′.
- Nomenclature: Root word + ane = Name of alkane. They mainly exhibit chain and conformational isomerism.

PHYSICAL PROPERTIES

- First four alkanes are gases, next thirteen are colourless liquids and rest higher ones are waxy solids.
- These are
  - insoluble in polar solvents (water)
  - soluble in non-polar solvents (alcohols, ethers, benzene)
- Their solubility decreases with increase in molecular weight.
- Dipole moments of all alkanes is zero.

POWER TIPS

➤ Stability order of conformers:
Staggered > *Skew* > Eclipsed > Fully eclipsed

CONFORMATIONS OR CONFORMERS

Definite infinite arrangement of atoms that can be converted into one another by rotation about single bonds.

01 STAGGERED
The most stable form in which groups are at maximum distance apart.

02 ECLIPSED
The least stable form in which the repulsion between groups is maximum.

03 SKEW OR GAUCHE
All possible conformations between fully eclipsed a staggered conformations.

REPRESENTATION

SAW HORSE PROJECTION

- Carbon-Carbon (C — C) bond is viewed from an oblique angle.
- All carbon-hydrogen (C — H) bonds are shown

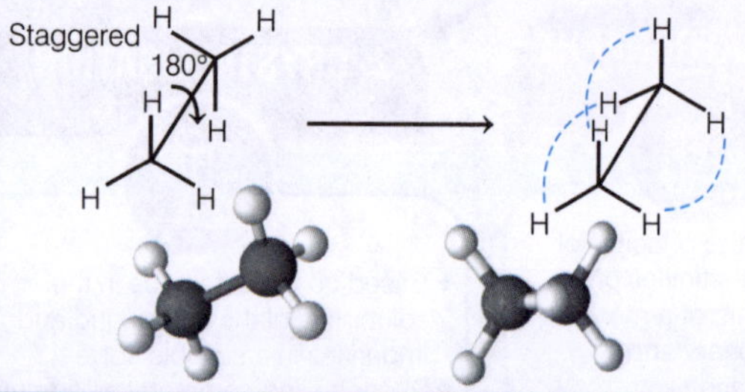

NEWMANN PROJECTION

- The C — H bonds of the front carbon are depicted from the centre of the point.
- The C — H bonds of the back carbon are drawn from the circumference of the circle.

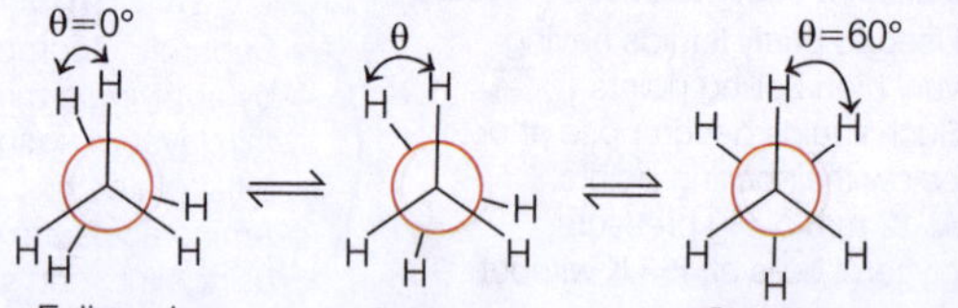

STABILITY OF CONFORMATIONS

Energy $\propto \frac{1}{\text{Stability}}$

BUTANE

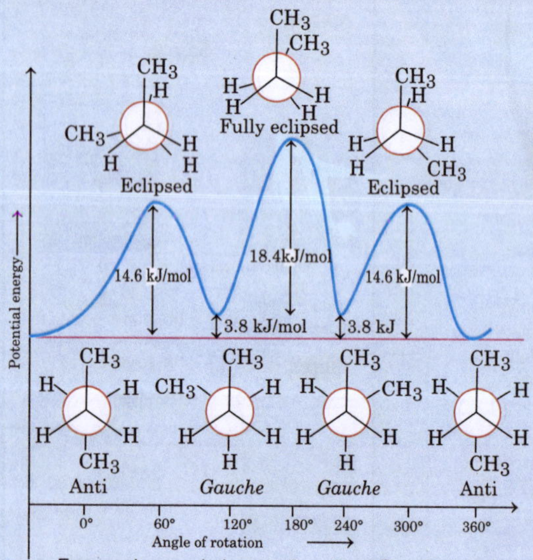

Energy change during rotation about $C_2 - C_3$ bond of *n*-butane

CYCLOHEXANE

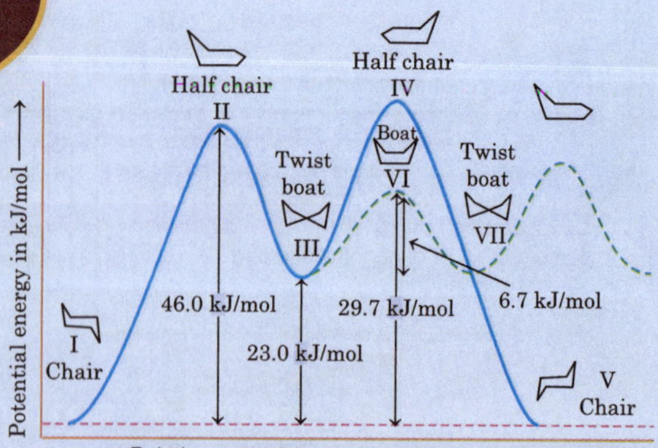

Relative potential energies of the various conformations of cyclohexane.

METHODS OF PREPARATION OF ALKANES

REDUCTION

Alcohols, Carboxylic Acids Their Derivatives and Alkyl Halides

- $CH_3COOH + 6HI \xrightarrow[425\ K]{Red\ P} CH_3-CH_3 + 2H_2O + 3I_2$
- $CH_3CH_2OH + 2HI \xrightarrow[425\ K]{Red\ P} CH_3-CH_3 + H_2O + I_2$
- $C_2H_5I + HI \xrightarrow{Red\ P} C_2H_6 + I_2$

Carbonyl Compounds (Aldehydes and Ketones)

- $>C=O + 6HI \xrightarrow[425\ K]{Red\ P} >CH_2 + H_2O + 3I_2$
- **CLEMMENSEN REDUCTION**

  $>C=O + [H] \xrightarrow[Conc.HCl]{Zn(Hg)} >CH_2 + H_2O$
- **WOLFF-KISHNER REDUCTION**

  $>C=O + NH_2NH_2 \xrightarrow{-H_2O} >C=N-NH_2 \xrightarrow[-N_2]{C_2H_5ONa} >CH_2$

Hydrogenation or Catalytic Reduction (Sabatier-Sanderens Reaction)

$HC\equiv CH \xrightarrow[Ni/250°C]{H_2} H_2C=CH_2 \xrightarrow[Ni/250°C]{H_2} H_3C-CH_3$

Decarboxylation

$RCOO^-Na^+ + NaOH/CaO \xrightarrow{\Delta} RH + Na_2CO_3$

Kolbe's Electrolytic Method

$$\begin{matrix} CH_3COO^-K^+ \\ CH_3COO^-K^+ \end{matrix} \xrightarrow{Electrolysis} \underbrace{\begin{matrix} CH_3 \\ | \\ CH_3 \end{matrix} + 2CO_2\uparrow}_{At\ anode} + \underbrace{H_2\uparrow + 2KOH}_{At\ cathode}$$

From Grignard Reagent

$RMgX + HOH \rightarrow R-H$

$RMgX + R'OH \rightarrow R-H$

$RMgX + R'COOH \rightarrow R-H$

$RMgX + R'C\equiv CH \rightarrow R-H$

Wurtz Reaction

$R-X + 2Na + X-R \xrightarrow{Dry\ ether} R-R + 2NaX$

Corey House Synthesis

$R_2CuLi + R'X \xrightarrow{Dry\ ether} R'-R + RCu + LiX$

Frankland Reaction

$R-X + Zn + X-R \xrightarrow{Dry\ ether} R-R + ZnX_2$

CHEMICAL PROPERTIES

HALOGENATION

- Displaces one or more hydrogen of alkane by halogen.
- The order of reactivity of halogens: $I_2 > Br_2 > Cl_2 > F_2$
- Reactivity of sp^3 hybrid carbon atoms:
  tert-benzyl carbon > *sec*-benzyl carbon > *p*-benzyl carbon > *tert*-allylic carbon > *sec*-allylic carbon > *p*-allylic carbon > 3° > 2° > 1°

NITRATION

- Alkanes having more than five carbon atoms can be nitrated with fuming HNO_3.
- Liquid phase nitration:
  $C_6H_{14} + HNO_3 \longrightarrow C_6H_{13}NO_2 + H_2O$
- For lower alkanes vapour phase nitration is used.
- Nitration follows free radical mechanism.

SULPHONATION

- Given by alkanes with minimum 6 carbons.
- Lower alkanes except those with tertiary hydrogen atom can't be sulphonated.
- It is done by fuming sulphuric acid (H_2SO_4)
  $\underset{Iso\text{-}butane}{(CH_3)_3CH} + \underset{Oleum}{H_2S_2O_7} \longrightarrow \underset{t\text{-}butyl\ sulphonic\ acid}{(CH_3)_3CSO_3H} + H_2O$

ISOMERISATION

- It is due to molecular rearrangement-1, 2-hydride or methyl shift.
- $CH_3CH_2CH_2CH_3 \xrightarrow[270°C,\ 35\ atm]{Anhyd.\ AlCl_3/HCl} \underset{Iso\text{-}butane}{CH_3-\overset{\overset{CH_3}{|}}{CH}-CH_3}$

COMBUSTION

$C_nH_{2n+2} + \left(\frac{3n+1}{2}\right)O_2 \xrightarrow{Flame} nCO_2 + (n+1)H_2O + Heat$

CONTROLLED OXIDATION

- Alkanes with 3° hydrogens are oxidised by $KMnO_4$ or K_2CrO_7.
- Lower alkanes undergo restricted oxidation in the presence of metallic catalysts like Cu.

PYROLYSIS

- Thermal breaking of organic molecules.

$CH_3CH_2CH_3 \xrightarrow{773K} \begin{matrix} CH_3 \\ | \\ CH=CH_2 \end{matrix} + \begin{matrix} CH_2 \\ \| \\ CH_2 \end{matrix} + CH_3-CH_3 + CH_4 + H_2$

- The reaction proceeds by free-radical mechanism.
- Temperature required – 500-800°C

AROMATISATION

- *n*-alkanes having six or more carbons on heating to 773K at 10-20 atm pressure in the presence of Al_2O_3 or Cr_2O_3 or V_2O_5 undergo aromatisation.

$CH_3CH_2CH_2CH_2CH_2CH_3 \xrightarrow[773K,\ 20\ atm]{Cr_2O_3/V_2O_5/Mo_2O_3}$ 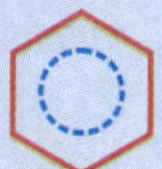

Benzene

ALKENES

- Unsaturated hydrocarbons characterised by the presence of a double bond between two adjacent carbons (>C=C<).
- The general formula C_nH_{2n}
- Nomenclature:
  Root word + 'ene' = alkene
- It has trigonal planar shape with bond angle of 120°.

PHYSICAL PROPERTIES

- First three alkenes are gases, next fourteen are liquids and rest are solids.
- All alkenes are colourless and odourless except ethene which has faint sweet smell.
- Boiling point increases with increase in molar mass.
  Boiling point of *cis*-isomer is higher than *trans*-isomer.
- Insoluble in water but soluble in non-polar solvents.

METHODS OF PREPARATION

CONTROLLED HYDROGENATION

- **Lindlar's catalyst** Pd poisoned with $BaSO_4$ or $CaCO_3$ in quinoline or xylene.

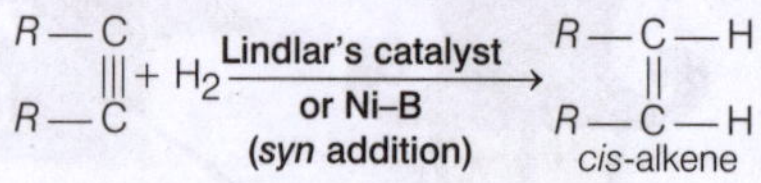

- **Birch reduction** Na in liquid NH_3.

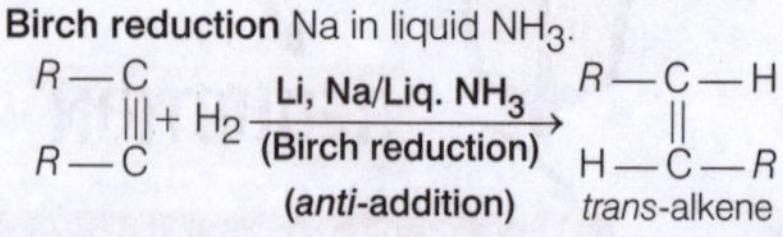

HYDROBORATION

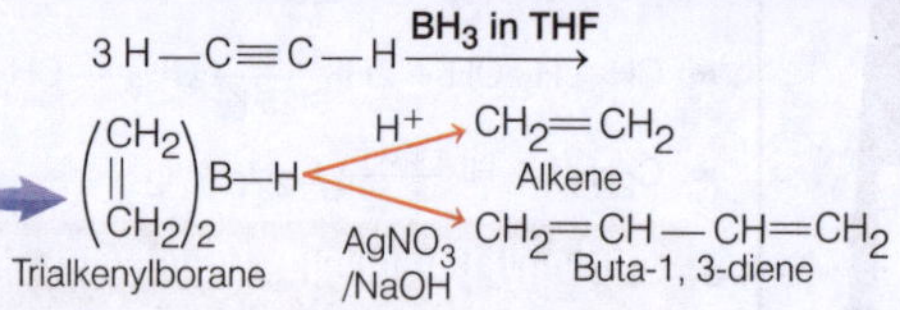

WITTIG REACTION

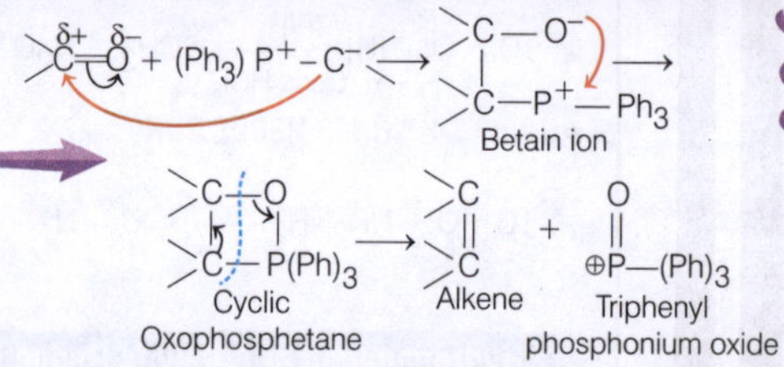

KOLBE'S ELECTROLYTIC METHOD

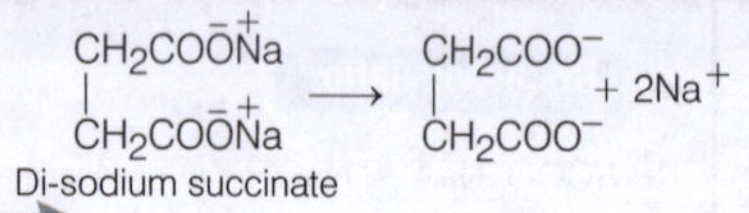

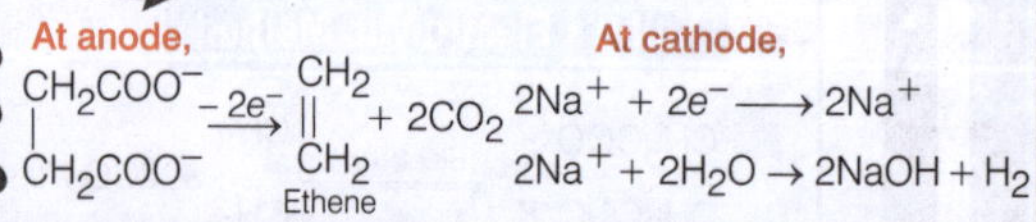

COPE REACTION

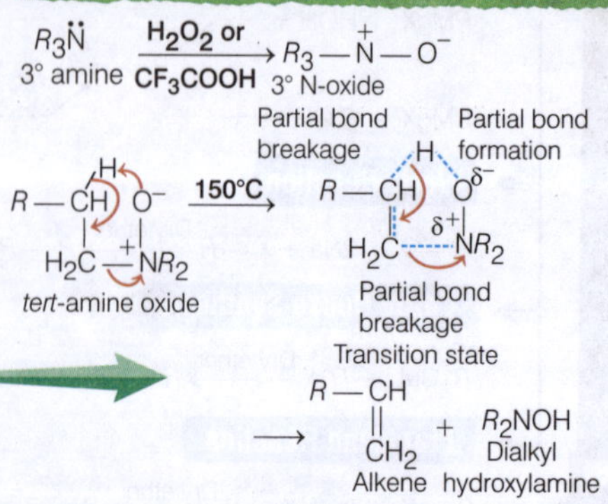

DEHYDROHALOGENATION

$$CH_3CH_2Br \xrightarrow[\Delta]{\text{Alc.KOH}} CH_2 = CH_2 + HBr + H_2O$$

- E_2 elimination occur in primary alkyl halides with β-carbon (1° or 2°) with reagents NaH, $NaNH_2$, KNH_2 etc.
- Ease of dehydrohalogenation: 3° > 2° > 1° (alkyl halide)
- **SAYTZEFF RULE** In elimination reactions, when alternatives are available, then the H-atom will be removed from carbon atom containing lesser number of hydrogen.

DEHYDRATION OF ALCOHOLS

$$CH_3CH_2OH \xrightarrow[170°C]{\text{Conc.}H_2SO_4} CH_2 = CH_2 + H_2O$$

- 1° alcohols follow E_2 mechanism, 3° alcohols follow E_1 mechanism while 2° alcohols follow both E_1 and E_2 mechanism.
- Ease of dehydration : 3° > 2° > 1°
- The reaction is also possible with Al_2O_3, P_2O_5, H_3PO_4, $POCl_3$ in pyridine.
- The reaction follows Saytzeff rule.

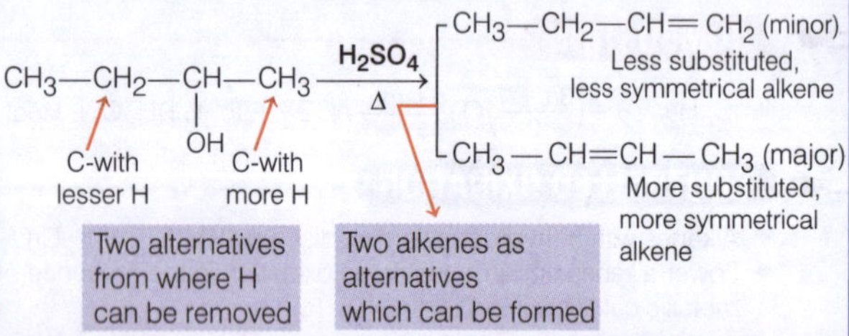

DEHALOGENATION

Geminal **Dihalides**

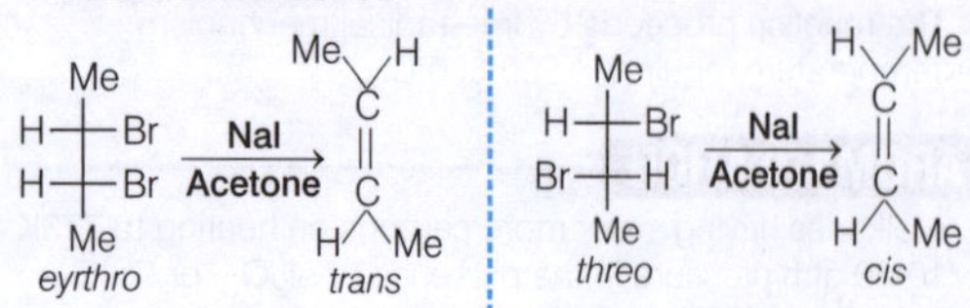

Vicinal **Dihalides**

$$BrCH_2—CH_2Br + Zn \xrightarrow{C_2H_5OH} CH_2{=}CH_2 + ZnBr_2$$

Vic-dihalide

CHEMICAL PROPERTIES

1 Addition of Hydrogen or Hydrogenation

$$-\overset{|}{C}=\overset{|}{C}- + H-H \longrightarrow -\underset{H}{\overset{|}{C}}-\underset{H}{\overset{|}{C}}-$$

- Wilkinson catalyst, $RhCl(C_6H_5)_3P)_3$ Raney Ni are used for hydrogenation.
- Birch reagent, i.e. Na in liq. NH_3 with C_2H_5OH or CH_3OH works only on terminal double bonds in aliphatic alkenes.

2 Addition of Halogens (Halogenation)

$$CH_2=CH_2 + Br_2 \xrightarrow{CCl_4} CH_2(Br)-CH_2(Br)$$

- The reaction is stereo-selective and predominantly *anti*.
- Relative rates of reaction in Br_2/CH_3OH Ethene< 1-butene < *trans* -2-butene < 2-methyl-1- butene < 2, 3 -dimethyl 2-butene.

3 Reaction with Hydrogen Halides

- **Markovnikov's Addition**
  Negative part of the addendum gets attached to that carbon atom which possesses lesser number of hydrogen atom.

$$H_3C-CH=CH_2 + HBr \rightarrow H_3C-CH(Br)-CH_3$$

2-bromopropane

- **Anti-Markovnikov's Addition**
  In the presence of peroxides (Kharasch effect) free radical mechanism is followed.

$$ROOR \longrightarrow 2RO^{\bullet}$$

$$RO^{\bullet} + HBr \longrightarrow R-OH + Br^{\bullet}$$

$$RCH=CH_2 + Br^{\bullet} \rightarrow R-CH(Br)-\dot{C}H_2 \text{ (1°, less stable)}$$

$$RCH=CH_2 + Br^{\bullet} \rightarrow R-\dot{C}HCH_2Br \text{ (2°, more stable)}$$

4 Reaction with water (Hydration)

- **With dil. H_2SO_4**

$$CH_2=CH_2 \xrightarrow{\text{Dil. } H_2SO_4} CH_3-CH_2HSO_4 \xrightarrow[\text{Warm}]{H_2O} CH_3CH_2OH$$

The reaction follows Markovnikov's addition

- **Hydroboration oxidation**

$$CH_2=CH_2 + BH_3 \rightarrow (CH_3CH_2)_3B \xrightarrow{H_2O_2,\ H_2O,\ NaOH} 3CH_3CH_2OH + H_3BO_3$$

It is a two step reaction
(i) *syn*-addition of borane to double bond
(ii) oxidative hydrolysis to get alcohol

- **Oxymercuration demercuration**

$$(CH_3)_3CCH=CH_2 \xrightarrow[\text{THF, } H_2O]{Hg(OCOCH_3)_2} \xrightarrow{NaBH_4/NaOH} (CH_3)_3C\cdot CH(OH)CH_3$$

5 Reaction with Hypohalous Acid (HOX)

$$CH_2=CH_2 + H\bar{O}X^{+} \longrightarrow CH_2(OH)-CH_2(X)$$

- Markovnikov's rule is followed in case of unsymmetrical alkene.
- Stereo-selective reaction, anti-addition occurs.
- Order of reactivity of different X_2,H_2O : $Cl_2/H_2O > Br_2/H_2O > I_2/H_2O$

6 Ozonolysis

$$(H_3C)(H)C=C(CH_3)(H) \xrightarrow[\text{(ii) } H_2O_2, H_2O]{\text{(i) } O_3} 2\ (CH_3)(H)C=O$$

$$(H_3C)_2C=C(H)(CH_3) \xrightarrow[\text{(ii) } H_2O/H_2O_2]{\text{(i) } O_3} (H_3C)_2C=O + O=C(H)(CH_3)$$

Ketone → No effect

Aldehyde $\xrightarrow{[O]}$ $O=C(OH)(CH_3)$ Acid

7 Hydroxylation (Insertion of — OH groups)

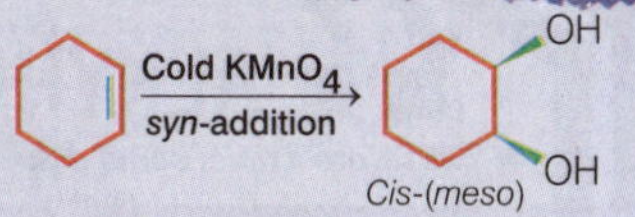

- Baeyer's reagent: $KMnO_4/NaOH$
- Hydroxylation is *syn.*
- OsO_4/H_2O: *anti*-addition
- I_2/CH_3COO Ag : *syn*-addition

8 Diels-Alder reaction

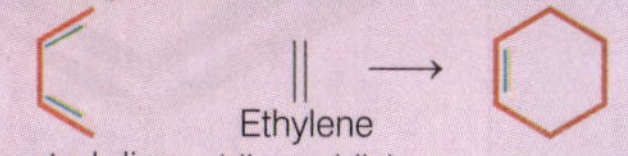

- This reaction is also called cycloaddition.
- Attachment of electron attracting groups in dienophile or electron releasing group in conjugated diene, increases the rate of reaction.
- Alkynes, benzynes and allenes can be used as dienophile.
- Benzene, naphthalene and phenanthrene are quite unreactive as such are not commonly used in reaction.
- The reaction is stereo-specific.

9 Polymerisation

- $nCH_2=CH_2 \longrightarrow -[CH_2-CH_2]_n-$
  Ethene → Polyethene
- $CH_2=CH-CH=CH_2 \longrightarrow -[CH_2-CH=CH-CH_2]_n-$
  1,3-Butadiene → Polybutadiene
- $CH_2=C(CH_3)-CH=CH_2 \longrightarrow -[CH_2-C(CH_3)=CH-CH_2]_n-$
  Isoprene → *cis*-polyisoprene (Natural rubber)

POWER TIPS

USES OF ETHENE

- Used to make polymers, such as polyethene.
- Used to ripen fruits, vegetables and flowers.
- Used in combination with oxygen to create an oxyethylene flame for cutting and welding.
- Used to make other compounds, such as ethylene glycol, ethanol etc.

CHEMICAL TESTS FOR UNSATURATION

BAEYER'S TEST

Decolourisation of pink colour indicates unsaturation

$$2KMnO_4 + H_2O \longrightarrow 2KOH + 2MnO_2 + 3[O]$$

$$>C=C< + [O] + H_2O \rightarrow >C(OH)-C(OH)<$$

BROMINE WATER TEST

Decolourisation of brown colour indicates unsaturation

$$>C=C< + Br_2 \xrightarrow{CCl_4} >C(Br)-C(Br)<$$

ALKYNES

- *These are triple bonded sp-hybridised, linear shaped with 180° bond angle.*
- *Hydrocarbons with two p-bonds and a bond between two carbon atoms.*
- *Nomenclature:*
  Root word + yne = Alkyne
- *General formula: C_nH_{2n-2}*

PHYSICAL PROPERTIES

- First three members of alkynes are gases, next eight are liquids and higher alkynes are solids.
- All alkynes are colourless and odourless except acetylene, has garlic odour.
- The melting point, boiling point and densities of alkynes are slightly higher than corresponding alkenes and alkanes.
- These are insoluble in water and soluble in non-polar solvents like benzene, ether etc.

METHODS OF PREPARATION

01 BY HYDROLYSIS OF METAL CARBIDES

- Metal carbides of group II elements on treatment with H_2O gives alkynes.

$$\left.\begin{matrix} MgC_2 \\ CaC_2 \\ SrC_2 \\ BaC_2 \end{matrix}\right\} + 2H_2O \longrightarrow C_2H_2 + \text{Metal hydroxide } [M(OH)_2]$$

$$Mg_2C_3 + 4H_2O \longrightarrow CH_3C{\equiv}CH + 2Mg(OH)_2$$

02 DEHALOGENATION

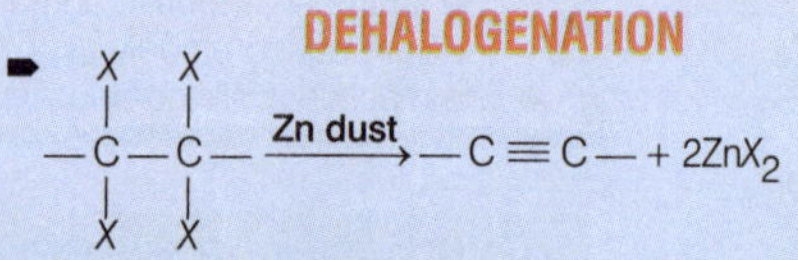

- In case of trihalides Ag is used.

$$CH X_3 + 6\,Ag + X_3 CH \xrightarrow{\Delta} CH{\equiv}CH + 6\,AgX$$

03 DEHALOGENATION OF 1, 2-DIHALIDES

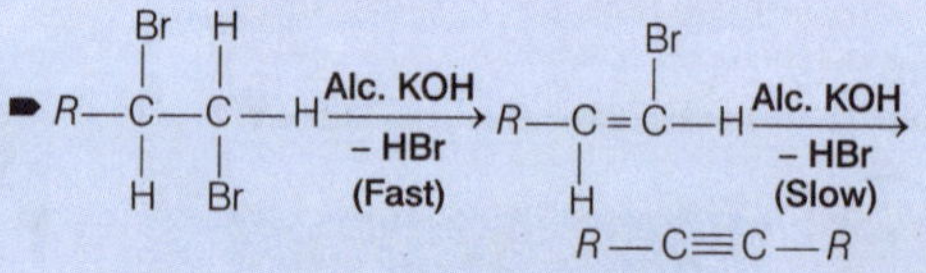

- Sodamide instead of alc. KOH is also used for direct preparation of alkynes.

04 KOLBE'S ELECTROLYTIC METHOD

- Potassium fumerate

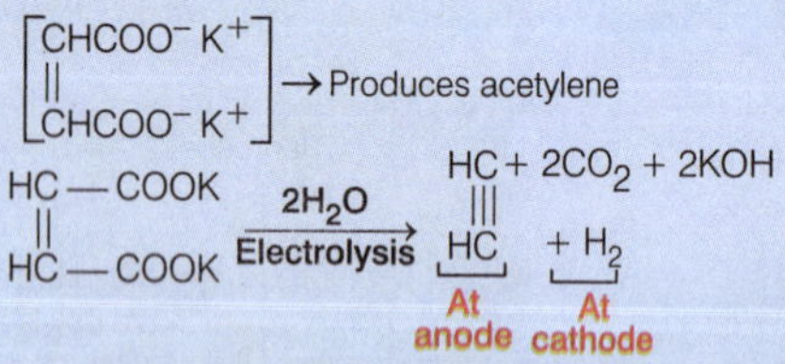

05 FROM SODIUM ACETYLIDE

- It is used to prepare higher alkynes from lower alkynes.
- $HC{\equiv}CH + Na \xrightarrow{liq.NH_3} HC{\equiv}C^{\ominus}Na^{\oplus} \xrightarrow[-NaX]{RX}$

$$\xleftarrow[-NaX]{R'X} Na^{+}\,C^{\ominus}{\equiv}CR \xleftarrow{\text{Na in liq.}NH_3} HC{\equiv}CR$$

$$R'-C{\equiv}C-R$$

06 FROM GRIGNARD REAGENT

- It is used for preparation of higher alkynes from terminal alkynes.
- $HC{\equiv}CH + RMgX \longrightarrow HC{\equiv}C^{\ominus}Mg^{\oplus}X^{\ominus}$

$$\downarrow RX$$

$$HC{\equiv}C-R + MgX_2$$

07 FROM OTHER METHODS

- By passing electric discharge through graphite electrodes in atmosphere of hydrogen.

$$2C + H_2 \xrightarrow{1200°C} CH{\equiv}CH$$

- By controlled partial oxidation of methane.

$$3CH_4 + 3O_2 \xrightarrow{1500°C} CH{\equiv}CH + CO + 5H_2O$$

POWER TIPS

USES OF ACETYLENE

- Used to produce polyethylene plastics, PVC and PVDF.
- Used to vulcanize rubber.
- Used in the production of aspirin, acetaminophen etc.
- Used in the production of wide range of insecticide.

CHEMICAL PROPERTIES

Electrophilic Addition Reactions

01 HYDROGENATION

- $CH_3-C\equiv CH + 2H_2 \xrightarrow{\text{Ni or Pt or Pd}} CH_3CH_2CH_3$
- $CH_3-C\equiv C-CH_3 + H_2$

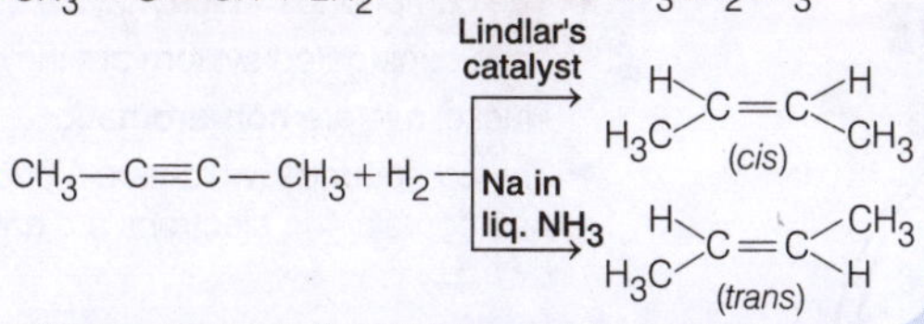

02 HALOGENATION

- Br_2 water is considered as a test for unsaturation of alkynes.

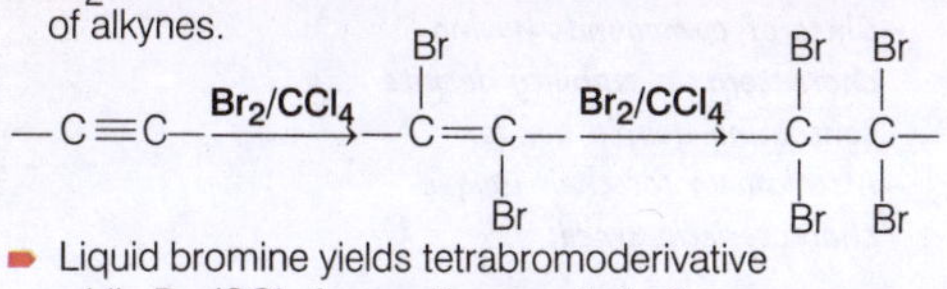

- Liquid bromine yields tetrabromoderivative while Br_2/CCl_4 forms dibromo derivative.

03 ADDITION OF HALOGEN ACIDS

- Markovnikov's addition gives *Geminal* dihalides.

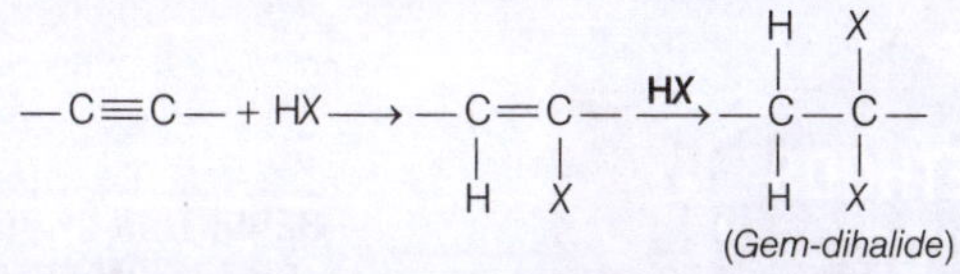

04 ADDITION OF HYPOHALOUS ACIDS

- Halohydrin formed initially is converted into halogen derivative of carbonyl compound.

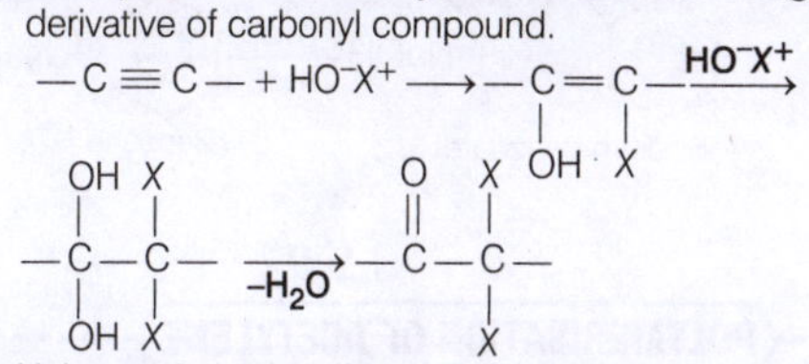

- Halogen derivative of carbonyl compound.

05 HYDRATION

- Among alkynes only acetylene gives aldehydes, rest all alkynes gives ketones as final product.

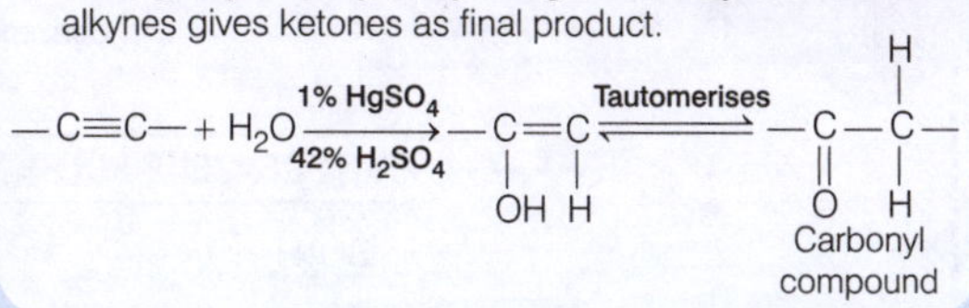

06 ADDITION OF HCN

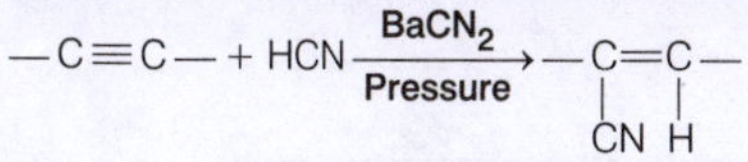

OZONOLYSIS

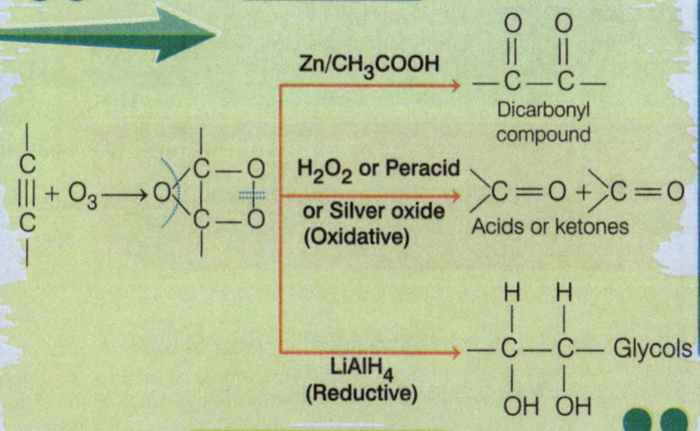

ADDITION OF ARSENIC TRICHLORIDE

Reaction occurs in the presence of $AlCl_3$ (anhydrous) to yield lewisite, a poisonous gas, used as a chemical weapon in World War II.

$$CH\equiv CH + AsCl_3 \xrightarrow{\text{Anhyd.}AlCl_3} ClCH=CH.AsCl_2$$

Lewisite

REACTIONS DUE TO ACIDIC CHARACTER OF ALKYNES

- Acidic nature of alkynes is due to *sp*-hybridisation, because of which the electrons of C—H bond are held more strongly towards C-nucleus.
- Reaction with Na in liquid NH_3:

$$H-C\equiv C-R + Na \xrightarrow[NH_3]{\text{In liquid}} Na^+C^-\equiv C-R + \frac{1}{2}H_2\uparrow$$

- Reaction with Tollen's reagent ($AgNO_3$).
- Used to test the terminal alkynes.

$$H-C\equiv C-H + 2AgNO_3 + 2NH_4OH \longrightarrow Ag-C\equiv C-Ag + 2NH_4NO_3 + 2H_2O$$

Silver acetylide (white ppt.)

- **Fehling's solution** Terminal alkynes with Fehling's solution gives red precipitate of their Cu salts.

$$H-C\equiv C-H + Cu_2Cl_2 + 2NH_4OH \longrightarrow Cu-C\equiv C-Cu + 2NH_4Cl + 2H_2O$$

Copper acetylide (Red ppt.)

POLYMERISATION

Reaction takes place when vapours are passed through red hot Cu or Fe tube:

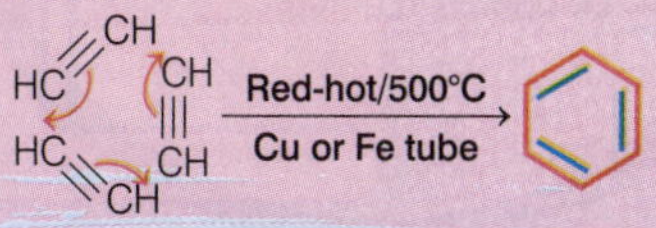

AROMATIC HYDROCARBONS

- Class of compounds having characteristic stability despite containing double bonds.
- Also known for their unique characteristic smell.

BENZENE

POWER TIPS

HUCKEL'S RULE

- A cyclic, conjugated, planar molecule is aromatic if it has $(4n+2)\pi$ electron, where n is a non-negative integer.
- The compounds which may be cyclic and may have conjugated system but they do not follow Huckel rule are **non-aromatic**.
- The compounds, which are monocyclic and contain $4n\pi$ electrons are **anti-aromatic**.

METHODS OF PREPARATION

DECARBOXYLATION

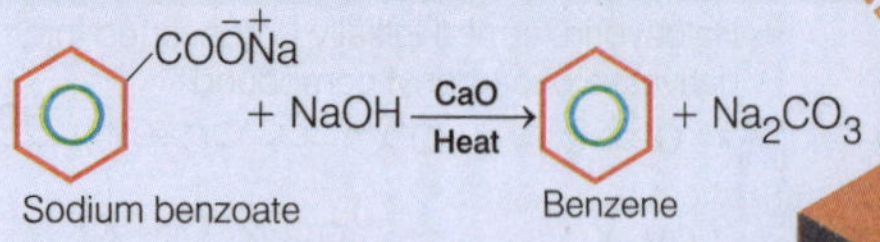

DEHYDROXYLATION

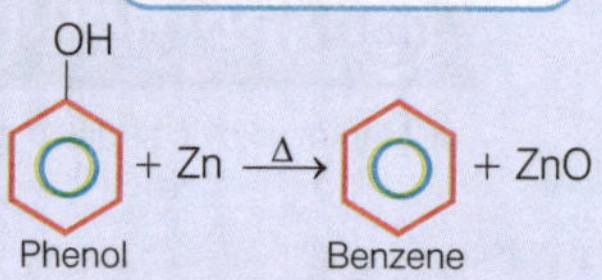

POLYMERISATION OF ACETYLENE

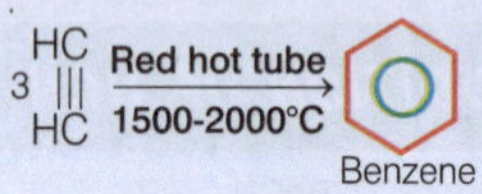

REDUCTION OF BENZENE DIAZONIUM CHLORIDE

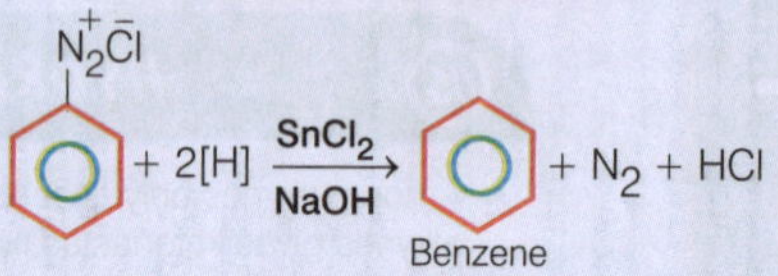

FROM CHLOROBENZENE

- ***By hydrogenation:***

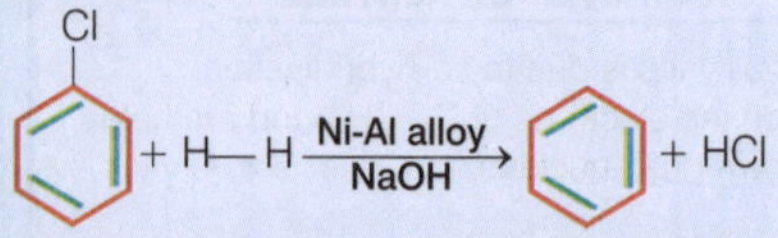

- ***From Grignard reagent formation followed by hydrolysis.***

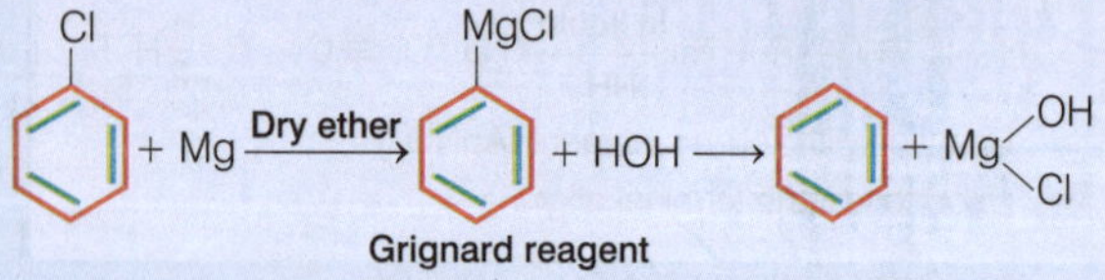

FROM BENZENE SULPHONIC ACID

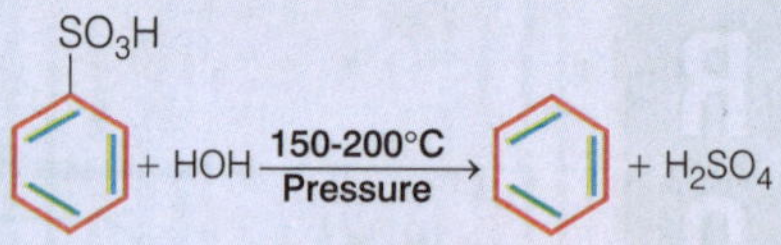

Aromatisation

- Hexane to higher alkane (upto decane) on aromatisation in the presence of Cr and Al oxides at high temperature gives benzene and its homologous.

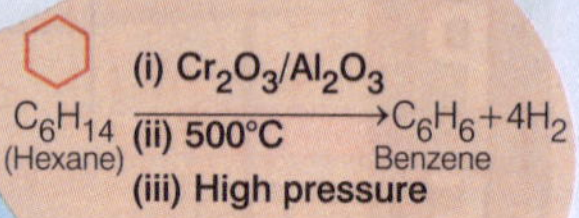

Distillation

- Benzene and its homologous are prepared by destructive distillation of wood.
- **Cracking of Petroleum** It is obtained through aromatisation of $C_6 - C_{10}$ fraction of petroleum naptha at high temperature and pressure.

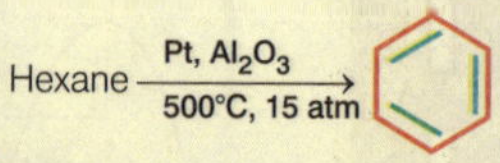

PHYSICAL PROPERTIES OF BENZENE

- A colourless inflammable liquid, insoluble in water, soluble in alcohol, ether and chloroform.
- Good solvent
- It burns with a luminous sooty flame and its vapours are highly toxic.
- Inhalation causes toxic effects in our body.
- Carcinogenic in nature.

VAPOUR PHASE OXIDATION

- The reaction is carried out at 770 K.
- Maleic acid is first produced which loses water to form maleic anhydride.

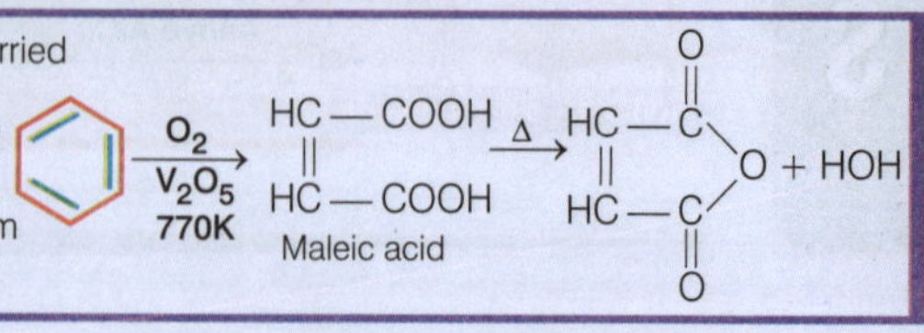

CHEMICAL PROPERTIES

ELECTROPHILIC SUBSTITUTIONS

01 HALOGENATION

- It undergoes chlorination when treated with Cl_2 in the presence of $AlCl_3$ or $FeCl_3$.

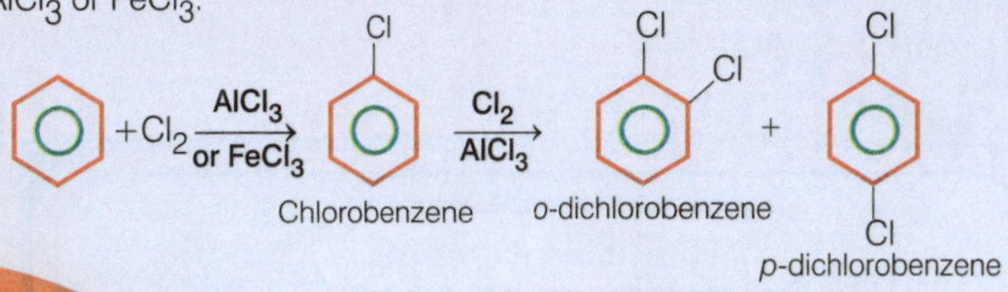

02 NITRATION

- It undergoes nitration when treated with conc. HNO_3 in the presence of H_2SO_4.

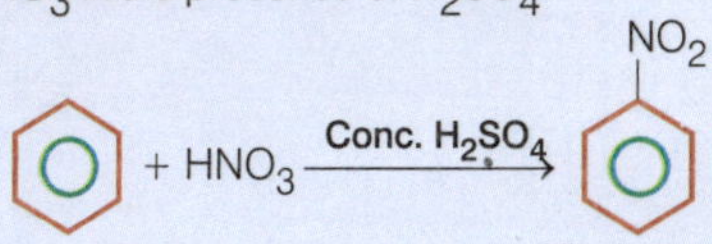

- On heating benzene with fuming HNO_3 and conc. H_2SO_4, 1, 3, 5-trinitrobenzene is formed.

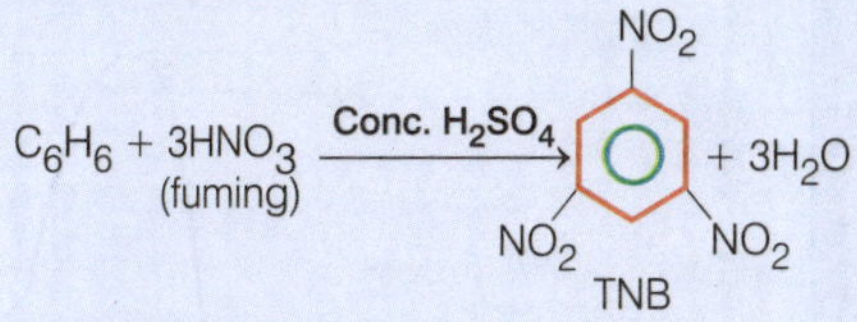

03 SULPHONATION

- It reacts with hot conc. H_2SO_4 to form benzene sulphonic acid, and *m*-benzene disulphonic acid with oleum.

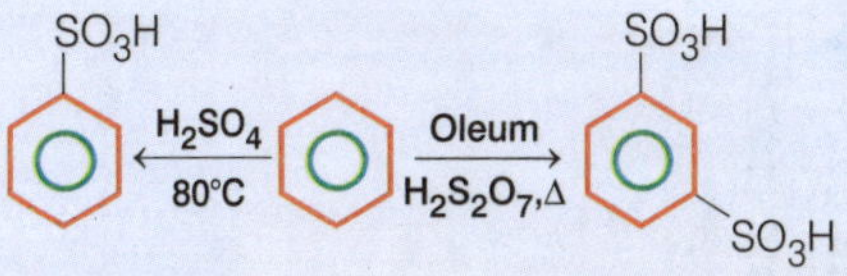

04 FORMYLATION

- It is the introduction of —CHO group into the benzene ring.
- **Gattermann-Koch Synthesis**

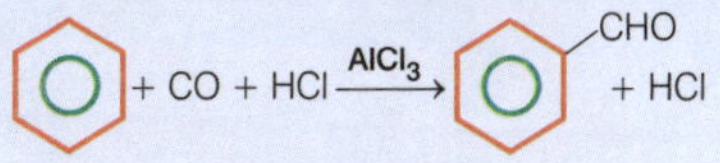

- **Gattermann Synthesis**

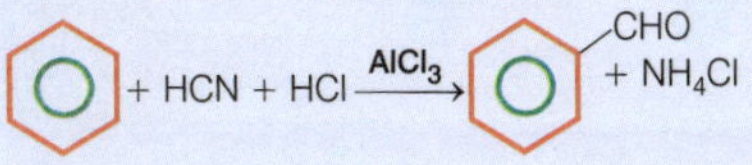

05 FRIEDEL-CRAFTS ALKYLATION, ACYLATION OR CARBOXYLATION

- The Lewis acid that can be used for these reactions are $AlCl_3$, $FeCl_3$, $SnCl_2$, $SnCl_4$, BF_3, HF etc.
- **Alkylation**

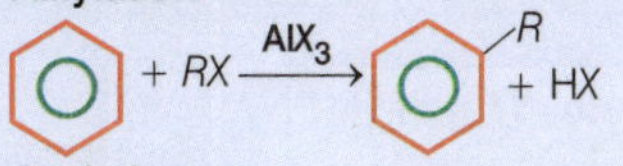

- **Acylation**

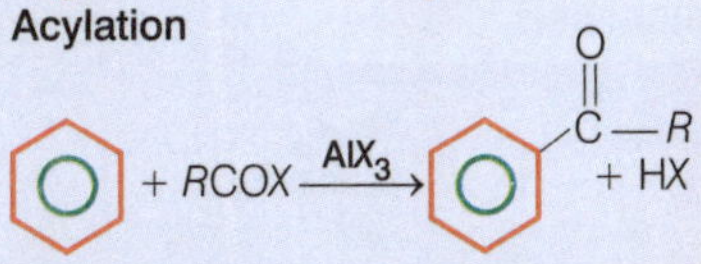

- **Carboxylation**

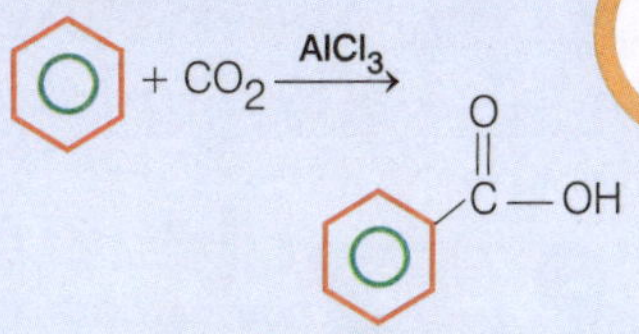

ADDITION REACTIONS

OXIDATION REACTIONS OF BENZENE

Ozonolysis Ozonide is formed in this reaction.

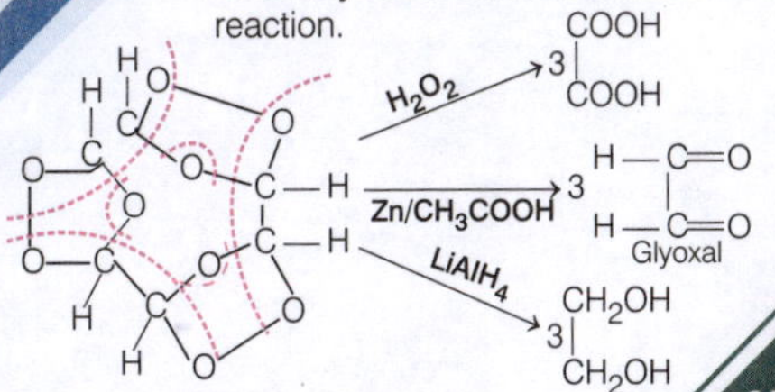

REDUCTION OR HYDROGENATION

This reaction is exothermic but it requires high temperature or pressure and an active catalyst.

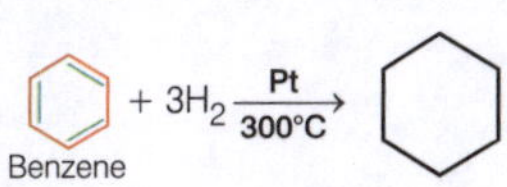

BIRCH REDUCTION

Catalyst used is a metal of group I, i.e. Li, Na and alcohol (CH_3OH or C_2H_5OH)

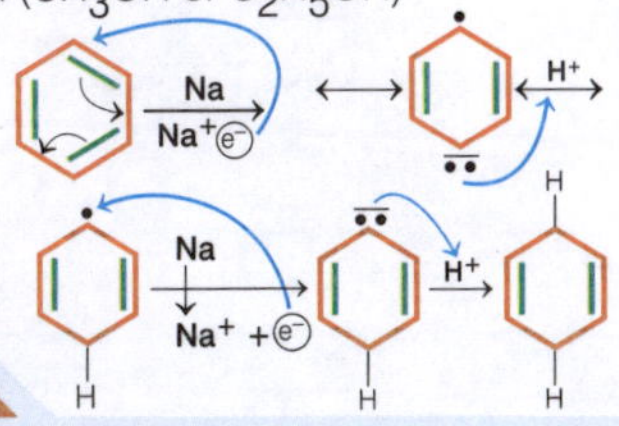

HALOGENATION

The product of halogenation is lindane or gammexane or 666 and is used as insecticide.

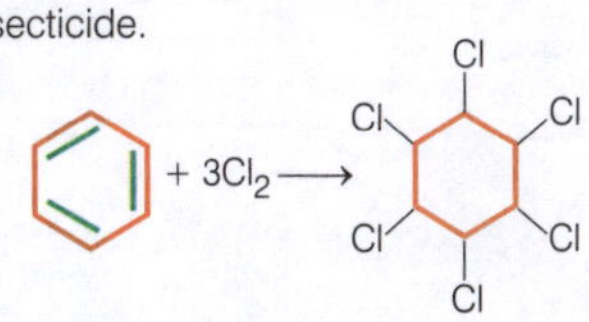

DIRECTIVE INFLUENCE OF GROUPS

***o/p* directing and activating group**

- Strongly activating: $—NH_2 > —NHR > —NR_2 > —OH > —O^-$
- Moderately activating: —NHCO*R* > —OCO*R*
- Weakly activating: $—R > -Ar > —CH = CR_2$
- Weakly deactivating: —F > —Cl > —Br > —I

***m*-directing and deactivating**

- Moderately deactivating: —CHO > —CO*R* > —COO*R* > —COOH
- Strongly deactivating: $—NO_2 > —\overset{+}{N}R_3 > —\overset{+}{N}HR_2 > —\overset{+}{N}H_2R > —NH_3 > —SO_3 > -CN$

Concept Map

Class 12th

Ch-1 to 12

Chapter 01 Solutions

DILUTE SOLUTIONS
The solution that contains relatively very small quantity of solute.

CONCENTRATED SOLUTIONS
The solution that contains relatively very large quantity of solute.

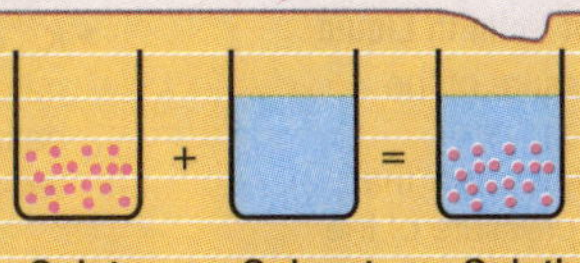

Solute + Solvent = Solution

On the Basis of State of Solute or Solvent

	SOLUTE	SOLVENT	EXAMPLES
SOLID SOLUTIONS	Gas	Solid	Solution of H_2 in palladium.
	Liquid	Solid	Amalgam of Hg with Na.
	Solid	Solid	Copper dissolved in gold.
LIQUID SOLUTIONS	Gas	Liquid	Oxygen dissolved in water.
	Liquid	Liquid	Ethanol dissolved in water.
	Solid	Liquid	Glucose dissolved in water.
GASEOUS SOLUTIONS	Gas	Gas	Mixture of oxygen and N_2 gases.
	Liquid	Gas	Chloroform mixed with N_2 gas.
	Solid	Gas	Camphor in nitrogen gas.

On the Basis of Amount of Solute Dissolved in Solvent

01 SATURATED SOLUTIONS
The point at which a liquid cannot dissolve more of the solute at constant temperature is called **saturation point** and such solution is called **saturated solution.**

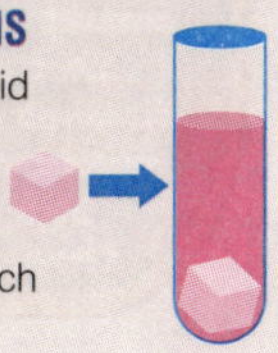

No more solute dissolves

02 SUPERSATURATED SOLUTIONS
A solution that contains more solute than would be necessary to saturate at a given temperature.

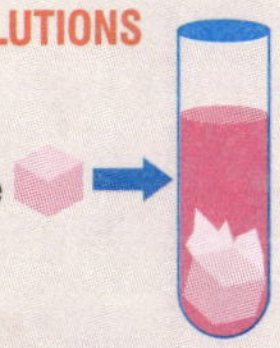

Becomes unstable, crystals form

03 UNSATURATED SOLUTIONS
Solution in which more solute can be dissolved at a given temperature.

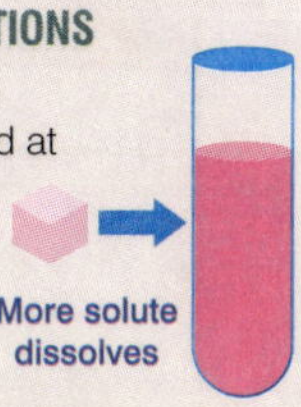

More solute dissolves

METHODS OF EXPRESSING THE CONCENTRATION OF SOLUTION

01 STRENGTH IN GRAM PER LITRE
- Represent the number of grams present in 1L of solution.
- Strength of solution $= \dfrac{\text{Mass of solute (in g)}}{\text{Volume of solution (in L)}}$

02 MASS PERCENTAGE
- Amount of solute present in 100 g of the solution.
- Percent by mass $= \dfrac{\text{Mass of solute (in g)}}{\text{Mass of solution (in g)}} \times 100$

03 PARTS PER MILLION (ppm)
- Amount of solute dissolved in one million part of the solution.
- ppm $= \dfrac{\text{Number of parts of components}}{\text{Total number of parts of all components of solution}} \times 10^6$

04 MASS BY VOLUME PERCENTAGE
- Mass of solute dissolved in 100 mL of the solution.
- Mass by volume percentage $= \dfrac{\text{Mass of solute (in g)}}{\text{Volume of solution (in mL)}} \times 100$

05 MOLE FRACTION
- The number of moles of one component divided by the total no. of moles of all the components present in the solution.
- Mole fraction of $A = \dfrac{n_A}{n_A + n_B}$
- Mole fraction of $B = \dfrac{n_B}{n_A + n_B}$

06 PARTS PER BILLION (ppb)
- The amount of solute, that is dissolved in 10^9 parts of a solution.
- ppb $= \dfrac{\text{Number of parts of components} \times 10^9}{\text{Total number of parts of all components of solution}}$

07 MOLALITY
- Number of moles of the solute dissolved per kg of the solvent.
- Molality $(m) = \dfrac{\text{No. of moles of solute}}{\text{Mass of solvent (in kg)}} \times 1000$
- Unit is moles/kg.

08 MOLARITY
- Number of moles of solute present in one litre of solution.
- Molarity $(M) = \dfrac{\text{No. of moles of solute}}{\text{Volume of solution (in L)}}$
- Unit is mol/L.

09 RELATION BETWEEN NORMALITY AND MOLARITY
- $\dfrac{\text{Normality}}{\text{Molarity}} = \dfrac{\text{No. of gram equivalent of solute}}{\text{No. of moles of solute.}}$

10 NORMALITY
- The number of gram equivalents of substance dissolved per litre of the solution.
- Normality $(N) = \dfrac{\text{No. of gram equivalents of solute}}{\text{Volume of solution (in L)}}$

SOLUBILITY

The maximum amount of a solute that can be dissolved in a given amount of solvent at a given temperature.

VAPOUR PRESSURE

The pressure exerted by the vapours above the liquid surface in equilibrium with the liquid at a given temperature.

FACTORS AFFECTING VAPOUR PRESSURE

- Nature of liquid.
- Temperature
- Presence of non-volatile solute.

01 Vapour Pressure of Liquid - Liquid Solution

- For a solution of volatile liquids, partial vapour pressure ∝ mole fraction in solution
  $p_1 = p_1^\circ x_1 ; p_2 = p_2^\circ x_2$
- According to Dalton's law of partial pressure
  $p_{Total} = p_1^\circ + (p_2^\circ - p_1^\circ) x_2$

02 Vapour Pressure of Solution of Solid In Liquid

- Vapour pressure of the solution at a given temperature is lower than the vapour pressure of the pure solvent at the same temperature.

Henry's Law

- Mass of gas dissolved per unit volume of the solvent at a given temperature is proportional to the pressure of the gas in the equilibrium with the solution.
  $m \propto p$
  $m = K_H p$
- K_H is Henry's constant.
- K_H depends on the nature of the gas, nature of the solvent, temperature.

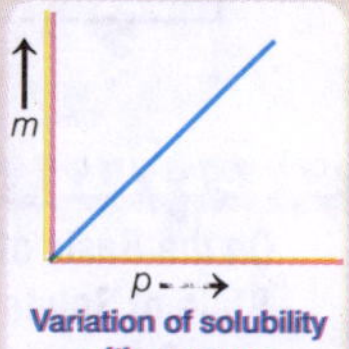

Variation of solubility with pressure

- $K_H \propto \frac{1}{\text{Solubility}} \propto$ Temperature

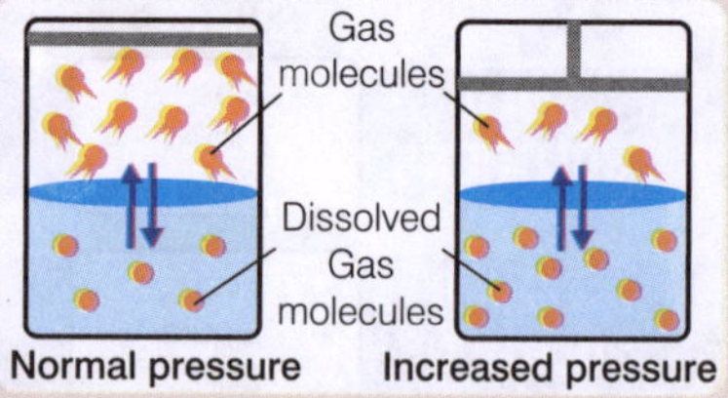

SOLUBILITY OF GAS IN LIQUID

- Expressed in terms of absorption coefficient.
- Absorption coefficient is the volume of gas (in mL) that can be dissolved by 1 mL of a liquid at STP.

FACTORS AFFECTING SOLUBILITY OF A GAS IN A LIQUID

Effect of Pressure
The solubility of a gas increase with increase in pressure.

Effect of Temperature
The solubility of a gas inverse related to temperature.

Nature of Gas
Gases which are easily liquified are more soluble in common solvents.

Nature of Solvent
Gases capable of forming ions in aqueous solution tend to be more soluble in water than other solvent.

Raoult's Law

$p_A = p_A^\circ x_A$, vapour pressure of the volatile components is directly proportional to the mole fraction of that component in the solution.

Ideal and Non-ideal Solutions

Ideal Solution

$A - B \approx A - A \approx B - B$
$\Delta_{mix}V = 0, \Delta_{mix}H = 0$

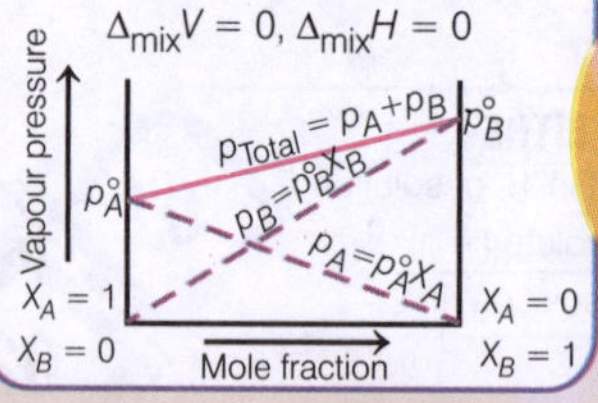

Non-ideal Solution

- $A - B \neq A - A \neq B - B$
- $\Delta V_{mix} \neq 0, \Delta H_{mix} \neq 0$
- These solutions do not obey Raoult's law.

Non-ideal Solution Showing Positive Deviation

- Observed vapour pressure is greater than predicted vapour pressure.
- e.g. $C_2H_5OH + H_2O$

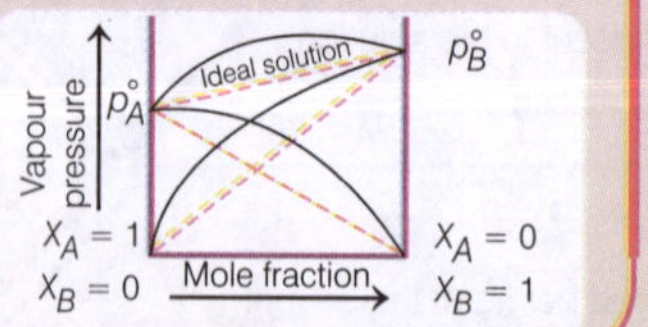

Non-ideal Solution Showing Negative Deviation

- Predicted vapour pressure is greater than observed vapour pressure.
- e.g. $CHCl_3 + CH_3COCH_3$

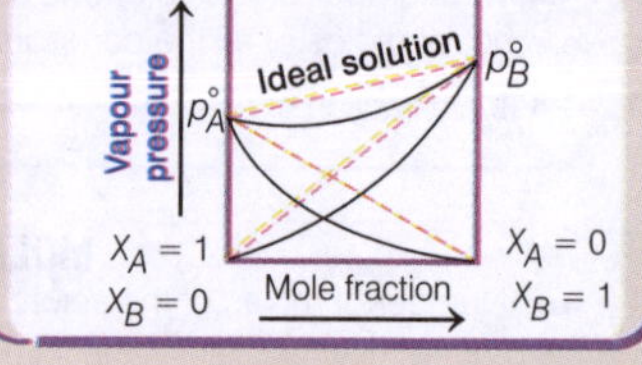

SOLUBILITY OF SOLIDS IN LIQUIDS

- Increases or decreases with, increase in temperature, depending on the nature of solute.
  Solute + Solvent ⇌ Solution

FACTORS AFFECTING SOLUBILITY OF SOLID IN LIQUID

Effect of Temperature
- For endothermic reaction direct relation.
- For exothermic reaction inverse relation.

Effect of Pressure
Pressure does not have any significant effect.

Nature of Solute and Solvent
Polar solute dissolves in polar solvents and non-polar solute dissolve in non-polar solvent.

AZEOTROPES

Mixture of liquids that boil at constant temperature like a pure liquid and possess same composition of components in liquid as well as vapour phase.

Maximum Boiling Azeotropes

- Formed by those liquid pairs that show negative deviations from ideal behaviour. e.g. Nitric acid-water mixture.

Minimum Boiling Azeotropes

- Formed by those liquid pairs that show positive deviations from ideal behaviour. e.g. Ethanol - water mixture.

COLLIGATIVE PROPERTIES

Relative Lowering of Vapour Pressure

Lowering in vapour pressure $= (p^\circ - p)$

Relative lowering in V.P. $= \dfrac{p^\circ - p}{p^\circ}$

By Raoult's law,

$$\frac{p_1^\circ - p_1}{p_1^\circ} = x_2 = \frac{n_2}{n_1 + n_2}$$

Or

$$\frac{p_1^\circ - p_1}{p_1^\circ} = \frac{n_2}{n_1} = \frac{w_2 \times M_1}{M_2 \times w_1}$$

Elevation of Boiling Point

- Boiling point of a solution containing a non- volatile solute is always higher than the boiling point of the pure solvent.
- $\Delta T_b = T_b - T_b^\circ$
- $\Delta T_b = K_b\left(\dfrac{w_2 \times 1000}{M_2 \times w_1}\right)$
- $T_b = T_b^\circ + K_b m$
- $K_b = \dfrac{MRT_b^2}{\Delta_{vap}H \times 1000}$

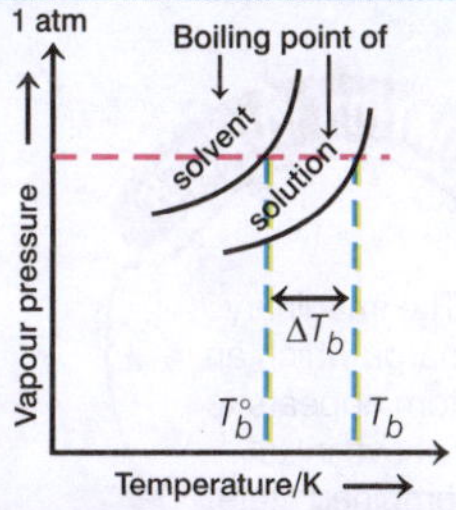

Osmotic Pressure

The amount of force applied to a solution that prevents solvent from moving across a semipermeable membrane.

- $\pi = CRT = \left(\dfrac{n_2}{V}\right)RT$
- $\pi V = \dfrac{w_2 RT}{M_2}$

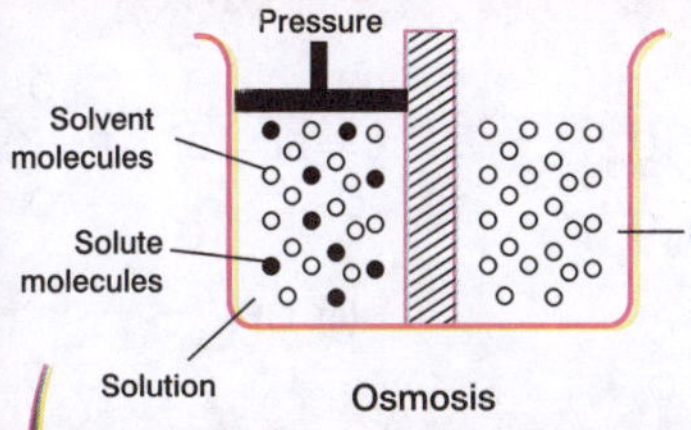

Depression of Freezing Point

- Freezing point of a solution containing a non-volatile solute is always less than the freezing point of the pure solvent.
- $\Delta T_f = T_f^\circ - T_f$
- $\Delta T_f = K_f\left(\dfrac{w_2 \times 1000}{M_2 \times w_1}\right)$
- $T_f = T_f^\circ - K_f m$
- $K_f = \dfrac{MRT_f^2}{\Delta_{fus}H \times 1000}$

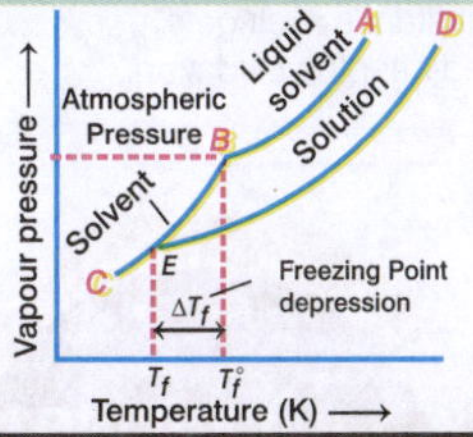

POWER TIPS

Modified Colligative Properties

- $\dfrac{p_A^\circ - p_A}{p_A^\circ} = ix_B$
- $\Delta T_f = iK_f m$
- $\Delta T_b = iK_b m$
- $\pi = iCRT$

DIRECTION OF MOVEMENT OF SOLVENT MOLECULES

Isotonic solutions — If two solutions of different substances have same osmotic pressure at same temperature.

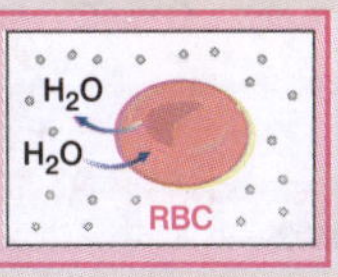

Hypertonic solutions — If a solution has higher osmotic pressure than the other solution.

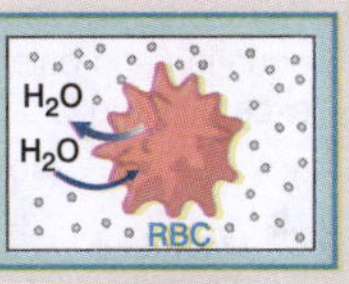

Hypotonic solutions — If a solution has lower osmotic pressure than the other solution.

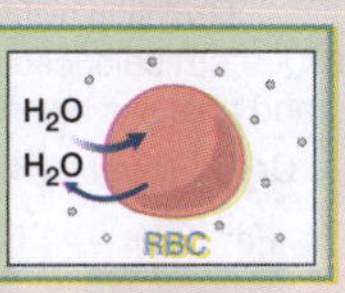

REVERSE OSMOSIS

Solvent will flow from the solution into the pure solvent through semipermeable membrane, when pressure higher than osmotic pressure is applied on solution.

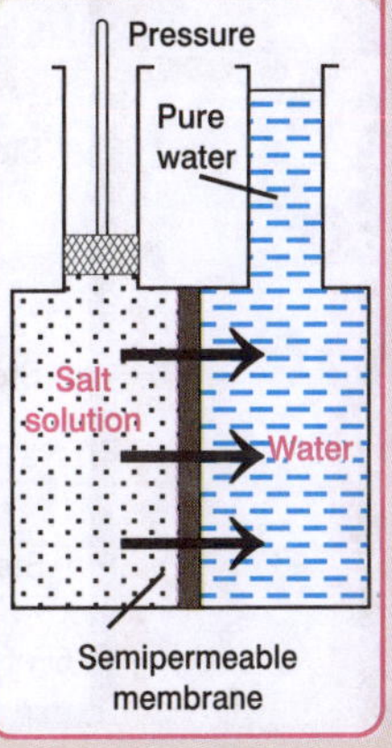

Abnormal Molecular Mass

- The molecular mass of a substance determined by any of the colligative properties comes out to be different than the expected value.
- Abnormal molecular masses are observed when the solution is non-ideal or solute undergoes association or dissociation.

VAN'T HOFF FACTOR (i)

- The ratio of the experimental value of the colligative property to the calculated value of the colligative property.
- $i = \dfrac{\text{Calculated molecular mass}}{\text{Observed molecular mass}}$

$= \dfrac{\text{Observed value of colligative property}}{\text{Calculated value of colligative property}}$

$= \dfrac{\text{Total number of moles of particles after association/dissociation}}{\text{Number of moles of particles before association/dissociation}}$

- For association $i < 1$, For dissociation $i > 1$.

van't Hoff factor and Degree of Dissocation (α)

If $A_n \rightarrow nA$

then, $\alpha = \dfrac{i-1}{n-1}$

van't Hoff factor and Degree of Association (α)

If $nA \rightarrow A_n$

then, $\alpha = \dfrac{i-1}{1/n-1}$

Chapter 02 Electrochemistry

REDOX REACTIONS

Reaction that involves oxidation and reduction as its two half reaction.

	OXIDATION	REDUCTION
MODERN CONCEPT	Loss of electron or increase in oxidation number.	Gain of electron or decrease in oxidation number.
CLASSICAL CONCEPT	➤ Addition of oxygen. ➤ Removal of hydrogen. ➤ Addition of an electronegative element. ➤ Removal of an electropositive element.	➤ Removal of oxygen. ➤ Addition of hydrogen. ➤ Removal of an electronegative element. ➤ Addition of an electropositive element.

OXIDATION NUMBER

The imaginary charge which an atom appears to have in its combined state.

REDUCING AGENT OR REDUCTANT

- Substance that supplies hydrogen or removes oxygen.
- The substance itself gets oxidised after the reduction.

OXIDISING AGENT OR OXIDANT

- Substance that supplies oxygen, removes hydrogen.
- The substance itself gets reduced after the oxidation.

RULES FOR ASSIGNING OXIDATION NUMBER

- Free elements have zero oxidation number.
- Oxidation number of F and O are respectively – 1 and –2.

Exception:

- Oxidation number of oxygen peroxide(–), superoxide(–1/2) and in oxygen difluoride is (+2).
- Oxidation number of hydrogen is – 1 in metallic hydride and + 1 in all other compound.

POWER TIPS — EXCEPTIONS

- Oxidation state of S in $Na_2S_4O_6$

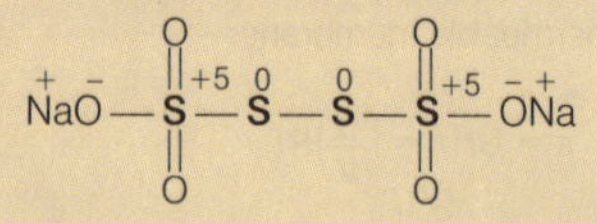

- Oxidation state of Cr in CrO_5,

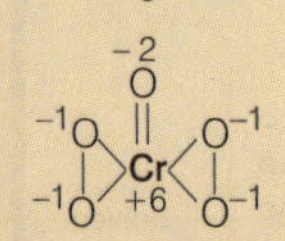

- Oxidation state of Br in Br_3O_8,

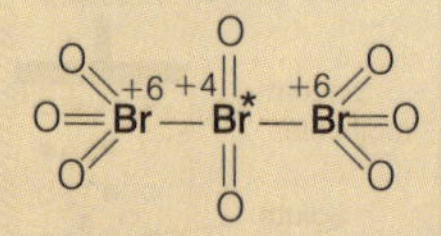

(I). H_2SO_5

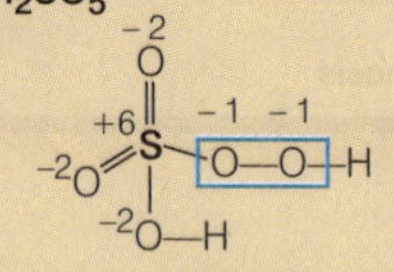

(ii). OF_2

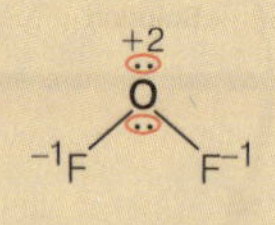

(iii). C_3O_2

$$\overset{-2}{O}=\overset{+2}{C}=\overset{0}{C^*}=\overset{+2}{C}=\overset{-2}{O}$$

BALANCING OF REDOX REACTION

OXIDATION NUMBER METHOD (METHOD 01)

Step I Write ionic equation of reaction.

$$\overset{+2}{Fe^{2+}} + \overset{+6}{Cr_2O_7^{2-}} \longrightarrow Fe^{3+}(aq) + Cr^{3+}(aq)$$

Step II Find change in oxidation number in each equation and balance atoms except H and O.

- $Fe^{2+} \longrightarrow Fe^{3+}$ .... Eq. 1

Change in oxidation number in each atom = 1

- $\overset{+6}{Cr_2O_7^{2-}} \longrightarrow 2Cr^{3+}$ .... Eq. 2

Change in oxidation number in each atom = 3 × 2 = 6

Step III To equalise the number of electron equation 1 multiply by 6.

$6Fe^{2+} \longrightarrow 6Fe^{3+}$ .... Eq. 3

Step IV Add eq. 2 with eq. 3 of reaction is carried out in acidic medium then firstly we balanced "O" by H_2O molecule and H atoms balanced by H^+ ions.

$$6Fe^{2+} + Cr_2O_7^{2-} + 14H^+ \longrightarrow 6Fe^{3+} + 2Cr(aq) + 7H_2O(l)$$

HALF REACTION METHOD (METHOD 02)

Step I Write ionic equation and split into two half equation and balance all other atom except H and O.

$$Fe^{2+}(aq) + Cr_2O_7^{2-}(aq) \longrightarrow Fe^{3+}(aq) + Cr^{3+}(aq)$$

$Fe^{2+}(aq) \longrightarrow Fe^{3+}(aq)$ — Oxidation half

$Cr_2O_7^{2-}(aq) \longrightarrow 2Cr^{3+}(aq)$ — Reduction half

Step II O- atom balanced by H_2O and H-atom by H^+ ions and charged balanced by electrons.

$$Cr_2O_7^{2-}(aq) + 14H^+ + 6e^- \longrightarrow 2Cr^{3+} + 7H_2O\ (l)$$

$$Fe^{2+}(aq) \longrightarrow Fe^{3+}(aq) + e^-$$

Step III To equalise the number of electron multiply by 6 in oxidation reaction and cancel the term common to both sides.

$$6Fe^{2+}(aq) + Cr_2O_7^{2-}(aq) \longrightarrow 6Fe^{3+}(aq) + 2Cr^{3+} + 7H_2O\ (l)$$

Step IV Verify balanced equation and convert ionic equation into molecular form.

$$6Fe^{2+}(aq) + Cr_2O_7\ (aq) + 14H^+ \rightarrow 6Fe^{3+}(aq) + 2Cr^{3+} + 7H_2O(l)$$

TYPES OF REDOX REACTION

01 Combination Reaction

- Combination of two or more atoms give a single product.
- Either one or both elements of the reactant must be in the elemental form.

e.g. $\overset{0}{C}(s) + \overset{0}{O_2}(g) \xrightarrow{\Delta} \overset{+4-2}{CO_2}(g)$

02 Decomposition Reaction

- Reactant breakdown into two or more components.
- At least one of the product must be in the elemental form.
- e.g. $\overset{+1+5-2}{2KClO_3}(s) \xrightarrow{\Delta} \overset{+1-1}{2KCl}(s) + \overset{0}{3O_2}(g)$

03 Disproportionation Reaction

- Same element is oxidised as well as reduced.
- e.g. $4K\overset{+5}{Cl}O_3 \longrightarrow 3K\overset{+7}{Cl}O_4 + K\overset{-1}{Cl}$

04 Displacement Reaction

Atom or ion in a compound is replaced by an ion/atom of another element.

$$X + YZ \longrightarrow XZ + Y$$

Metal Displacement

- One metal displaces the other metal.
- e.g. $Cu + \overset{+1-1}{2AgNO_3} \longrightarrow \overset{0}{2Ag} + \overset{+2-1}{Cu(NO_3)_2}$

Non - metal Displacement

- Non - metal is displaced by metal or non - metal.
- e.g. $\overset{0}{Zn}(s) + \overset{+1-1}{2HCl}(aq) \longrightarrow \overset{+2-1}{ZnCl_2}(aq) + \overset{0}{H_2}(g)$

LAW OF EQUIVALENCE

In a chemical reaction, the number of gram equivalents of reactants is equal to gram equivalents of products.

n-Factor

Equivalent = Mole × n-factor
$= M \times V \times n$-factor
$= N \times V$

- **For redox reaction**
  The number of e^- gained or lost per atom.
- **For disproportionation**

$$n_f = \frac{XY}{X+Y} \begin{bmatrix} X = n\text{-factor for alone oxidation} \\ Y = n\text{-factor for alone reduction} \end{bmatrix}$$

ELECTROCHEMICAL SERIES

- Arrangement of various elements in the order of increasing values of their standard reduction potentials.
- Negative E° means redox couple is stronger reducing agent than the H^+/H_2 couple.
- Positive E° means redox couple is weaker reducing agent than the H^+/H_2 couple.

Standard Electrode Potential (E°)

Potential difference developed between metal electrode and solution of its ions of unit molarity at 1 atm pressure and 25°C.

Reaction (Oxidised form + ne^-	→ Reduced form)	E°/V
$F_2(g) + 2e^-$	$\rightarrow 2F^-$	2.87
$Co^{3+} + e^-$	$\rightarrow Co^{2+}$	1.81
$H_2O_2 + 2H^+ + 2e^-$	$\rightarrow 2H_2O$	1.78
$MnO_4^- + 8H^+ + 5e^-$	$\rightarrow Mn^{2+} + 4H_2O$	1.51
$Au^{3+} + 3e^-$	$\rightarrow Au(s)$	1.40
$Cl_2(g) + 2e^-$	$\rightarrow 2Cl^-$	1.36
$Cr_2O_7^{2-} + 14H^+ + 6e^-$	$\rightarrow 2Cr^{3+} + 7H_2O$	1.33
$O_2(g) + 4H^+ + 4e^-$	$\rightarrow 2H_2O$	1.23
$MnO_2(s) + 4H^+ + 2e^-$	$\rightarrow Mn^{2+} + 2H_2O$	1.23
$Br_2 + 2e^-$	$\rightarrow 2Br^-$	1.09
$NO_3^- + 4H^+ + 3e^-$	$\rightarrow NO(g) + 2H_2O$	0.97
$2Hg^{2+} + 2e^-$	$\rightarrow Hg_2^{2+}$	0.92
$Ag^+ + e^-$	$\rightarrow Ag(s)$	0.80
$Fe^{3+} + e^-$	$\rightarrow Fe^{2+}$	0.77
$O_2(g) + 2H^+ + 2e^-$	$\rightarrow H_2O_2$	0.68
$I_2(s) + 2e^-$	$\rightarrow 2I^-$	0.54
$Cu^+ + e^-$	$\rightarrow Cu(s)$	0.52
$Cu^{2+} + 2e^-$	$\rightarrow Cu(s)$	0.34
$AgCl(s) + e^-$	$\rightarrow Ag(s) + Cl^-$	0.22
$AgBr(s) + e^-$	$\rightarrow Ag(s) + Br^-$	0.10
$\mathbf{2H^+ + 2e^-}$	$\mathbf{\rightarrow H_2(g)}$	**0.00**
$Pb^{2+} + 2e^-$	$\rightarrow Pb(s)$	−0.13
$Sn^{2+} + 2e^-$	$\rightarrow Sn(s)$	−0.14
$Ni^{2+} + 2e^-$	$\rightarrow Ni(s)$	−0.25
$Fe^{2+} + 2e^-$	$\rightarrow Fe(s)$	−0.44
$Cr^{3+} + 3e^-$	$\rightarrow Cr(s)$	−0.74
$Zn^{2+} + 2e^-$	$\rightarrow Zn(s)$	−0.76
$2H_2O + 2e^-$	$\rightarrow H_2(g) + 2OH^-$	−0.83
$Al^{3+} + 3e^-$	$\rightarrow Al(s)$	−1.66
$Mg^{2+} + 2e^-$	$\rightarrow Mg(s)$	−2.36
$Na^+ + e^-$	$\rightarrow Na(s)$	−2.71
$Ca^{2+} + 2e^-$	$\rightarrow Ca(s)$	−2.87
$K^+ + e^-$	$\rightarrow K(s)$	−2.93
$Li^+ + e^-$	$\rightarrow Li(s)$	−3.05

Increasing strength of oxidising agent (upwards) — Increasing strength of reducing agent (downwards)

1. A negative E° means that the redox couple is a stronger reducing agent than the H^+/H_2 couple.
2. A positive E° means that the redox couple is a weaker reducing agent than the H^+/H_2 couple.

POWER TIPS

- The greater the reduction potential of an element, the more easily it will be reduced and low reduction potential will get oxidised easily.
- On moving down in the electrochemical series the reducing strength increase and oxidising strength decreases.

ELECTROCHEMISTRY

- Deals with study of relationship between electrical energy and chemical energy.
- Interconversion of one form of energy into another.

ELECTROLYSIS AND ITS LAW

The process of decomposition of an electrolyte by the passage of electricity through aqueous solution or molten state.

1 Quantitative Electrolysis

- Study of amount of product formed at electrodes.

2 Qualitative Electrolysis

- Study of possible products formed at electrodes.

CONDUCTOR

Substance that allow the electric current to pass through them.

INSULATOR

Substance that do not allow the passage of current through them.

01 METALLIC CONDUCTOR

- Free electrons or holes are responsible for conduction.
- Conduction due to metallic conductor is called **electronic conductivity**. It depends upon
  - Nature and structure of metal.
  - Density of metal.
  - Number of valence electron per atom.
  - Temperature inverse relation.

02 ELECTROLYTIC CONDUCTOR

- Movement of ions is responsible for conduction.
- Conductivity depends upon
  - Nature of electrolyte
  - Nature of solvent and its viscosity
  - Concentration of the electrolyte
  - Temperature (direct relation)

STRONG ELECTROLYTES

- Have the ability to dissociate completely or almost completely.
- e.g. NaCl, HCl, H_2SO_4 etc.

WEAK ELECTROLYTES

- Have less ability to dissociate.
- e.g. H_2CO_3, $ZnCl_2$, $HgCl_2$ etc.

FARADAY'S LAW OF ELECTROLYSIS

FIRST LAW

- Amount of any substance deposited or liberated at any electrode is directly proportional to the quantity of electricity passed through the electrolytic solution.

$$W = Zit$$

W → Substance deposited; Z → Electrochemical Equivalent; it → Electricity passed per unit time

$$Z = \frac{\text{Equivalent wt. of substance}}{96500}$$

96500 → Faraday constant

SECOND LAW

- When same quantity of electricity is passed through solutions of different electrolytes connected in series, the weight of substance produced at the electrodes is directly proportional to their equivalent weights.

- $\frac{W_1}{W_2} = \frac{E_1}{E_2}$ or $\frac{Z_1 it}{Z_2 it} = \frac{E_1}{E_2}$

KOHLRAUSCH'S LAW

- The molar conductivity of an electrolyte at infinite dilution is the sum of molar conductivity of ions produced by the electrolyte at infinite dilution.

$$\mu^{\infty} = n^{+} \times \mu_c^{\infty} + n^{-} \times \mu_a^{\infty}$$

n^+ → Number of cation; μ_c^{∞} → Molar conductivity of cation; n^- → Number of anion; μ_a^{∞} → Molar conductivity of anion.

- The equivalent conductivity of an electrolyte at infinite dilution is the sum of two values one depending on cation and other on anion.

$$\lambda_{eq}^{\circ} = \lambda_c^{\circ} + \lambda_a^{\circ}$$

MOLAR CONDUCTIVITY

- The conducting power of all the ions produced by dissolving 1 mol of on electrolyte in solution.
- $\Lambda_m = \frac{\kappa \times 1000}{M}$

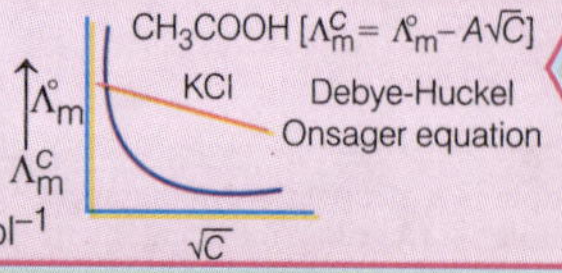

Unit S cm^{2}mol^{-1}

EQUIVALENT CONDUCTIVITY

- Conducting power of all the ions produced by dissolving 1g - equivalent of an electrolyte in the solution.
- λ_{eq} or $\Lambda = \frac{\kappa \times 1000}{C_{eq}\ (N)}$
- **Unit** Ω^{-1} cm^2 (eqv^{-1})

CONDUCTANCE IN ELECTROLYTIC SOLUTION

Conductance (C)
- Property of a medium which tells about ease with which current flow through medium.
- $C = \frac{1}{R}$

Resistivity (ρ)
- Resistance of a conductor of 1 cm length and have cross-sectional area of 1cm^2.
- $\rho = Rl/A$

Specific conductance (k)
- Reciprocal of specific resistance
- $k = \frac{1}{\rho} = C\frac{l}{a}$

Resistance (R)
- Hindrance in the flow of current through a conductor.
- $R = \frac{V}{I}$

Cell constant (G*)
- $G^* = \frac{l}{a}$
- Unit in cm^{-1} or m^{-1}

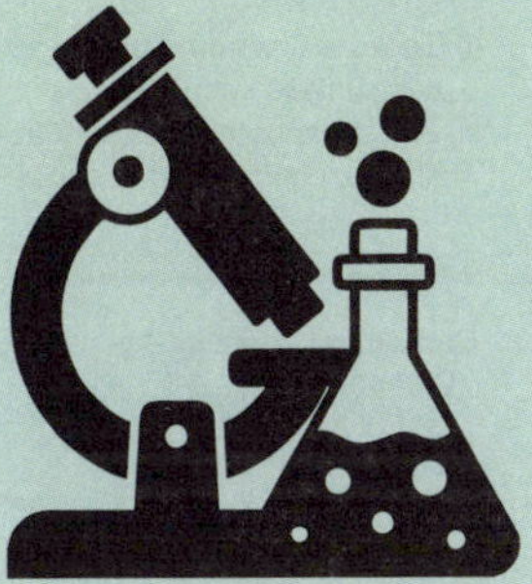

WHEATSTONE BRIDGE

Use to measure resistance of an electrolytic solution.

When null point is obtained,

$$\frac{R_1}{R_2} = \frac{R_3}{R_4}$$

Unknown resistance,

$$R_2 = \frac{R_1 R_4}{R_3}$$

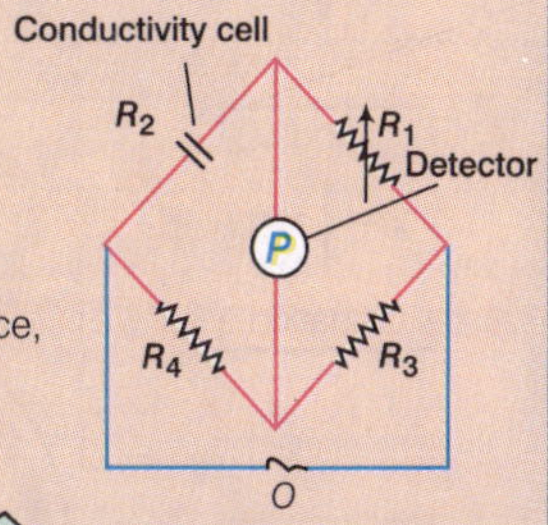

TYPES OF HALF-CELLS

Type	Example	Half cell reaction
Gas - Ion half-cell	$Pt(H_2)/H^+ (aq)$ $Pt (Cl_2)/Cl^- (aq)$	$1/2H_2(g) \rightarrow H^+(aq) + e^-$ $Cl^-(aq) \rightarrow 1/2\ Cl_2(g) + e^-$
Metal - Metal ion half cell	$Ag/Ag^+ (aq)$	$Ag(s) \rightarrow Ag^+(aq) + e^-$
Mercury - Mercury sulphate half cell	$Hg, HgSO_4/SO_4^{2-}(aq)$	$SO_4^{2-}(aq) + Hg(l) \rightarrow HgSO_4(s) + 2e^-$

ELECTRODE AND THEIR TYPES

- These are the material that conducts electricity to or from cell due to movement of electrons.
- Inert and attackable electrode.

01 Standard Hydrogen Electrode (SHE)

- Pressure of H_2 gas is maintained at 1atm.
- Concentration of H^+ in the solution is 1M.

02 Normal Hydrogen Electrode (NHE)

- Electrode potential of NHE is zero.
- Represented at Pt/H_2 (atm)/H^+(1M)

03 Calomel Electrode

- It is secondary reference electrode.
- Paste of mercury and mercurous chloride is used.

Effect of Nature of Electrolyte

- Conductivity of strong electrolyte is higher in comparison to weak electrolytes.

Variation of Conductivity with Dilution

- For both weak and strong electrolytes, the electrolytic conductance, the equivalent conductivity (Λ_{eq}) and molar conductivity (Λ_m) increases with dilution.
- Conductivity (or specific conductivity, K) always decreases with dilution, for both weak and strong electrolyte.

ELECTROCHEMICAL CELLS

Type	Energy Change	Anode	Cathode
Electrolytic cell	Electrical energy → Chemical energy	+	–
Galvanic (Voltaic) cell	Chemical energy → Electrical energy	–	+

DANIELL CELLS

- Anode is made up of Zn-rod and dipped in solution of $ZnSO_4$ (oxidation half-cell).
- Cathode is made up of Cu-rod and dipped in the solution of $CuSO_4$ (Reduction half-cell).
- Overall redox reaction,

$$Zn(s) + Cu^{2+}(aq) \longrightarrow Zn^{2+}(aq) + Cu(s)$$

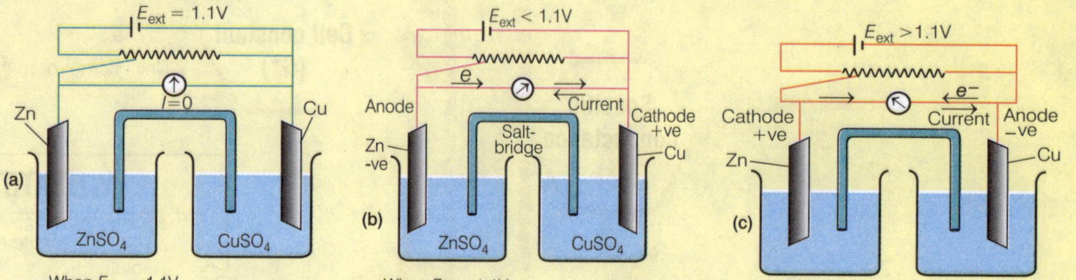

When $E_{ext} = 1.1V$
(i) No flow of electrons or current
(ii) No chemical reaction

When $E_{ext} < 1.1V$
(i) Electrons flow from Zn rod to Cu rod, hence current flows from Cu to Zn
(ii) Zn dissolves at anode and copper deposits at cathode

When $E_{ext} > 1.1V$
(i) Electrons flow from Cu to Zn and current flows from Zn to Cu.
(ii) Zinc is deposited at the zinc electrode and copper dissolves at copper electrode.

CELL REPRESENTATION

Anode

$X(s) \mid X^{n+}(aq)$

Oxidation

Cathode

$Y^{m+}(aq) \mid Y(s)$

Reduction

EMF OF CELL

$$E^\circ_{cell} = E^\circ_{right} - E^\circ_{left} = E^\circ_{cathode} - E^\circ_{anode}$$

Dry Cells

- **Anode** $Zn(s) \longrightarrow Zn^{2+} + 2e^-$
- **Cathode** $2MnO_2 + 2NH_4^+ + 2e^- \longrightarrow 2MnO(OH) + 2NH_3\uparrow$
- **Net reaction** $Zn(s) + 2NH_4^+(s) + 2MnO_2(s)$
  $\longrightarrow Zn^{2+}(aq) + 2MnO(OH) + 2NH_3$
- **Uses** In transistor and clock.

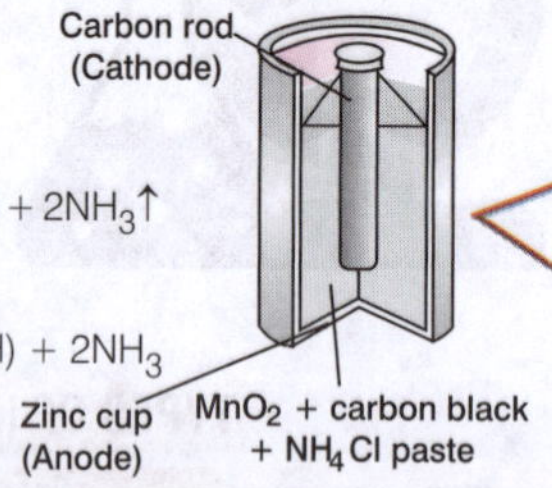

SALT BRIDGE

- Inverted U shaped tube that contains a mixture of *agar-agar* jelly and an electrolyte like KCN or KNO_3 etc.
- It connects the two solution of two half-cells, thus completes the cell circuit.
- Prevents diffusion of the solution from one half cell to other.
- Prevents liquid - liquid junction potential.

Lead Storage Cell

- **Anode** $Pb(s) + SO_4^{2-}(aq) \longrightarrow PbSO_4(s) + 2e^-$
- **Cathode** $PbO_2(s) + SO_4^{2-}(aq) + 4H^+(aq) + 2e^-$
  $\longrightarrow PbSO_4(s) + 2H_2O(l)$
- **Net Reaction** $Pb(s) + PbO_2(s) + 2H_2SO_4(aq)$
  $\longrightarrow 2PbSO_4(s) + 2H_2O(l)$
- Reverse reaction takes place during recharging.
- **Use** In automobile and inverter.

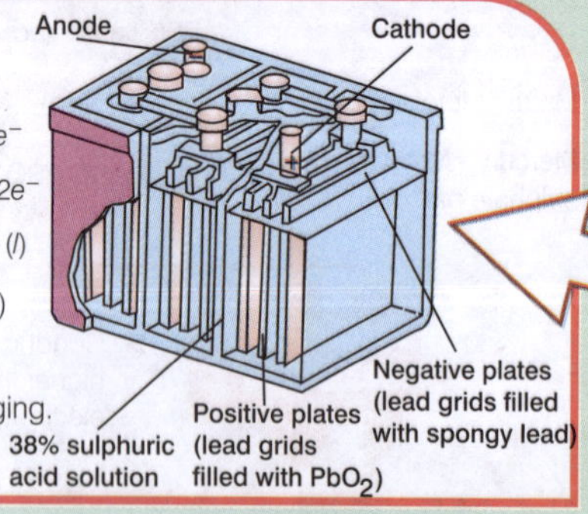

FUEL CELLS

- Cells that can convert energy of combustion of fuel into electrical energy.

- **Anode** $2H_2(g) + 4OH^-(aq) \longrightarrow 4H_2O(l) + 4e^-$
- **Cathode** $O_2(g) + 2H_2O(l) + 4e^- \longrightarrow 4OH^-(aq)$
- **Net reaction** $2H_2(g) + O_2(g) \longrightarrow 2H_2O(l)$
- **Uses** In automobiles on experimental basis, producing electricity in apollo space program.

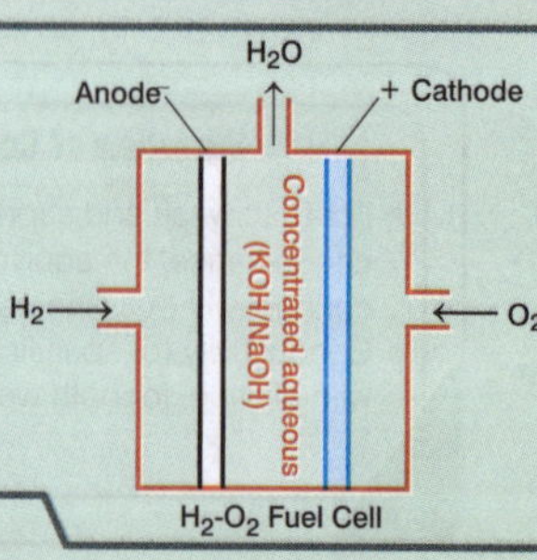

01 Equilibrium constant from Nernst Equation

$$E^\circ_{cell} = \frac{0.0591}{n} \log K_C$$

02 Relationship between cell potential and Gibbs free energy

$$\Delta G = -nFE_{cell}$$
$$\Delta G^\circ = -nFE^\circ_{cell}$$

03 Relation between cell potential (E°_{cell}), free energy (ΔG°) and Equilibrium Constant, K_c

$$\Delta G^\circ = -2.303\, RT \log K_C$$
$$E^\circ_{cell} = \frac{2.303RT}{nF} \log K_C$$

NERNST EQUATION

- Relationship between electrode potential and concentration of solution.
- For reduction half reaction, Nernst equation is

$$E_{M^{n+}/M} = E^\circ_{(M^{n+}/M)} - \frac{2.303\, RT}{nF} \log \frac{[M(s)]}{[M^{n+}(aq)]}$$

ELECTRODE POTENTIAL (E)

It is the measure of the tendency of an electrolyte to gain or lose electrons in a half-cell.

- Oxidation potential - Tendency of an electrode to lose electron.
  $M(s) \rightleftharpoons M^{n+}(aq) + ne^-$
- Reduction potential - Tendency of an electrode to gain electron.
  $M^{n+}(aq) + ne^- \rightleftharpoons M(s)$

POWER TIPS

NERNST EQUATION FOR CONCENTRATION CELLS

Electrode is reversible wrt cation. $Zn|Zn^{2+}(C_1)||Zn^{2+}(C_2)|Zn$

- $E_{cell} = \frac{0.0591}{2} \log \frac{C_2}{C_1}$
- For reaction to be spontaneous $C_2 > C_1$

Electrode is reversible wrt anion. $Pt(Cl_2)|Cl^-(C_1)||Cl^-(C_2)|Pt(Cl_2)$

- $E_{cell} = \frac{0.0591}{n} \log \frac{C_1}{C_2}$
- For reaction to be spontaneous $C_1 > C_2$

Electrode at different concentration are dipped into same electrolyte.

- $E_{cell} = E^\circ_{cell} - \frac{0.0591}{n} \log \frac{p_2}{p_1}$
- Cell is spontaneous, if p_1 (LHS) > p_2 (RHS)

MEASUREMENT OF ELECTRODE POTENTIAL

- Measurement of absolute value of electrode potential is not possible.
- Difference of potentials between 2 electrodes can be measured.
- For indirect measurement, reference electrode is used.

BATTERY

Arrangement of one or more cells connected in series.

Primary Batteries

Cells once exhausted cannot be used again.

Mercury Cell

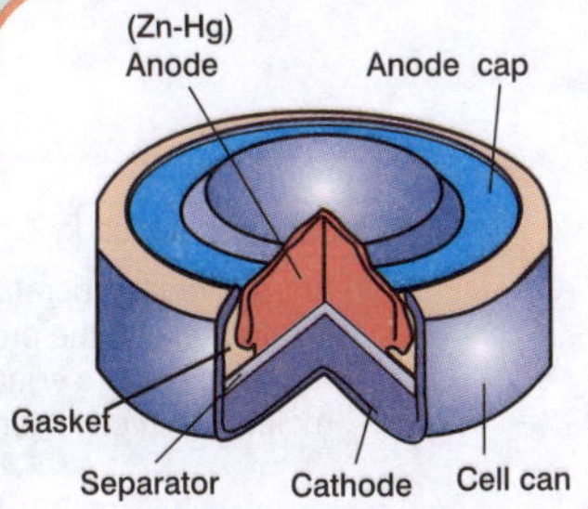

- **Anode** $Zn(Hg) + 2OH^-(aq) \longrightarrow ZnO(s) + H_2O(l) + 2e^-$
- **Cathode** $HgO(s) + 2H_2O(l) + 2e^- \longrightarrow Hg(l) + 2OH^-(aq)$
- **Net reaction** $Zn(Hg) + HgO(s) \longrightarrow ZnO(s) + Hg(l)$
- Cell potential is 1.55 V.
- **Use** In watch and hearing aid.

Secondary Batteries

Cells that can be used again and again.

Nickel-Cadmium Cell

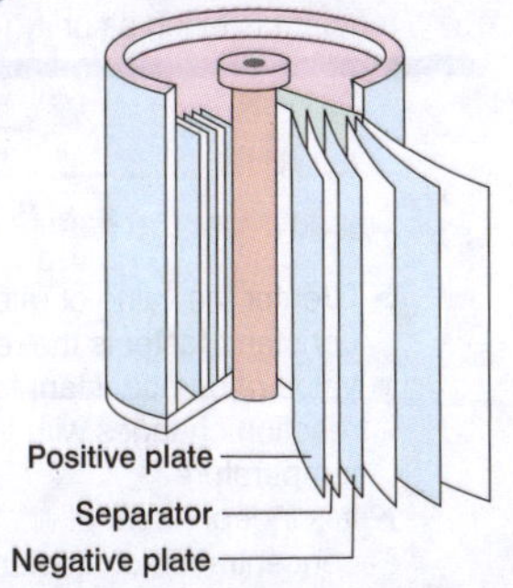

- **Cathode** $2Ni(OH)_3(s) + 2e^- \longrightarrow 2Ni(OH)_2(s) + 2OH^-(aq)$
- **Anode** $Cd(s) + 2OH^-(aq) \longrightarrow CdO(s) + H_2O(l) + 2e^-$
- **Net reaction** $Cd(s) + 2Ni(OH)_3(s) \longrightarrow CdO(s) + 2Ni(OH)_2(s) + H_2O(l)$
- **Use** In portable electronic device, emergency lighting, photography equipment.

Chapter 03

Chemical Kinetics

CHEMICAL KINETICS

The branch of science that deals with-

- The speed or the rate of chemical reactions.
- Factors affecting the rate of reactions.
- Mechanism by which reaction proceeds.

RATE OF CHEMICAL REACTION

- The change in concentration of any one of the reactants or products per unit time.
- Rate of reaction

$$= \frac{\text{Decrease in concentration of reactant}}{\text{Time taken}}$$

$$= \frac{\text{Increase in concentration of product}}{\text{Time taken}}$$

Average Rate of Reaction

The average value during a large time interval.

$$r_{av} = \frac{-\Delta[R]}{\Delta t} = \frac{\Delta[P]}{\Delta t}$$

Instantaneous Rate of Reaction

The rate of reaction at a particular instant of time, i.e. when Δt approaches zero.

$$r_{inst} = -\frac{d[R]}{dt} = \frac{d[P]}{dt}$$

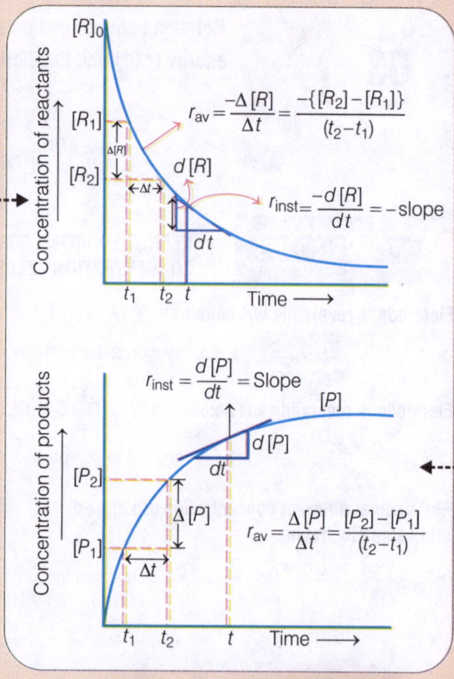

CHEMICAL REACTIONS

One or more substances undergoes a change that result in the formation of new product that differ from original one in composition.

Instantaneous/Very Fast Reactions

- Reaction complete in less than 10^{-12} s.
- e.g. Ionic reactions.

Very Slow Reactions

- Reactions which complete in some days or years.
- e.g. Weathering of rocks.

Moderately Slow Reactions

- Reactions which are intermediate between very slow and very fast reactions.
- e.g. Hydrolysis of esters .

Elementary Reaction

- The reactions that takes place in one step.

Complex Reactions

- A chemical reaction that occur in multiple steps.
- Different step of complex reactions are elementary reactions.

FACTORS AFFECTING RATE OF REACTION

Concentration of Reaction

- Greater the concentration, faster is the reaction, as the number of collision increases.

Nature of Reactant

- The reactant with weak bonds react quickly.
- The reactants with strong bond react slowly.

Surface Area of Reactant

- Greater the surface area faster is the reaction.

Catalyst

- Substance that increases the reaction rate without undergoing a chemical change itself.
- It lowers the activation energy for a chemical reaction.

Temperature

- As temperature increases, kinetic energy also increases.

RATE LAW AND RATE CONSTANT

Law of Mass Action

For a given temperature, the rate of reaction is directly proportional to the product of the active mass of the reactant raised to powers equal to the number of their respective molecules in stoichiometric equation.

01 Rate Constant

Rate of the reaction when the concentration of each reactant is taken as unity.

02 Rate Law Expression

The mathematical relation between the rate of reaction and the concentration of the reactant.

Characteristics of Rate Constant

- Greater the value of rate constant, faster is the reaction.
- Value of rate constant for same reaction changes with temperature.
- It is independent of concentration of reactant.

Units of Rate Constant

For n^{th} order of a reaction,

$$nA \longrightarrow \text{Product}$$

$$\text{Rate} = k[A]^n$$

$$k = \frac{\text{Rate}}{[A]^n}$$

$$= [\text{Concentration}]^{1-n}\,[\text{Time}]^{-1}$$

$$= (\text{mol})^{1-n}\,\text{L}^{n-1}\,\text{s}^{-1}$$

ORDER OF A REACTION

- Experimental quantity, cannot be calculated.
- Order can be 0, 1, 2, 3 or fractional.
- Applicable to elementary and complex reactions
- For complex reaction, order is given by slowest step.

- It is the sum of powers of the concentration of the reactants in the rate law expression.
- e.g. For a reaction, $aA + bB \rightarrow cC + dD$

Rate = $k\,[A]^x[B]^y$ — Their sum will give order of reaction.

Zero Order

$H_2 + Cl_2 \xrightarrow{\text{Sunlight}} 2HCl$

Rate = $k\,[H_2]^0[Cl_2]^0 = k$

First Order

$2N_2O_5 \longrightarrow 4NO_2 + O_2$

Rate = $k[N_2O_5]$

Second Order

$H_2 + I_2 \longrightarrow 2HI$

Rate = $k\,[H_2][I_2]$

Third Order

$2NO + O_2 \longrightarrow 2NO_2$

Rate = $k\,[NO]^2\,[O_2]$

Fractional Order

$CH_3CHO \longrightarrow CH_4 + CO$

Rate = $k\,[CH_3CHO]^{3/2}$

MOLECULARITY

- Can be calculated by adding molecules in the slowest step.
- It is always a whole number.
- For complex reaction, molecularity has no significance.
- The number of reacting species (atoms, ions or molecules) that takes part in an elementary reaction, which must collide simultaneously in order to bring a chemical reaction.

Unimolecular Reaction

- One reacting species is involved.
- e.g. Decomposition of ammonium nitrite .

$NH_4NO_2 \longrightarrow N_2(g) + 2H_2O(g)$

Bimolecular Reaction

- Involves simultaneous collision between two species.
- e.g. Dissociation of HI.

$2HI \longrightarrow H_2 + I_2$

Trimolecular Reaction

- Involves collision among three species.
- e.g. Reaction between NO and O_2.

$2NO + O_2 \longrightarrow 2NO_2$

Pseudo-Unimolecular Reaction

- Reactions which are not truly of the first order but under certain conditions becomes reactions of the first order.
- e.g. Acid hydrolysis of ethyl acetate, Acid catalysed inversion of cane sugar.

$CH_3COOCH_2CH_3 + H_2O \xrightleftharpoons{H^+} CH_3COOH + CH_3CH_2OH$

METHODS OF DETERMINATION OF ORDER OF REACTIONS

Hit and Trial Method

- General equation, $nA \rightarrow$ products $\quad X_n = \dfrac{1}{t(n-1)}\left[\dfrac{1}{(a-x)^{n-1}} - \dfrac{1}{a^{n-1}}\right]$
- Equation is applicable for all order except first.

Half-Life Method or Fractional Change Method

- $t_{1/2} \propto [A]_0$ (For zero order)
- $t_{1/2} = \dfrac{0.693}{k}$ (For 1st order)
- For gaseous reaction, $n = \dfrac{1 + \log (t_{1/2})_1/(t_{1/2})_2}{\log (P_2/P_1)}$

Initial Rate Method

- Determined by varying the concentration of one of the reactant.
- The concentration of other reactant are kept constant.

Ostwald Isolation Method

- Used to determine the order of complicated reaction by isolating one of the reactants.
- It involved isolating and varying the concentration of one reactant while keeping the concentration of other reactants constant.

Order	Rate Law	Integrated Rate Law	Half-Life	Unit of Rate Constant	Graph
0	Rate = $k[A]^0$	$[A]_t = -kt + [A]_0$	$t_{1/2} = \dfrac{[A]_0}{2k}$	mol $L^{-1}\,s^{-1}$	$[A]$ vs t slope = $-k$
1	Rate = $k[A]^1$	$ln[A]_t = -kt + ln[A]_0$	$t_{1/2} = \dfrac{0.693}{k}$	s^{-1}	$ln[A]$ vs t slope = $-k$
n	Rate = $k[A]^n$	$(n-1)kt = \dfrac{1}{[A]^{n-1}} - \dfrac{1}{[A]_0^{n-1}}$	$t_{1/2} = \dfrac{2^{n-1}-1}{k(n-1)[A]_0^{n-1}}$	$(\text{mol } L^{-1})^{1-n}\,s^{-1}$	$\dfrac{1}{[A]^{n-1}}$ vs t slope = k

POWER TIPS

Graphical Method

- The values of $\Delta x/\Delta t$ at different interval is calculated by plotting a curve between x & time t.
- The value of $\Delta x/\Delta t$ at a particular time corresponds to particular value of $(a-x)$ is given by slope of the curve at that curve.

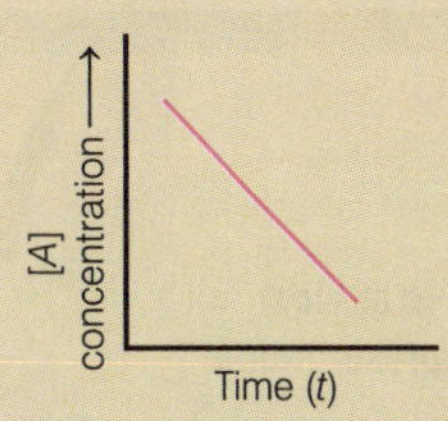

For zero order

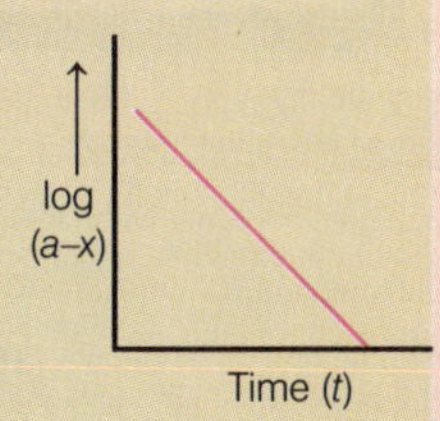

For first order

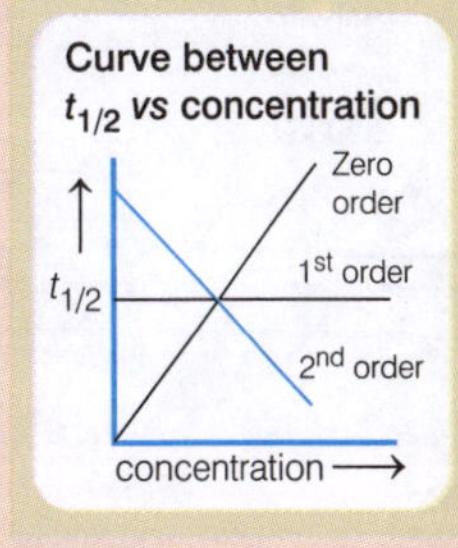

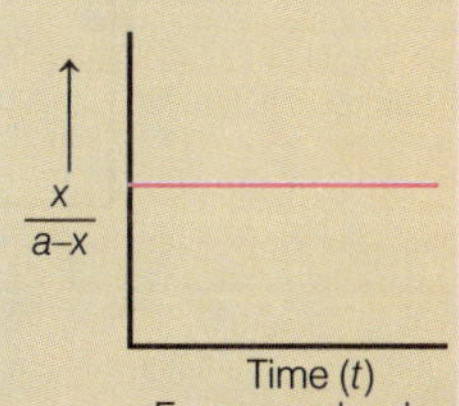

For second order

Molecular and Energetic Aspects of Reaction

Molecular Orientation

Molecules with proper orientation during collisions determines whether a reaction occurs.

Energy Distribution

Only molecule with energy greater than E_a contribute to the reaction.

Temperature

Higher temperature increases molecular kinetic energy leading to more effective collisions.

Rate of Catalyst

Lowers the activation energy, increasing the number of effective molecular collisions.

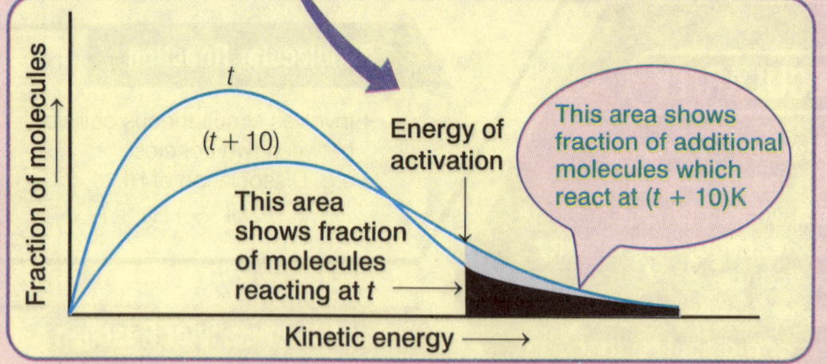

Arrhenius Equation

$$k = A(e^{-E_a/RT})$$

Energy of Activation (E_a); Gas Constant (R); Boltzmann Factor ($e^{-E_a/RT}$); Frequency Factor/Collision Number (A)

- Different reactions have different rates.
- Lesser is the activation energy, faster is the reaction rate.
- Activation energy can never be zero.
- As $T \to \infty$, the rate constant becomes equal to frequency factor (A).

Activation Energy

The minimum amount of energy required to break the bonds of the reactants and allow them to form new products.

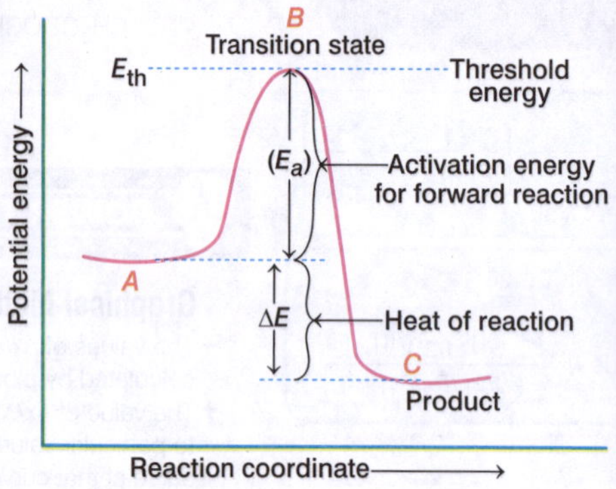

Graphical representation

$$\log k = \log A - \frac{E_a}{2.303RT}$$

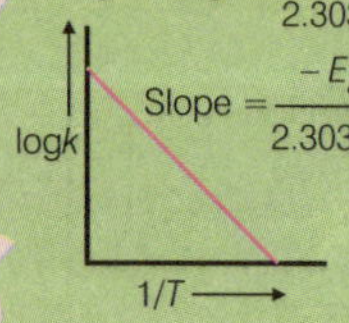

Calculation

$$\log \frac{k_2}{k_1} = \frac{E_a}{2.303R}\left[\frac{T_2 - T_1}{T_1 T_2}\right]$$

$$\frac{d[\log k]}{dT} = \frac{E_a}{RT^2}$$

POWER TIPS

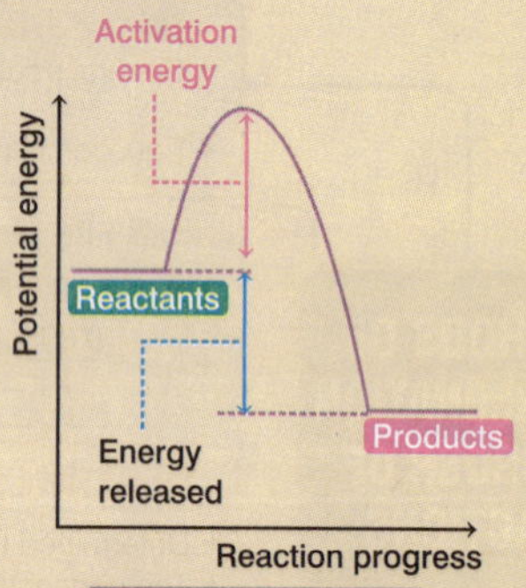

Exothermic Reaction

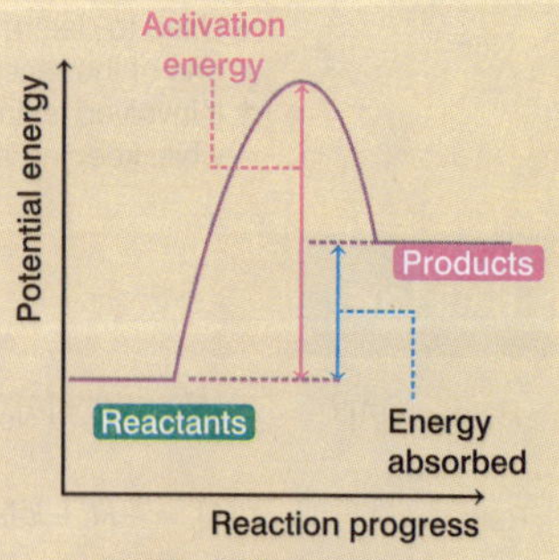

Endothermic Reaction

THEORIES OF RATE OF REACTION

Collision Theory of Bimolecular Reactions

- If two molecules are react together, they must collide with each other.
- Collision between all molecules do not lead to chemical reaction.
- To make effective collision, colliding molecules must possess the threshold energy.
- Rate constant is given by $k = PZ_{AB}e^{-E_a/RT}$

✸ Effective orientation of collision

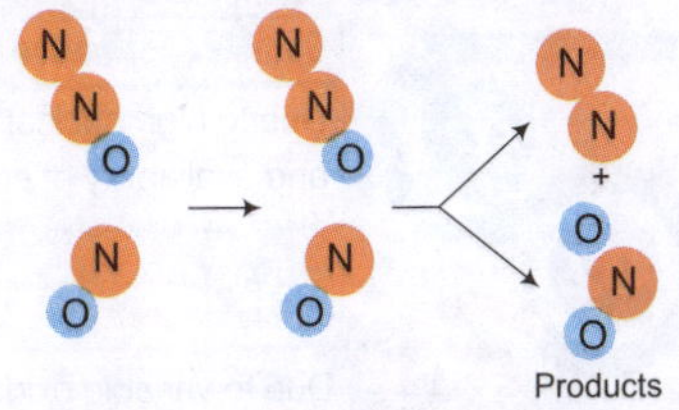

✸ Ineffective orientation of collision

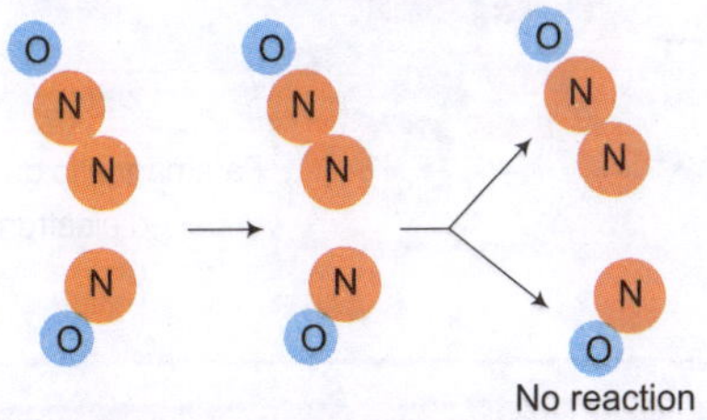

Transition State Theory

- Theory is based on bond breaking and bond making involved in a chemical reaction must occur simultaneously.
- Reactant molecule must come together to form an activated complex, whose energy is higher than the reactant molecule.
- Activated complex is in equilibrium with the reactant molecules.
- The complex is unstable and has transient existence and its potential energy is maximum.
- Energy of activation is the additional energy that the reacting molecule must acquire to form the activated complex.

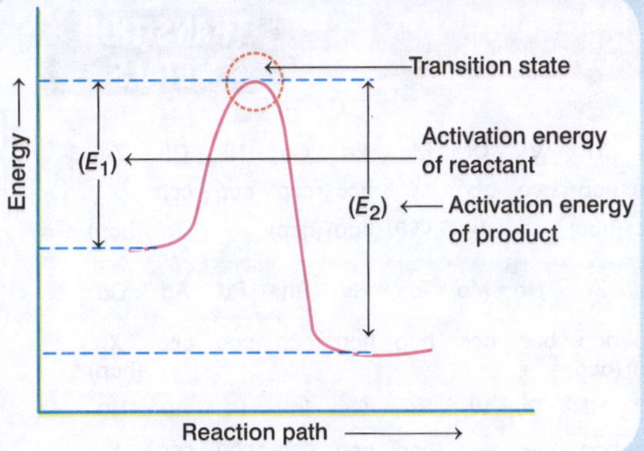

Action of Catalyst

A catalyst speed up the reaction lowering the potential energgy barrier and thus by decreasing the activation energy.

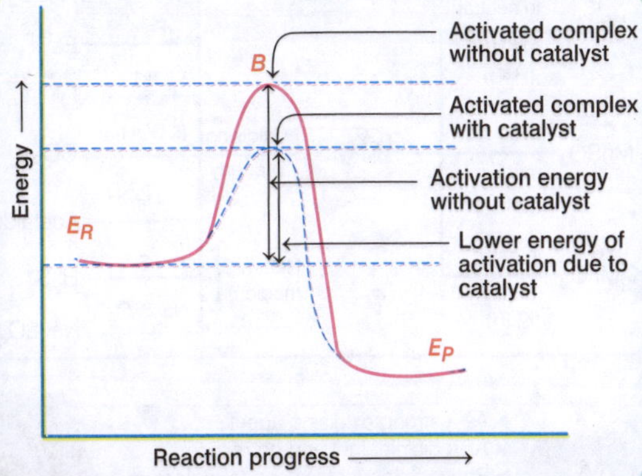

POWER TIPS

1. Rate law equation for parallel reactions

(i) Parallel reaction

$$A \xrightarrow{k_1} B, \quad A \xrightarrow{k_2} C$$

$$\text{Rate} = (k_1+k_2)[A]$$

Fraction Yield of 'A' $= \dfrac{k_1}{k_1+k_2}$ Fraction Yield of 'B' $= \dfrac{k_2}{k_1+k_2}$

(ii) Consecutive reaction

$$A \xrightarrow{k_1} B \xrightarrow{k_2} C$$

Concentration of 'A' at t, $[A]_t = [A]_0\, e^{-k_1 t}$

2. The rate of reaction increases with increase in temperature because of the increase in the effective number of collisions.
3. Molecularity of a reaction is mostly lie between 1 to 3, but never be zero. It is rare that molecularity exceeds to 3.

Chapter 04 *d*-and *f*-Block Elements

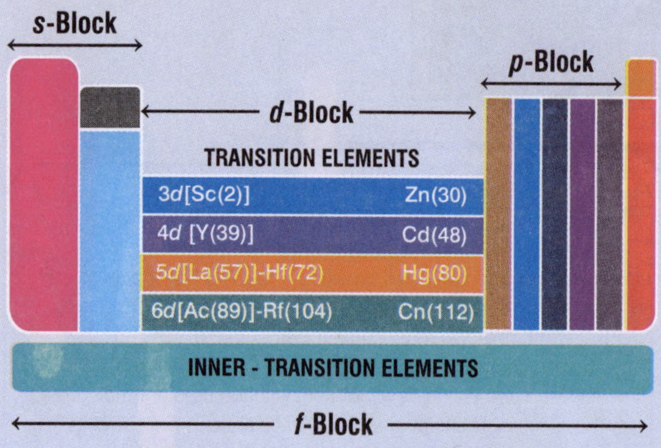

d-Block Elements

- They have completely filled outermost shell and incompletely filled inner shell.
- Last electron enter into $(n-1)$ *d*-orbital.
- Placed from group 3 to 12. Also called as **transition elements.**
- Zinc, cadmium and mercury have completely filled $(n-1)d$ subshell. They are called as **non-typical transition elements.**

General Characteristics

TRANSITION METALS

Lattice Structure of Transition Metals

Sc	Ti	V	Cr	Mn	Fe	Co	Ni	Cu	Zn
hcp (bcc)	hcp (bcc)	bcc	bcc	X (bcc,ccp)	bcc	ccp (hcp)	ccp (hcp)	ccp	X (hcp)
Y	**Zr**	**Nb**	**Mo**	**Tc**	**Ru**	**Rh**	**Pd**	**Ag**	**Cd**
hcp (bcc)	hcp (bcc)	bcc	bcc	hcp	hcp	hcp	ccp	ccp	X (hcp)
La	**Hf**	**Ta**	**W**	**Re**	**Os**	**Ir**	**Pt**	**Au**	**Hg**
hcp (ccp, bcc)	hcp (bcc)	bcc	bcc	hcp	hcp	ccp	ccp	ccp	X

Chemical Properties

01 **Complex Formation**: Due to high nuclear charge, small size and availability of empty *d*-orbitals.

02 **Form Coloured Compounds**: Due to *d-d* transition and charge transfer.

03 **Catalytic Behaviour**: Due to variable oxidation states and ability to form complexes.

04 **Alloy Formation**: Due to similar atomic size.

05 **Magnetic Behaviour**: Paramagnetic due to presence of unpaired electrons.

POTASSIUM DICHROMATE ($K_2Cr_2O_7$)

Prepared from chromite or ferrochrome or chrome iron ($FeCr_2O_4$ or $FeO{\cdot}Cr_2O_3$).

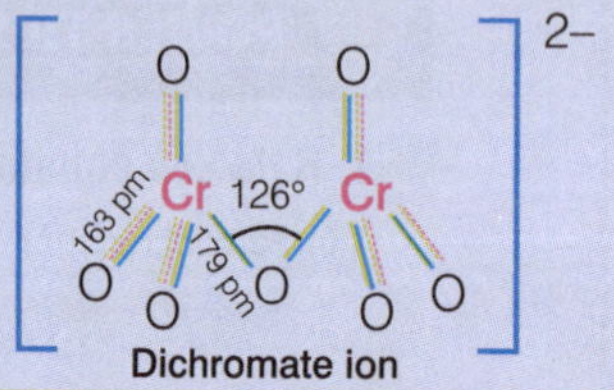

Dichromate ion

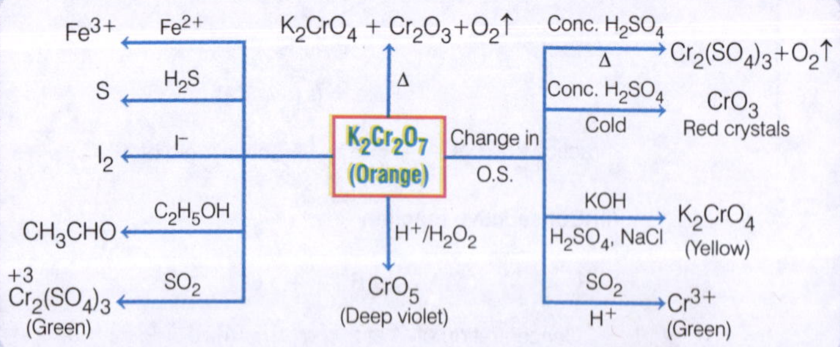

Uses

- In volumetric analysis, for estimation of iron and iodine in redox titration.
- In chrome tanning in leather industry.
- In photography for hardening gelatine film.

POTASSIUM PERMANGANATE ($KMnO_4$)

- Prepared from MnO_2.
- Powerful oxidising agent in solution state and acts as a strong bleaching agent.

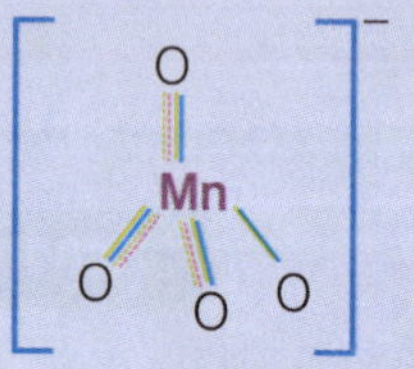

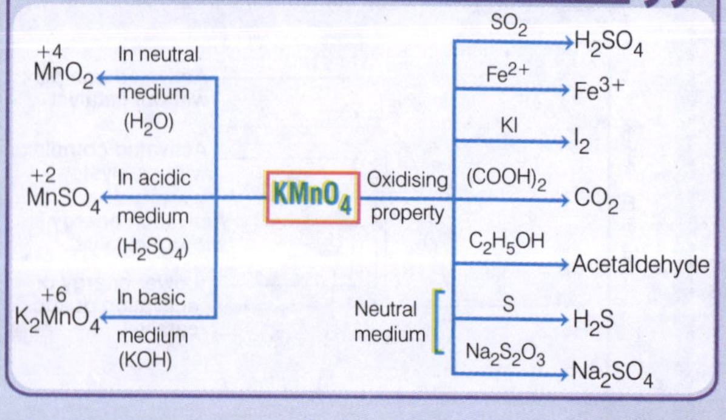

Uses

- As a strong oxidising agent.
- As a disinfectant and germicide.
- Baeyer's reagent is used for detecting unsaturation in an organic compound.

GENERAL AND PHYSICAL PROPERTIES

01 Molar Volume and Density

- Molar volume of *d*- and *f*-block elements are much lower than those of *s*-elements of neighbouring groups.
- Density increases on moving from left to right.

02 Enthalpy of Atomisation

- Possess high enthalpy of atomisation.
- Metals of 2nd and 3rd series have greater enthalpies of atomisation than the corresponding element of first series.

03 Nature of Bond

- Have tendency to form covalent bond along with ionic bond.
- Compounds with lower valency form ionic compound.
- Compounds with higher valency form covalent compound.

04 Interstitial Compound

- Have tendency to trap small atoms like H, B, N etc in the interstitial space to form interstitial or non-stoichiometric compound.

05 Oxidation State

- Variable oxidation states arise due to participation of $(n-1)d$ and ns electrons.
- In +2 and +3 O.S, the bonds formed are mostly ionic.
- Low oxidation state, such as +1, 0 or negative are also possible.

06 Electronic Configuration

- General electronic configuration is $(n-1)d^{1-10}ns^{1-2}$.
- Do not show a regular trend of physical and chemical properties like *s*- and *p*-block elements.
- Half and completely filled sets of orbitals are relatively more stable.

07 Standard Reduction Potential (SRP)

- Negative standard reduction potential ∝ stability of transition metal.

Trends in $E^{\circ}_{M^{2+}/M}$

- No regular trend
- Except copper, all other elements have negative reduction potential values.

Trends in $E^{\circ}_{M^{3+}/M^{2+}}$

- Stability of Sc^{3+} is more than Sc^{2+} due to noble gas configuration.
- E° values for the redox couple M^{3+}/M^{2+} indicate Mn^{3+} and Co^{3+} are strongest oxidising agents.

08 Atomic and Ionic Size

- Atomic radii first decreases at the middle becomes almost constant and then increases towards the end of the period.
- Members of 4*d* and 5*d*-series exhibit similar radii which is due to lanthanoid contraction.

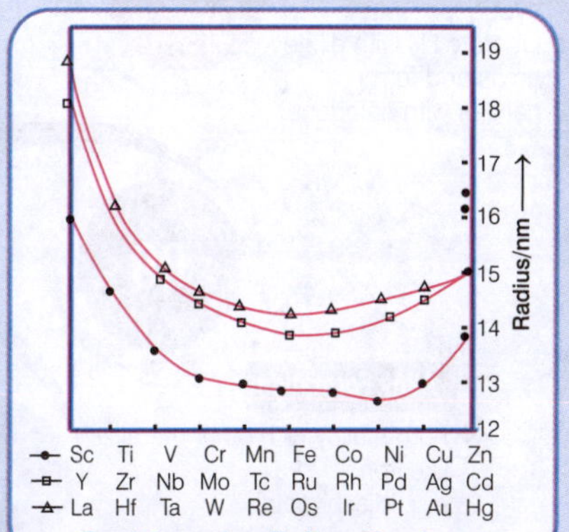

Trends in atomic radii of transition elements

09 Formation of Compounds

- Form binary compounds with non-metals.
- Metals of first transition series form oxides of general formula MO, M_2O_3, M_2O_5 and MO_3 at high temperature.
- Acidic strength of transition metal increases with increase in oxidation number.

10 Ionisation Enthalpy

- I.E of *d*-block is higher than those of *s*-block elements and lower than *p*-block elements.
- Extra stability of half filled and fully filled orbitals give rise to high I.E.

4*f*-SERIES OR LANTHANOIDS

- The last electron occupies the 4*f*-orbital.
- Includes elements from Ce (Z = 58) to Lu(Z=71).

f-BLOCK ELEMENTS

- Elements in which last electron enter into *f*-orbitals of the anti-penultimate shell are *f*-block elements.
- Have incomplete *d* and *f*-subshells.
- Elements after uranium are called **'transuranic elements'**.
- Depending upon the nature of *f*-orbitals of the antipenultimate shell, they are divided into 4*f* and 5*f*-series.

POWER TIPS

Some Reaction of lanthanoids

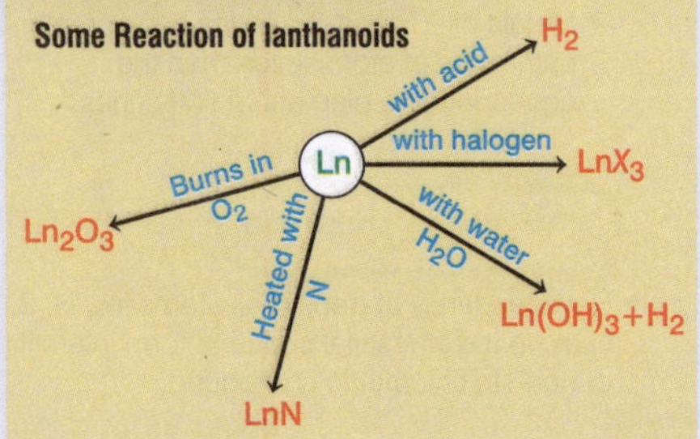

GENERAL AND PHYSICAL PROPERTIES

01 Electronic Configuration

- General electronic configuration is $[Xe]4f^{1-14}\ 5d^{0-1}\ 6s^2$
- **Exception**
  $Gd_{64} = [Xe]4f^7 5d^1 6s^2$
  $Lu_{71} = [Xe]4f^{14} 5d^1 6s^2$

02 Atomic and Ionic Radii

- As atomic number increases from La to Lu, the atomic and ionic radii decreases gradually.
- The decrease in atomic and ionic size is due to lanthanoid contraction. The contraction is due to imperfect shielding of electrons of *f*-orbital.

03 Oxidation State

- Shows variable valency or oxidation state +3 oxidation state is most stable.
- Higher oxidation state is not possible due to large energy gap between 4*f* and 5*d* orbital.

04 Electronegativity

- Increases from La to Lu for trivalent ions.

05 Ionisation Energy

- Have low ionisation energy.
- Have high electropositive character.

06 Colour

- Mostly trivalent lanthanoid ions are coloured in solid and aqueous solution.
- Colour of ions is due to *f*-*f* transition.
- Ce^{3+}, Gd^{3+}, Yb^{3+} and Lu^{3+} do not show colour.

07 Magnetic Properties

- Lanthanoid ions are generally paramagnetic
- Except Lu^{3+}, Yb^{3+}, Ce^{4+}

08 Complex Formation

- Have less tendency to form complexes.
- Have low charge density.
- Form complex with strong chelating agent but not with π-bonding ligands.

09 Alloy Formation

- Forms alloy with other metal like iron. e.g. Misch metal.

10 Reactivity

- Easily combined with hydrogen to form hydrides.
- Liberate H_2 with dilute acids and form halides with halogens.

11 Basic Nature

- Oxides (M_2O_3) and hydroxides [$M(OH)_3$] are stable.
- The hydroxides are ionic and basic.
- Basic strength decreases from $Ce(OH)_3$ to $Lu(OH)_3$.

5f-SERIES OR ACTINOIDS

- The last electron occupies the 5*f*-orbital.
- Includes elements from thorium ($Z = 90$) to lawrencium ($Z = 103$).
- Thorium, protactinium and uranium are radioactive.

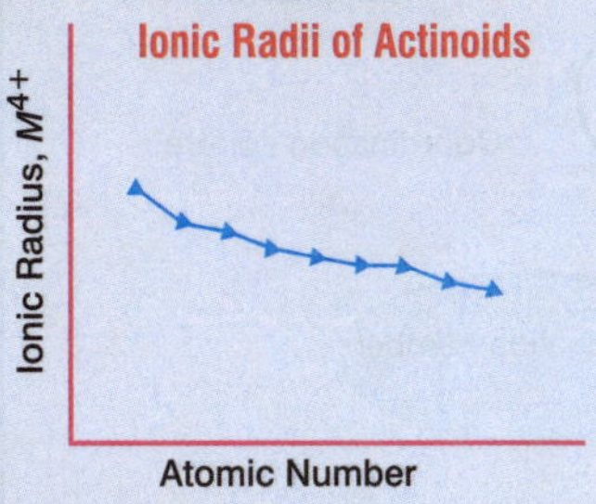

POWER TIPS

First 3 actinoides (Th, pa, u) are natural and $_{93}Np - _{103}Lr$ are man-made element.

Lanthanoids Contraction

- Poor shielding of the 6s electron from nuclear charge by the 4*f*-electron makes the atom smaller than expected.

Actinoid Contraction

- Poor shielding of the 7*s*-electron from nuclear charge by the 5*f*-electron makes the atom smaller than expected.

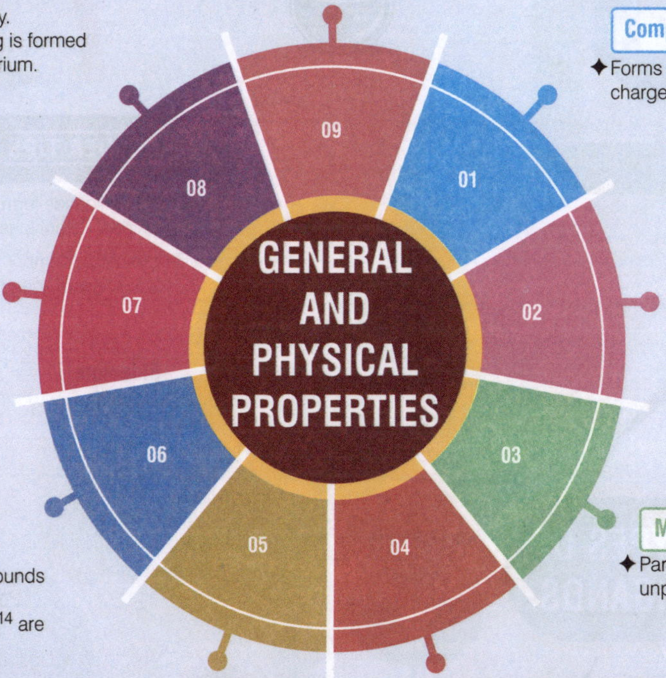

Basic Nature

- Their hydrides are non-stoichiometric.
- They do not react with alkalies like NaOH.
- Reacts with non-metals at moderate temperature.

Reactivity

- Increases with increase in atomic number.
- They tarnish rapidly.
- Protective covering is formed only in case of thorium.

Complex Formation

- Forms complex due to higher nuclear charge and small size.

Ionisation Energy

- I.E. are lower than lanthanoids.
- Have high electropositive character and behave as strong reducing agents.

Atomic and Ionic Size

- There is a gradual decrease in the size of atom or M^{3+} ions across the series due to actinoid contraction.
- It is due to poor shielding by 5*f*-electrons.

Colour

- These are coloured compounds due to $f-f$ transition.
- Ions having $5f^0$, $5f^7$ and $5f^{14}$ are colourless.

Magnetic Property

- Paramagnetic in nature due to presence of unpaired 5*f*-electrons.

Oxidation State

- Shows greater range of oxidation state.
- Maximum oxidation state increases from +4 in Th to +5 in Pa, +6 in U and +7 in Np and Pu and then decreases in succeeding elements.

Electronic Configuration

- The general electronic configuration is (Rn) $5f^{1-14}\,6d^{0-1}\,7s^2$.

Uses

- *Thorium is used in atomic reactor and in the treatment of cancer.*
- *U is used as nuclear fuel.*
- *Pu is used as fuel for atomic reactor.*

Chapter 05 Coordination Compounds

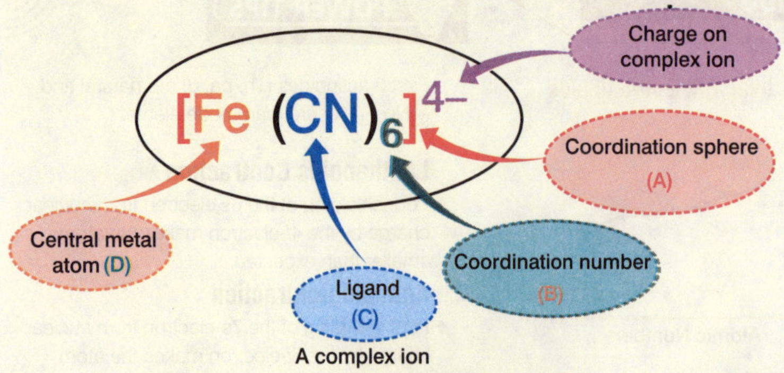

A complex ion

(A) Square bracket enclosing the central atom and the ligands directly attached to it.

(B) The total number of ligands attached to the central metal ion through coordinate bond.

(C) The donor atom, molecules or anions which donate a pair of electrons to the metal atom or ion and form a coordinate bond.

(D) Metal atom to which ligands are attached.

DOUBLE SALTS

- Compounds formed by combination of two or more simple compounds, that is stable only in solid state.
- In solution, it breaks into component ions.
- e.g. $KCl \cdot MgCl_2 \cdot 6H_2O$ (carnallite)

COMPLEX COMPOUNDS

- Molecular compounds in which central metal atom or ion is coordinated by number of ions/groups in a definite geometrical arrangement.
- When dissolved, do not break up completely into individual ions.
- e.g. $[Cu(NH_3)_4]SO_4 \xrightarrow{Aq.} [Cu(NH_3)_4]^{2+} + SO_4^{2-}$

POWER TIPS — Chelating Effect

- Chelating ligands form more stable complexes than the unidentate analogs.
- Co-ordination number $= \sum$ Number of ligands $\times$ Dentate character of ligand

TYPES OF LIGANDS

ON THE BASIS OF CHARGE

01 Negative ligands - F^-, Cl^-, Br^-, I^-

02 Neutral ligands - H_2O, NH_3, CO, NO

03 Positive ligands - NO^+

ON THE BASIS OF DENTICITY

Unidentate ligands

- Ligands with one donor site.
- e.g. H_2O, PH_3, NH_3, $P(Ph)_3$, NO, NO^+, NO_2^+, CO etc.

Bidentate ligands

- Ligands which have two donor atoms at two positions.
- e.g. oxalate $C_2O_4^{2-}$, Ethylenediamine, glycenato (gly) $^{-2}$

Polydentate ligands

- Ligands that have several donor atom.
- e.g. $[EDTA]^{-4}$

Ambidentate ligands

- A unidentate ligand that can coordinate through two different sites but one at a time.
- e.g. NO_2^-, SCN^- etc.

HOMOLEPTIC COMPLEXES

- Metal atom/ion is bonded to only one kind of ligands.
- e.g. $[Co(NH_3)_6]^{3+}$

HETEROLEPTIC COMPLEXES

- Metal atom/ion is bonded to more than one kind of ligands.
- e.g. $[Co(NH_3)_4Cl_2]^+$

WERNER'S THEORY OF COORDINATION COMPOUNDS

- Explains the nature of bonding in complexes.
- Metals show two different types of linkages.

Primary Valency

- Equal to oxidation state of the central metal ion satisfied by negative ions.
- Ionisable.

Secondary Valency

- Equal to the coordination number of the metal satisfied by neutral or negative ligand.
- Non-ionisable.

Ionisation of the coordination compound is written as

$[Co(NH_3)_6]Cl_3 \rightleftharpoons [Co(NH_3)_6]^{3+} + 3Cl^-$

EFFECTIVE ATOMIC NUMBER (EAN)

They generally coincides with the atomic number of next inert gas in some cases.

$$EAN = (z - x) + n \times y$$

- z – Atomic number of central metal atom
- x – Oxidation state of the central metal ion
- n – Number of ligands
- y – Number of electrons donated by one ligand

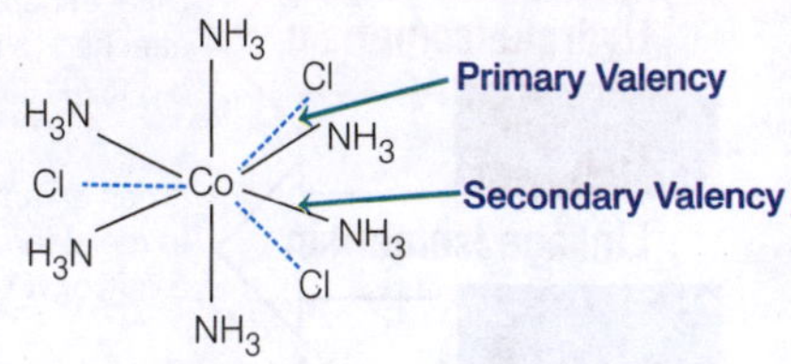

$[Co(NH_3)_6]Cl_3$

e.g. $K_4[Fe(CN)_6] \Rightarrow$ O.S of Fe $\Rightarrow +2$

E.A.N $= 26 - (+2) + 2 \times 6 = 36$ [Kr = 36]

SIDGWICK RULE

➤ If EAN of central metal atom in metal carbonyl is equal to atomic number of nearest inert gas then the stability of metal is high.

e.g. (a) $[Mn(CO)_5] < [Mn(CO)_5]^-$ = stability

EAN = 35   EAN = 36

(b) $[V(CO)_6] \xrightarrow[\text{Reduction}]{+e^-} [V(CO)_6]^-$

EAN = 35   EAN = 36 (more stable)

[Sidgwick rule is applicable only for metal carbonyl]

IUPAC Nomenclature of Coordination

(i) **Name the cation before the Anion.**

(ii) **Ligand** (+) **Metal (O.S in Roman Numbers**

Ligand

Anionic ligand

end with –ido

e.g. N^{3-} → Azido

Cl^- → Chlorido

O_2^{2-} → Peroxido

NH_2^- → Amido

Neutral ligand

Same name

Except

- H_2O → Aqua
- NH_3 → Ammine
- CO → Carbonyl
- NO → Nitrosyl

Positive ligand

end with –ium

e.g. NO^+ → Nitrosonium

$NH_2NH_3^+$ → Hydrazinium

Metal

When complex ion is cation, same metal name.

e.g. Co → Cobalt

Pt → Platinum

When complex ion is anionic, metal name are used in latin.

e.g. Fe → Ferrate

Co → Cobaltate

IUPAC Name of Coordination Complex

➡ $[Cr(NH_3)_3(H_2O)_3Cl_3$ – Triamminetriaquachromium (III) chloride.
[Cationic complex]

➡ $[Pt(NH_3)_2Cl(NO_2)]$ – Diammine chloridonitrito-N-platinium(II)
[Neutral complex]

➡ $K_3[Fe(CN)_6]$ – Potassium hexacyanido ferrate (III)
[Anionic complex]

ISOMERISM

STRUCTURAL ISOMERISM

Ionisation Isomerism
Compounds that give different ions in solution due to exchange of ions in coordination sphere and counter ion
e.g. $[CoBr(NH_3)_5]SO_4$, $[CoSO_4(NH_3)_5]Br$

Hydrate Isomerism
Differ in number of water molecule attached to metal atom.
e.g $[Cr(H_2O)_6]Cl_3$, $[Cr(H_2O)_5Cl]Cl_2 \cdot H_2O$

Linkage Isomerism
When an ambidentate ligand is attached to metal through different atom.
e.g $[Co(NO_2)(NH_3)_5]Cl$, $[Co(ONO)(NH_3)_5]Cl$

Coordination Isomerism
When both positive and negative ions of a salt are complex ion.
e.g $[Co(NH_3)_6][Cr(CN)_6]$, $[Co(CN)_6]$ $[Cr(NH_3)_6]$

STEREOISOMERISM

Geometrical or *cis-trans*

✦ If two identical ligands occupy adjacent position-*cis*.
✦ If occupy opposite positions-*trans*.

In square planar
Shown by
➤ MA_2X_2
➤ $MABX_2$
➤ MA_2XY

e.g. $[Pt(NH_3)_2Cl_2]$

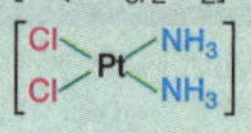

In octahedral
Shown by

MA_4X_2
↓

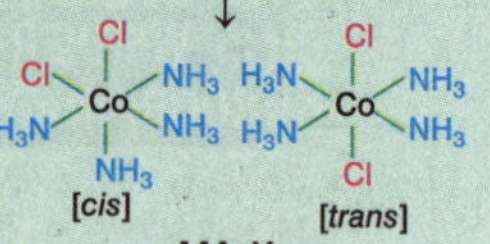

MA_3X_3
↓

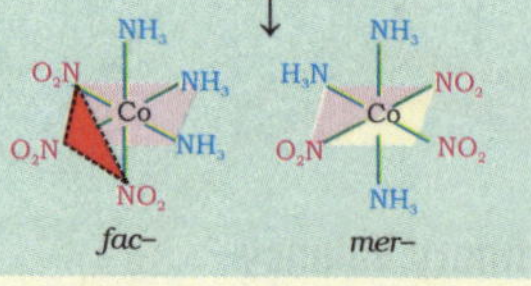

Optical

✦ Arises due to non-superimposable mirror images.
✦ In octahedral complex with 2 or 3 bidentate ligands

cis — Optically active: *d*-form, *l*-form
trans — Optically inactive

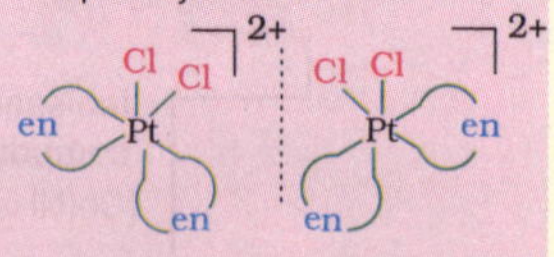

Valence Bond Theory (VBT)

- Describes the bonding in terms of hybridised orbitals of the central metal atom or ion.
- Explains the shapes of complexes and relation between the observed magnetic behaviour and bond type.

POSTULATES

➤ The central metal atom/ion makes available a number of vacant orbitals equal to its coordination number which hybridise together.
➤ The vacant hybrid orbitals form coordinate bond with ligands. These bonds are equal strength and directional in nature.

LIMITATIONS

➤ Could not explain the colour and electronic spectra of complexes.
➤ Could not explain pairing of electrons in the presence of strong ligands and the structure of $[Cu(NH_3)_4]^{2+}$ ion.

HYBRIDISATION AND GEOMETRY

COORDINATION NUMBER	TYPES OF HYBRIDISATION	GEOMETRY OF COMPLEX
4	sp^3	Tetrahedral
4	dsp^2	Square planar
5	sp^3d	Trigonal bipyramidal
6	sp^3d^2	Octahedral
6	d^2sp^3	Octahedral

SPECTROCHEMICAL SERIES

➤ Arrangement of ligands in the order of increasing field strength.
➤ $I^- < Br^- < SCN^- < Cl^- < S^{2-} < F^- < OH^- < C_2O_4^{2-} < H_2O < NCS^- < EDTA^{4-} < NH_3 < en < CN^- < CO$

⟶ increasing order of CFSE (Δ_o)

➤ If $\Delta_o < P$, then complex is high spin.
➤ If $\Delta_o > P$, then complex is low spin.

POWER TIPS

➤ **Magnetic moment**
$$\mu = \sqrt{n(n+2)}\ \text{B.M}\ (n = \text{unpaired electron})$$
➤ **Ferromagnetic** Fe, Co.

CRYSTAL FIELD THEORY (CFT)

- Under the influence of ligand field, degeneracy of *d*-orbitals is destroyed and they split into two or more energy levels.
- The extent of splitting depends upon the strength of ligands.

OCTAHEDRAL COMPLEX

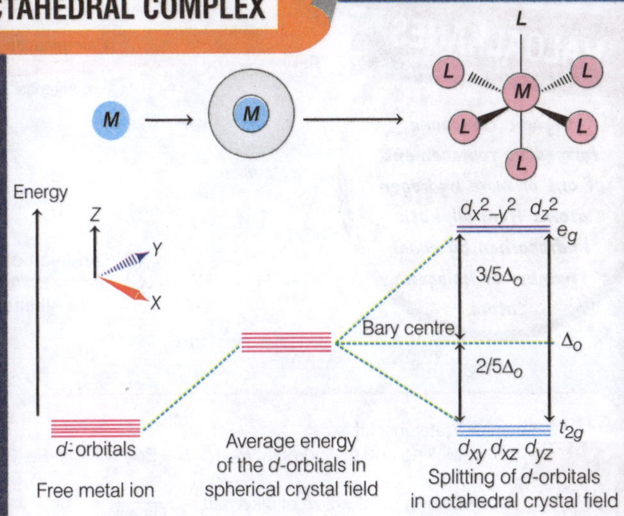

***d*-orbital splitting in a octahedral crystal field**

John Teller Effect

Distortion in octahedral geometry due to unsymmetrical e^- closed in e_g set of orbitals

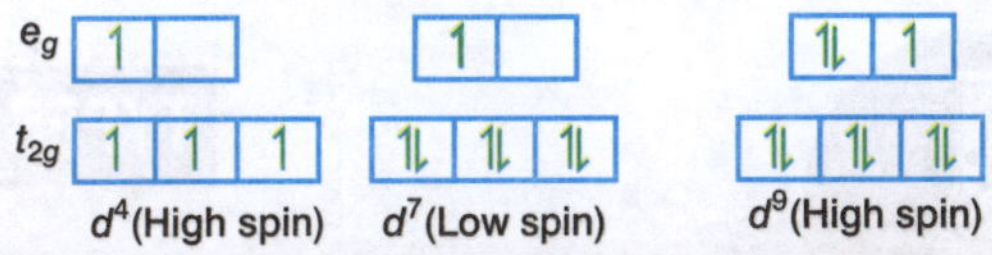

TETRAHEDRAL COMPLEX

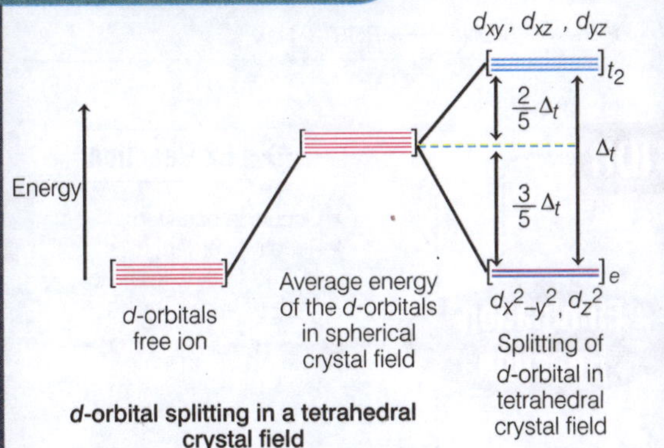

***d*-orbital splitting in a tetrahedral crystal field**

Factor Affecting Splitting Energy

01. $3d < 4d < 5d$
02. $\Delta_o \propto$ Strength of ligand
03. Geometry of complex $\Delta_{sp} > \Delta_o > \Delta_t$
04. $\Delta_o \propto Z_{eff}$ of central metal atom
05. $\Delta_o \propto$ Charge of central metal atom

ORGANOMETALLIC COMPOUND

- Homoleptic carbonyls are formed by most of the transition metals.
- Metal-carbon bond posses both σ and π character.

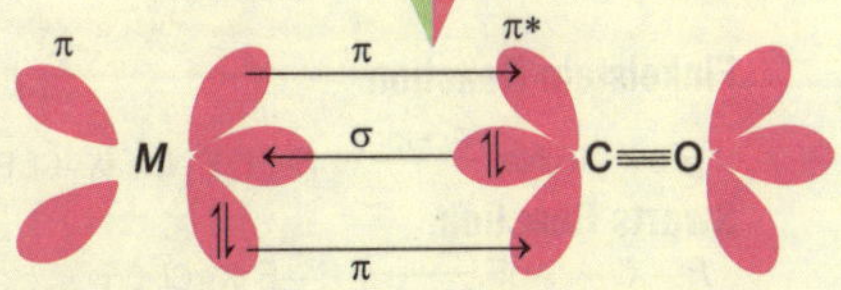

Example of synergic bonding interactions in a carbonyl complex.

POWER TIPS

- $\Delta_t = \frac{4}{9}\Delta_0$
- Complexes possessing d^0 or d^{10} configuration of a metal ion are always diamagnetic.
- Colour of some compound is due to charge transfer formation to metal ion.
- $KMnO_4$ – Purple, $K_2Cr_2O_7$ – Orange, CrO_2Cl_2 – Blood red
- $[EDTA]^{-4}$ is used for estimation and removal of hardness of H_2O.
- Wilkinson catalyst $RhCl(PPh)_3$ is used for hydrogenation of alkene.

Chapter **06**

Haloalkanes and Haloarenes

HALOALKANES

Organic compound formed by replacement of one or more hydrogen atoms from aliphatic hydrocarbon by equal number of halogen atom.

METHODS OF PREPARATION

- Halogenation of Alkanes: $RH + X_2 + h\nu$
- Borodine-Hunsdiecker (CCl_4): $CH_3COOAg + Br_2$
- Addition of HX of Alkenes: $R-CH=CH_2 + \overset{\oplus\ominus}{HX}$
- Substitution of OH group:
  - R—OH with PX_3 or PX_5
  - R—OH with Conc. HCl / Anhy. $ZnCl_2$
  - R—OH with HX
  - R—OH with $SOCl_2$

Physical Properties

- Water insoluble
- Melting and boiling point $R-I > R-Br > R-Cl > R-F$
- Boiling point $\propto$ size of alkyl part $\propto \frac{1}{\text{branching}}$
- Bond strength $CH_3F > CH_3Cl > CH_3Br > CH_3I$
- Stability of $R-X$ bond $\rightarrow R-F > R-Cl > R-Br > R-I$

Chemical Properties

- $R-X + Mg \xrightarrow{\text{Dry ether}} R-Mg-X$ (Grignard's reagent)
- $R-X + NaCN \xrightarrow{C_2H_5OH-H_2O} R-CN$

  $AgCN \longrightarrow R-N \overset{\rightarrow}{=} C$
- $R-I + AgNO_2 \xrightarrow[-\ AgI]{\text{Alcohol}} RNO_2$ (Nitro alkane)
- $R-X + R'ONa \longrightarrow ROR' + NaX$

TYPES OF REACTION

Nucleophilic Substitution Reaction

S_N1

- Rate $\propto$ [Substrate]
- Carbonium ion formation takes place. Occurs in two step.
- **Step I**-Formation of carbonium ion (slow).
- **Step II**- Attack of nucleophile.
- Racemic mixture is obtained.
- 3° alkyl halide is most favourable.

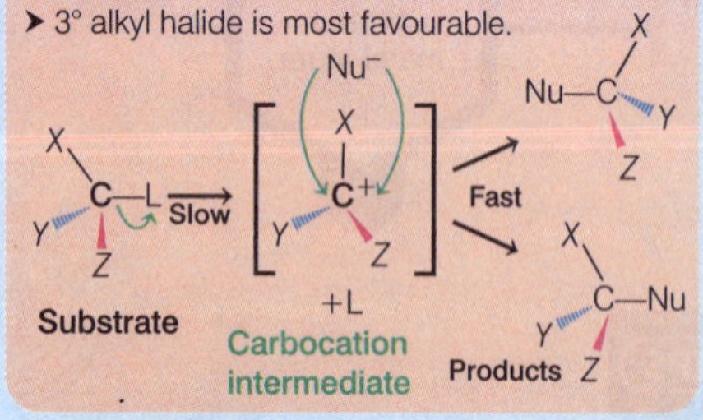

S_N2

- Rate $\propto$ [alkyl halide] [nucleophile]
- Occurs in single step.
- Walden inversion occurs.
- 1° alkyl halide is most favourable.
- Favoured in non-polar solvent.

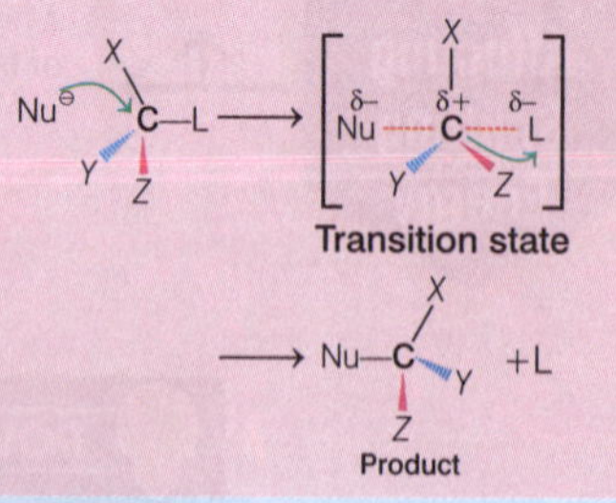

Elimination Reaction

E2 Reaction

- Occurs in one step.
- Reactivity order: 1° > 2° > 3° (alkyl halide)

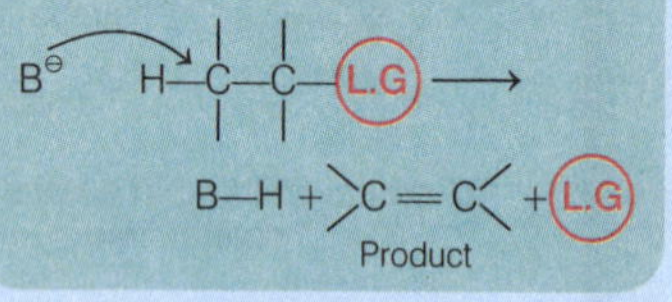

E1 Reaction

- Occurs in two steps.
- Reactivity order: 3° > 2° > 1° (alkyl halide)

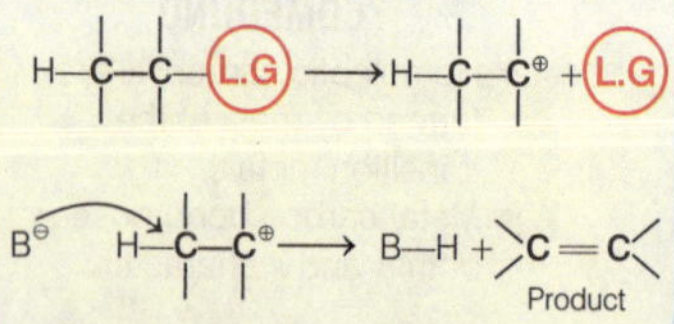

Substitution

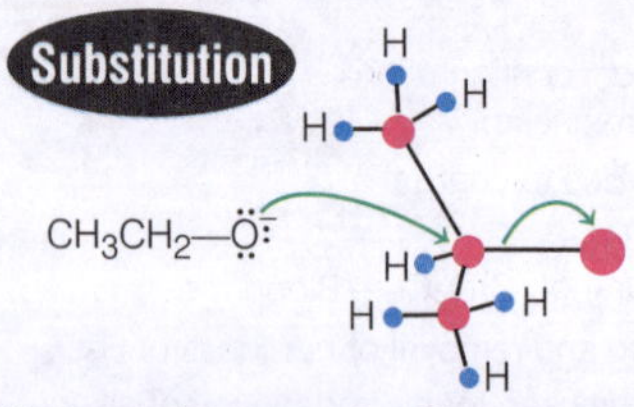

This is small base so it will attack on 3° H site.

Elimination

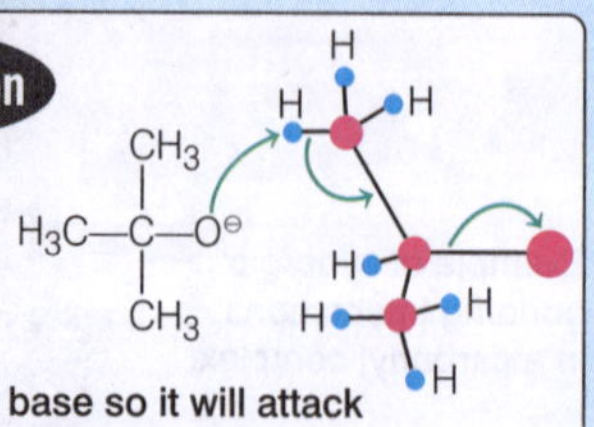

This is Bulky base so it will attack on less Hindrance site.

POWER TIPS

Halogen Exchange Reaction

Finkelstein Reaction

$R-X + NaI \xrightarrow{\text{Acetone}} R-I + NaX$ (X=Cl, Br)

Swarts Reaction

$R-X + AgF \longrightarrow R-F$ (X=Cl, Br)

RACEMIC MIXTURE

- Both *d* and *l* enantiomers present in equal amount (50-50%).
- The mixture is optically inactive due to external compensation.

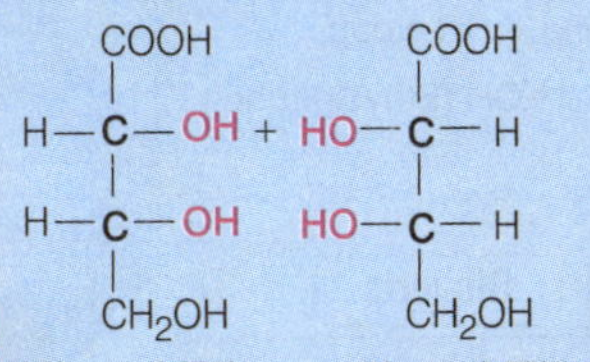

Resolution of Racemic Mixture

- Process of separation of racemic mixture into *d* and *l*-forms.

Racemisation

- It is conversion of (+) or (–) isomer into its racemic mixture.
- Reverse of resolution.

HALOARENES

- Organic compounds formed by the replacement of one or more hydrogen atom from the aromatic hydrocarbons by equal number of halogen atom.
- Also called as aryl halides.

Physical Properties

- Boiling point of isomers dihalobenzenes are nearly same.
- Melting point of isomers dihalobenzenes is $-p > -o > -m$.
- **Boiling point**
  Iodoarenes > Bromoarenes > Chloroarenes > Fluoroarenes.

Chemical Properties

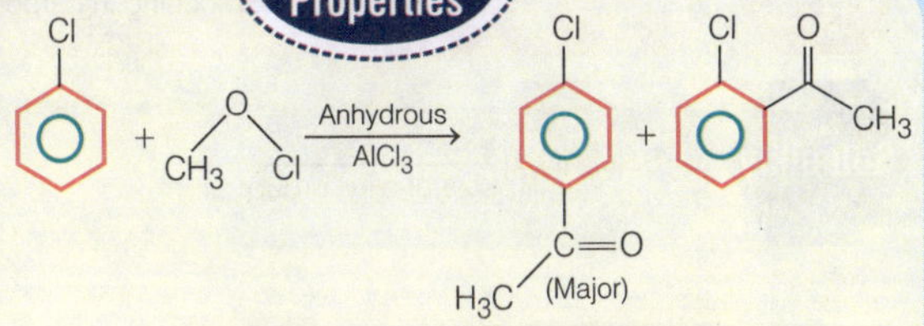

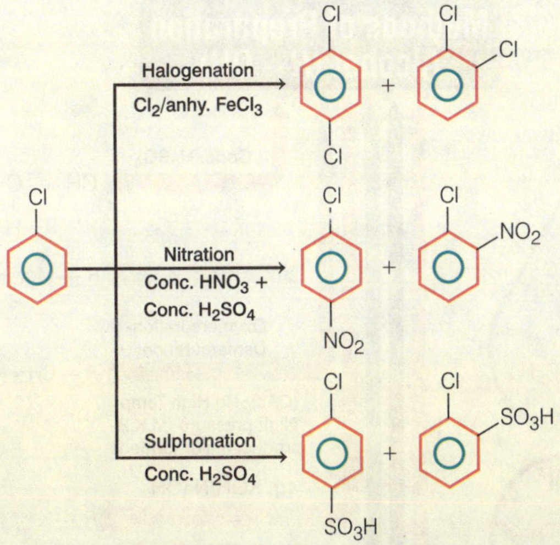

METHODS OF PREPARATION

Halogenation

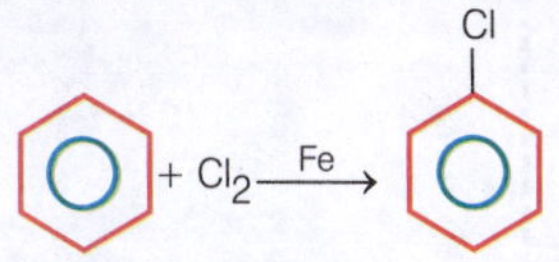

Decomposition of Diazonium Salt

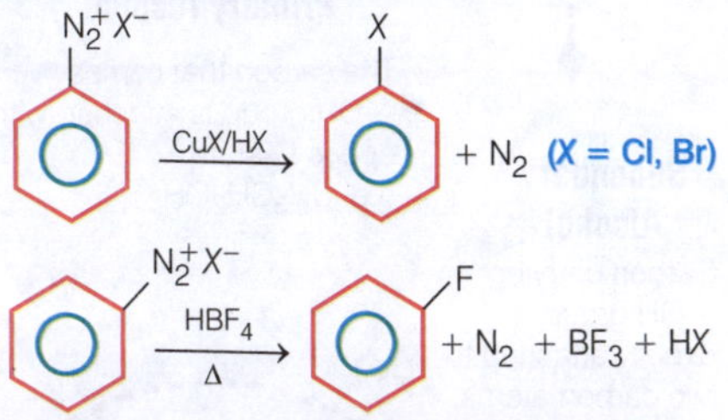

From Aromatic Amino and Nitro Compounds

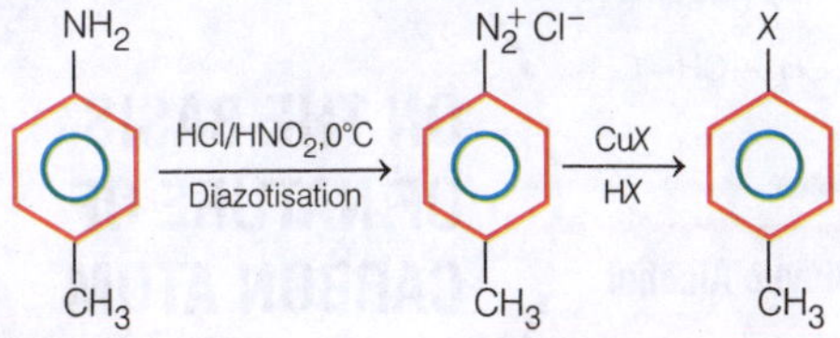

Raschig Process

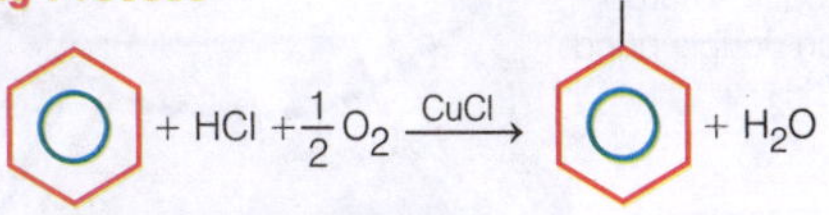

Borodine Hunsdiecker Reaction

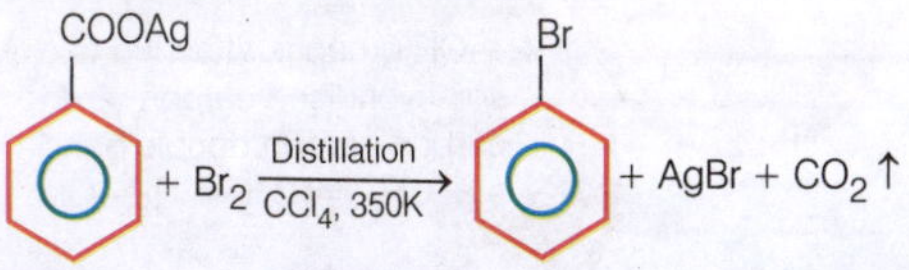

POLYHALOGEN COMPOUNDS

Carbon Tetrachloride

Prepared by chlorination of alkane, chloroform, carbon disulphide under different reaction condition.

DDT

Prepared by heating chloral with two moles of chlorobenzene in the presence of conc. H_2SO_4.

Freons

They are chlorofluorocarbon (CFC). Produced as a volatile derivative of methane and ethane.

Chapter 07

Alcohols, Phenols and Ethers

ALCOHOLS

Hydroxy derivatives of alkanes having general formula $C_nH_{2n+1}OH$.

R—O—H (bond angle 108.9°)

Classification

On the Basis of Number of —OH Group

Monohydric

- Has one —OH group.
- e.g. C_2H_5OH **(Ethyl alcohol)**

Dihydric

- Have two —OH group.
- e.g. CH_2OH—CH_2OH **(Ethylene glycol)**

Trihydric

- Have three —OH group
- e.g. CH_2OH—CH_2OH—CH_2OH **(Glycerol)**

Polyhydric

- Have many —OH group attached to aliphatic chain
- e.g. CH_2OH—$(CHOH)_4$—CH_2OH **(Sorbitol)**

ON THE BASIS OF NATURE OF CARBON ATOM

Primary Alcohol

- The carbon that carries —OH group is attached with or one C-atom.
- e.g. CH_3CH_2OH

Secondary Alcohol

- Carbon carrying —OH group is directly attached to two carbon atoms, which may or may not be same.
- e.g. CH_3—CH(OH)—CH_3

Tertiary Alcohol

- Carbon carrying —OH group is joined directly attached to three carbon atoms, which may or may not be same.
- e.g. H_3C—C(CH_3)(OH)—CH_3

Vinylic Alcohol

- —OH group is bonded to a carbon-carbon double bond.
- e.g. $CH_2=CH$—OH

Benzylic Alcohol

- — OH group is attached to sp^3-hybridised carbon atom next to an aromatic ring.
- e.g.

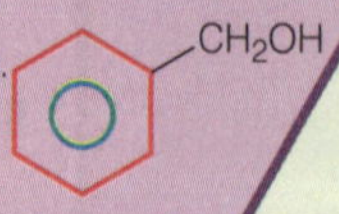

Allylic Alcohol

- —OH group is attached to a sp^3-hybridised carbon next to carbon-carbon double bond.
- e.g. $CH_2=CH$—CH_2—OH

Physical Properties

Physical States

- Lower alcohols are colourless liquid with characteristic smell.
- Higher alcohols are colourless, odourless waxy solids

Boiling Points

$$\text{B.P} \propto \text{no. of carbon atoms} \propto \frac{1}{\text{Branching in carbon chain}}$$

Solubility

$$\text{Solubility} \propto \frac{1}{\text{size of alkyl group}}$$

Methods of Preparation Alcohol (R—OH)

- CH_3—CH=CH_2 —(Conc. H_2SO_4)→ Alcohol
- $\bar{R}$—$\overset{+}{Mg}X$ + R—CH=O → Alcohol
- R—CH=CH_2 —(Oxymercuration-Demercuration; $(OAc)_2Hg$ High Temp. High pressure (M.K.R product major formed))→ Alcohol
- R—X —(aq. KOH/NaOH)→ Alcohol
- R—CH_2—CHO —($NaBH_4$)→ Alcohol
- R—CH_2—COOH —($LiAlH_4$)→ Alcohol
- R—CH=CH_2 —(Hydroboration oxidation; B_2H_6 in THF (A.M.K.R. product formed))→ Alcohol

(A.M.K.R) The hydrogen attaches to least substituted carbon.
(M.K.R) The hydrogen attaches to more substituted carbon.

Chemical Properties

Reaction Involving the Cleavage of Both the Alkyl and Hydroxyl Group

Dehydration

$$R\text{—}CH_2\text{—}CH_2OH \xrightarrow[\Delta]{\text{Conc. } H_2SO_4} R\text{—}CH{=}CH_2$$

Alcohol → Alkene

Oxidation

$$CH_3\text{—}CH_2\text{—}OH \xrightarrow{[O]} CH_3\text{—}CHO \xrightarrow{[O]} CH_3\text{—}COOH$$

Alcohol → Aldehyde → Acid

Dehydrogenation

$$CH_3\text{—}CH_2\text{—}OH \xrightarrow[-H_2]{Cu/300^\circ C} CH_3\text{—}CH{=}O$$

Ethanol → Ethanal

REACTIONS INVOLVING CLEAVAGE OF O—H BOND

- Order of reactivity (1°>2°>3°).
- Alcohols act as nucleophiles.
- E.W.G. increase the acidity and E.D.G. decrease.

R—OH

- $\xrightarrow{\text{Na or K}}$ $RO\text{—}Na + H_2$
- $\xrightarrow{Al}$ $(RO)_3Al + H_2$
- $\xrightarrow{MH}$ $RO\text{—}M + H_2$
- $\xrightarrow{NaNH_2}$ $RO\text{—}Na + NH_3$
- $\xrightarrow{RCOOH/H^+}$ $RO\text{—}COR + H_2O$
- $\xrightarrow{RCOCl/\text{Pyridine}}$ $RO\text{—}COR + HCl$
- $\xrightarrow{(RCO)_2O/H^+}$ $RO\text{—}COR + RCOOH$
- $\xrightarrow{\text{Conc. } HNO_3}$ $RO\text{—}NO_2 + H_2O$

REACTIONS INVOLVING CLEAVAGE OF C—O BOND

- Order of reactivity (3°>2°>1°)
- Alcohols act as electrophiles.
- Reaction depends on C^+ stability.

R—OH

- $\xrightarrow[\Delta]{HX/\text{Anhy. } ZnCl_2}$ $R\text{—}X + H_2O$
- $\xrightarrow{PX_3}$ $R\text{—}X + H_3PO_3$
- $\xrightarrow{PX_5}$ $R\text{—}X + POX_3 + HX$
- $\xrightarrow[\Delta]{\text{Red } P/X_2}$ $R\text{—}X + H_3PO_3$
- $\xrightarrow[\text{Pyridine}]{SOCl_2}$ $R\text{—}Cl + SO_2\uparrow + HCl$
- $\xrightarrow[CrO_3\cdot C_5H_5N\cdot HCl]{PCC}$ $RCHO$
- $\xrightarrow[\text{443 K or Conc. } H_3PO_4]{\text{Conc. } H_2SO_4}$ $\rangle C{=}C\langle + H_2O$
- $\xrightarrow[\text{Conc. } H_2SO_4/\Delta]{RCOOH}$ $RCOOR + H_2O$

Identification of Primary, Secondary and Tertiary Alcohol

01 Lucas Test - Reagent (Conc. HCl and $ZnCl_2$)

- 1° alcohol $\xrightarrow{\text{Lucas reagent}}$ No reaction
- 2° alcohol $\xrightarrow{\text{Lucas reagent}}$ Turbidity appears in 5 minute
- 3° alcohol $\xrightarrow{\text{Lucas reagent}}$ Turbidity appears immediately

02 Victor-Meyer Test

- 1° alcohol gives red colour.
- 2° alcohol gives blue colour.
- 3° alcohol remains colourless.

POWER TIPS — COMMERCIALLY IMPORTANT ALCOHOLS

- **Methanol** Produced by catalytic hydrogenation of CO in the presence of $ZnO\text{—}Cr_2O_3$ as catalyst at high temperature and pressure.
- **Ethanol** Commercially manufactured by using fermentation of sugar present in molasses, sugarcane or fruits such as grapes.

PHENOLS

- Aromatic compounds in which hydroxyl group is directly attached with benzene.
- General formula C_6H_5OH.
- —OH group is attached to sp^2-hybridised C-atom of an aromatic ring.

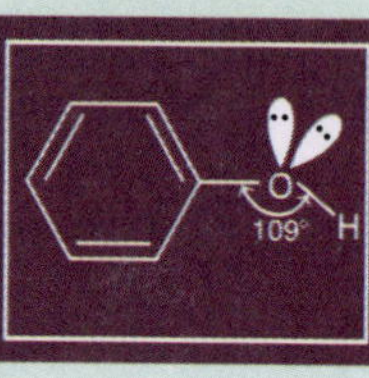

Methods of Preparation

From Haloarenes

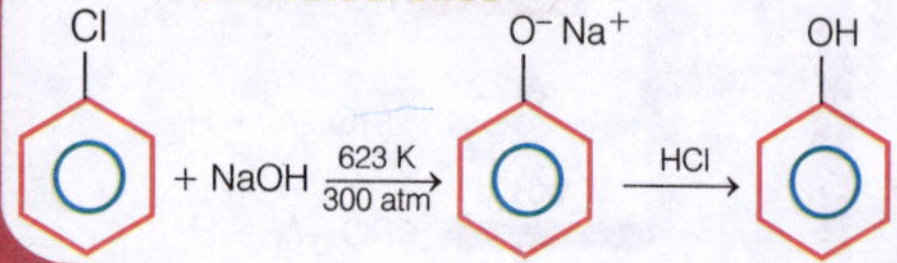

From Benzene Sulphonic Acid

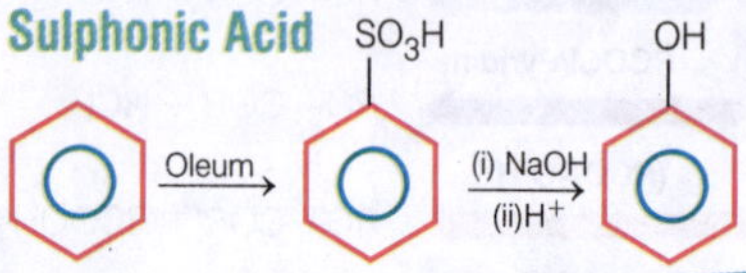

From Diazonium Salts

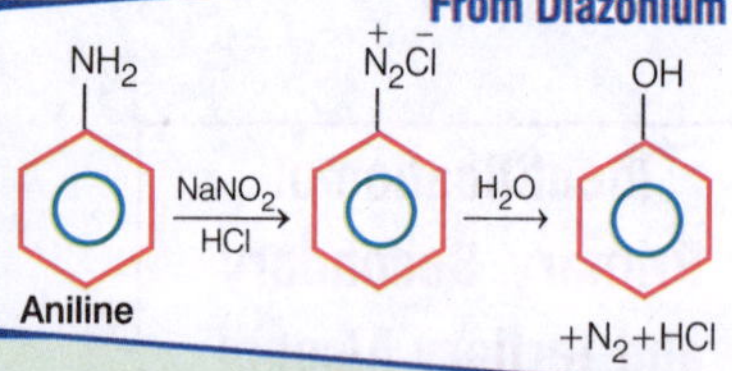

Aniline

From Cumene

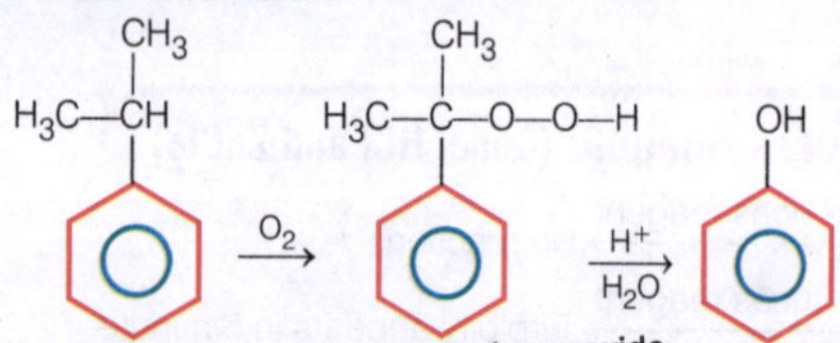

Cumene — Cumene hydroperoxide

Other Reactions of Phenol

Oxidation

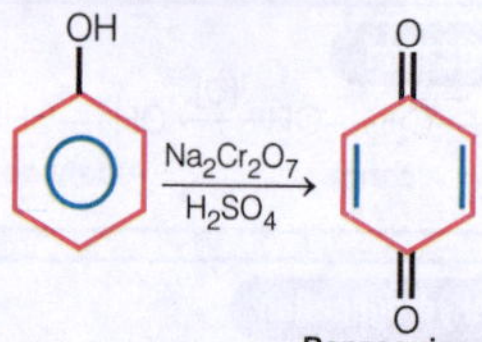

Benzoquinone

Reduction

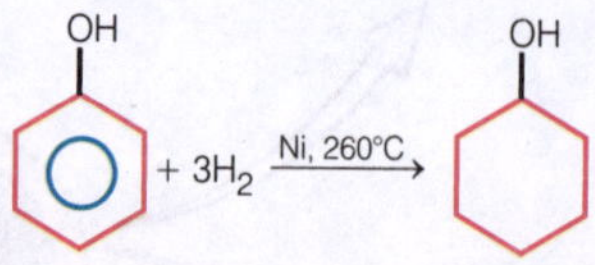

Cyclohexanol

Phthalein Reaction

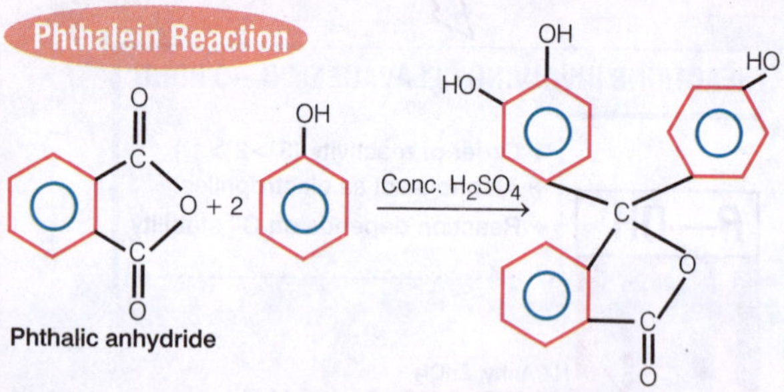

Phthalic anhydride — Phenolphthalein

Condensation with Formaldehyde

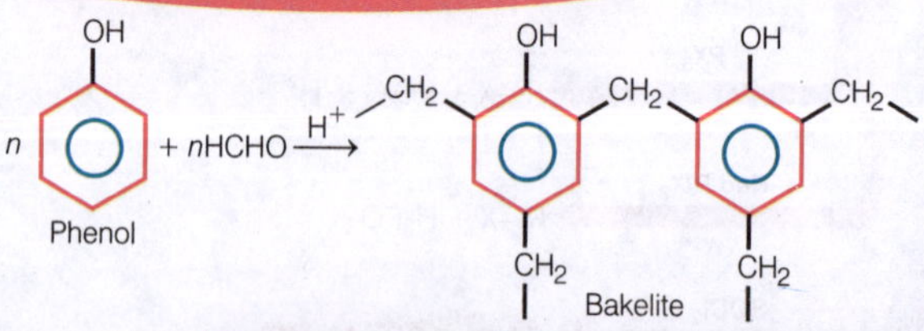

Phenol — Bakelite

PHYSICAL PROPERTIES

Physical State

- Phenols are colourless crystalline solids or liquids.
- Have characteristics phenolic odour.

Boiling Points

- B.P of phenol >> B.P of aromatic hydrocarbon or haloarenes.

Solubility

- Soluble in water.
- Phenols are less soluble than alcohol.

POWER TIPS

Test for Phenols

Test	Observation
$FeCl_3$ test	Violet colour
Br_2 water	White ppt.
Lebermann's nitroso test	Deep blue green colour that changes to violet or red on dilution
Azo dye Test	Orange colour

CHEMICAL PROPERTIES

Acidity of Phenols

- Weakly acidic due to polar O—H bond directly attached to sp^2-hybridised C-atom.
- Does not react with Na_2CO_3 and $NaHCO_3$.
- Acidic Strength : Carboxylic acid > Phenol > Alcohol.
- EWG increases the acidic strength while EDG decreases it.

Reaction with Metals

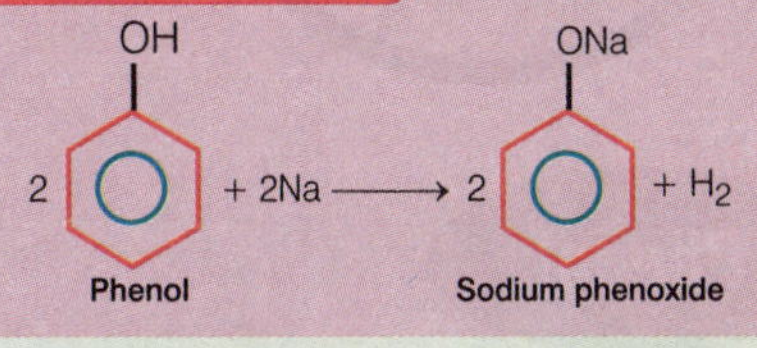

Esterification

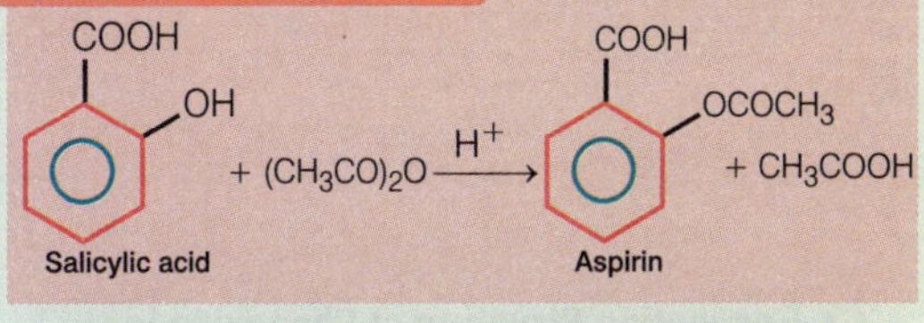

Electrophilic Substitution Reactions

01 Kolbe's Reaction

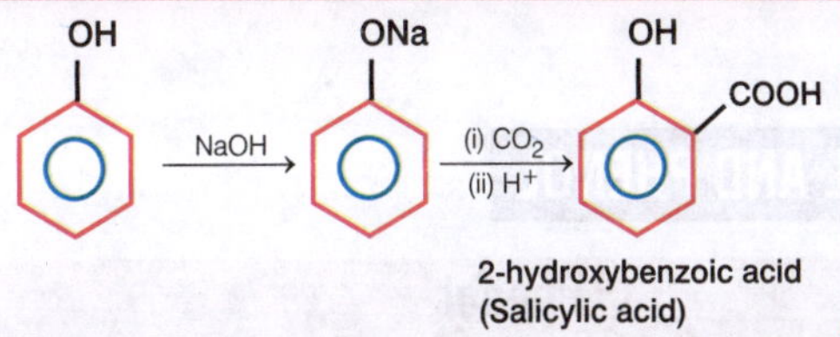

02 Riemer-Tiemann Reaction

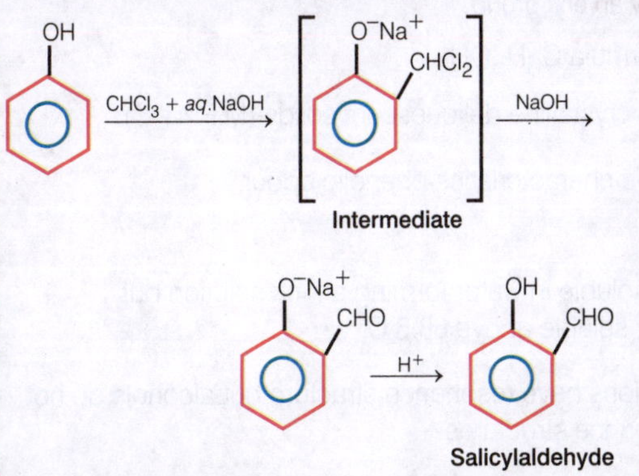

03 Nitration

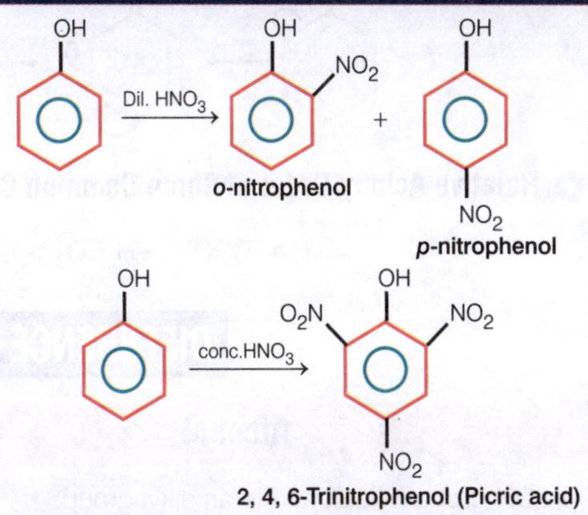

04 Halogenation

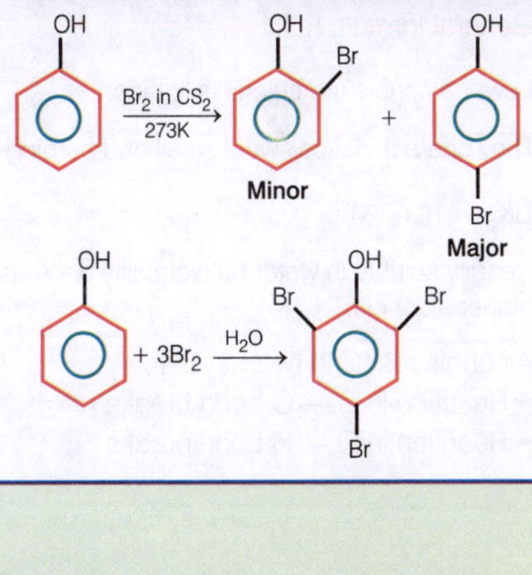

PHENOL ATOMIC ORBITAL

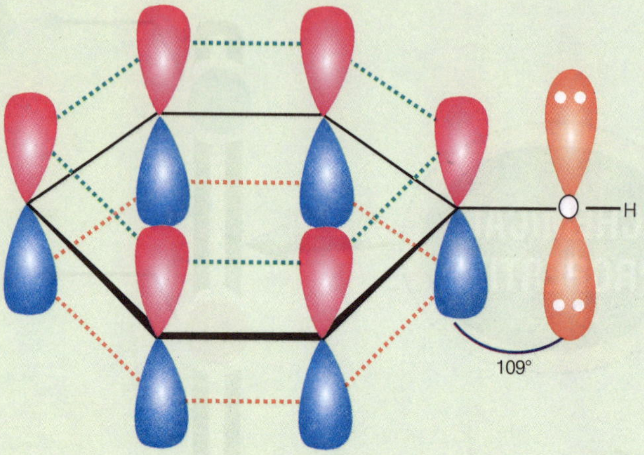

Phenol

Due to resonance O atom acquires a partial positive charge and hence attracts electron pair of O — H bond leading to the release of H^+.

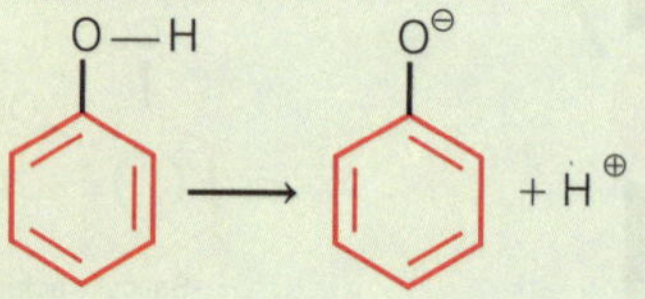

Phenoxide-ion

Resonating Structure of Phenoxide Ion

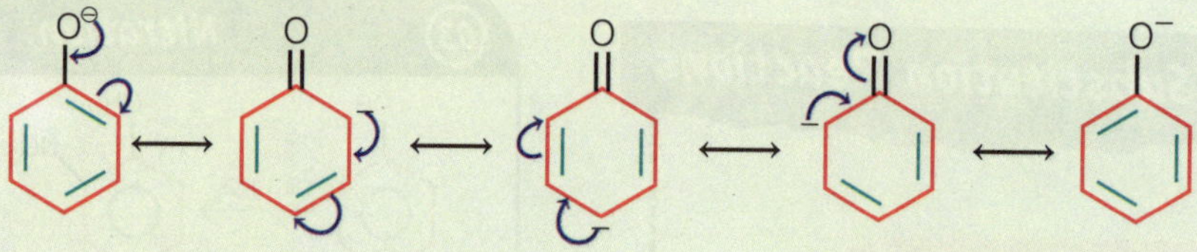

Relative Acidity Order of Some Common Compounds

$$R—COOH > H_2CO_3 > C_6H_5OH > H_2O > ROH$$

DIFFERENCE BETWEEN ALCOHOL AND PHENOL

Alcohol	Phenol
✦ OH group is attached to an alkyl group.	✦ OH group is attached to an aryl group.
✦ Hydroxyl derivatives of alkane.	✦ Hydroxyl derivatives of benzene.
✦ The compounds in which one hydrogen of water is replaced by an alkyl group.	✦ The compounds in which one hydrogen of water is replaced by an aryl group.
✦ General formula ROH.	✦ General formula C_6H_5OH.
✦ Lower alcohols are colorless liquids.	✦ Colourless crystalline deliquescent solids (M.P 41°C).
✦ They characteristics sweet smell and burning taste.	✦ They have a characteristics phenolic odour.
✦ pK_a = 16 to 20	✦ pK_a =10
✦ Readily soluble in water but solubility decreases in higher alcohols.	✦ Sparingly soluble in water forming a pink solution but completely soluble above 68.5 C.
✦ Alcohols reacts in two ways ➡Reaction in C — O bond breaks ➡Reaction in O — H bond breaks	✦ Phenolate ions have resonance structure but alcohols do not have resonance structures.

Classification

Simple or Symmetrical
Same alkyl groups are attached to oxygen, *ROR*.

Mixed or Unsymmetrical
Different alkyl groups are attached to oxygen, *ROR′*.

Aliphatic Ethers
R and *R′* both are alkyl groups.

Aromatic Ethers
Either one or both *R* and *R′* are aryl groups.

POWER TIPS

- Aromatic ethers are relatively less reactive towards electrophilic ring substitution than phenols.
- Ethers can form co-ordinate complexes with Lewis acids like BF_3, $AlCl_3$ etc.

Physical Properties

- C—O bonds are slightly polar.
- Boiling point are lower than isomeric alcohols.
- Solubility $\propto \frac{1}{\text{molecular mass}}$
- Fairly soluble in all organic solvent.

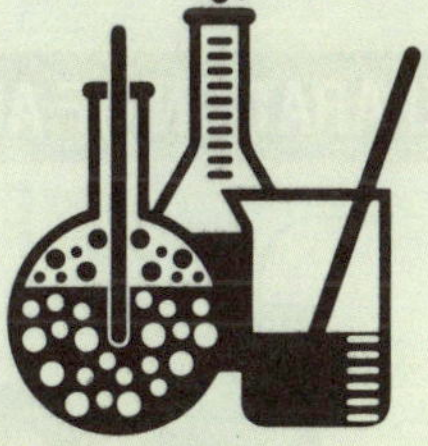

ETHERS

Organic compounds in which two alkyl or aryl group are attached to a divalent oxygen.

General Formula $C_nH_{2n+2}O$

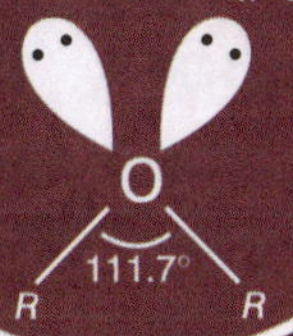

Methods of Preparation

Williamson Synthesis

- $RO^-Na^+ + R'X \longrightarrow ROR' + Na^+X^-$
- Reaction of alkyl halide with dry silver.
- $2RX + Ag_2O \longrightarrow ROR + 2AgX$
- By dehydration of alcohol

$$CH_3CH_2OH \xrightarrow[443\ K]{H_2SO_4} CH_2{=}CH_2 \text{ (Ethene)}$$

$$CH_3CH_2OH \xrightarrow[413\ K]{H_2SO_4} C_2H_5{-}OC_2H_5 \text{ (Diethyl ether)}$$

From Alkenes

(i) By adding alcohols

$$CH_3{-}\underset{}{\overset{CH_3}{\overset{|}{C}}}{=}CH_2 + H{-}OCH_3 \xrightarrow{\text{Conc. } H_2SO_4} H_3C{-}\overset{CH_3}{\overset{|}{\underset{CH_3}{\underset{|}{C}}}}{-}OCH_3$$

(ii) By alkoxy mercuration-demercuration

$$\text{Alkene} + \text{Alcohol} \xrightarrow[\text{(ii) } NaBH_4/OH^-]{\text{(i) Hg (OAc)}_2} \text{Ether}$$

By action of diazomethane on alcohols

$$ROH + CH_2N_2 \xrightarrow{HBF_4} R{-}O{-}CH_3 + N_2\uparrow$$

USES

- Ethers are used as a solvent for oils, fats and Grignard reagent.
- Provide inert and moisture free medium for various reactions.
- As a general anaesthetic.

CHEMICAL PROPERTIES

Reaction Involving Alkyl Group

- Formation of peroxide with air and light.
- Substitution products obtained on halogenation.

Reaction of Ethereal Oxygen

$ROR + HCl \text{ (Conc.)} \longrightarrow$

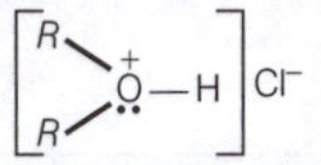

Electrophilic Substitution Reactions

Aryl alkyl ethers give *o*- and *p*-substituted products due to + *R* effect of alkoxy group (—*OR*).

Cleavage of C—O Bond

- $ROR + HX \xrightarrow{373\ K} R{-}OH + R{-}X$
- $ROR + H_2O \xrightarrow{\text{Dil. } H_2SO_4} 2R{-}OH$
- $ROR + PCl_5 \xrightarrow{\Delta} 2R{-}Cl$

Chapter 08

Aldehydes, Ketones and Carboxylic Acids

CARBONYL COMPOUNDS

Organic compound that contains carbon-oxygen double bond.

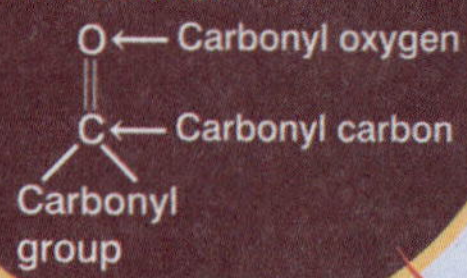

Nature and Structure of Carbonyl Group

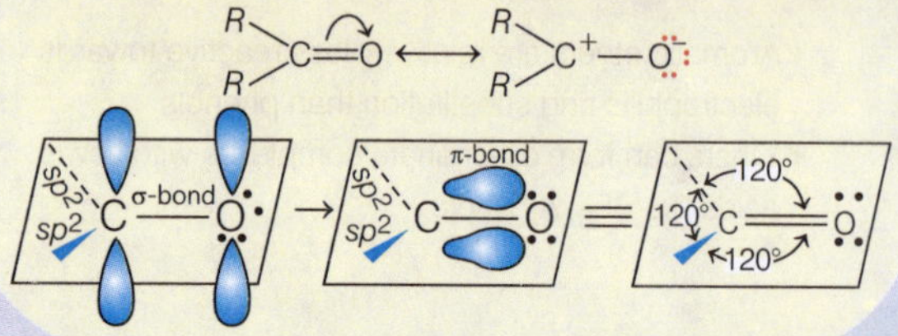

Ketones

- Carbonyl group is attached to two carbon atoms of an alkyl/aryl group
- **IUPAC Name** Alkanones
- **General Formula** $C_nH_{2n+1}COC_nH_{2n+1}$

$R_2C{=}O$

Aldehydes

- Contains carbonyl group attached to either two H-atoms or one H-atom and one C-atom of an alkyl/aryl group.
- **IUPAC Name** Alkanals
- **General Formula** $C_nH_{2n+1}CHO$

$R(H)C{=}O$

METHODS OF PREPARATION OF ALDEHYDES AND KETONES BOTH

Hydrolysis of *Gem*-Dihalides

- $R-CHX_2 \xrightarrow[-H_2O]{\text{Aq. NaOH/KOH}} R-CHO$ (Aldehyde)
- $R-CX_2-R \xrightarrow[-H_2O]{\text{Aq. NaOH/KOH}} R-CO-R$ (Ketone)

By Oxidation of Alcohols

- $R-CH_2-OH + [O] \xrightarrow[\text{Alkaline } KMnO_4]{\text{Acidified } K_2Cr_2O_7} R-CO-H + H_2O$ (1° alcohol → Aldehyde)
- $R_2CH-OH + [O] \xrightarrow[\text{Alkaline } KMnO_4]{\text{Acidified } K_2Cr_2O_7} R_2C=O + H_2O$ (2° alcohol → Ketone)

Catalytic Dehydrogenation of Alcohols

- $RCH_2OH \xrightarrow[300°C]{Cu} RCHO + H_2\uparrow$ (1° alcohol → Aldehyde)
- $RR'CH-OH \xrightarrow[300°C]{Cu} RR'C=O + H_2\uparrow$ (2° alcohol → Ketone)

Catalytic Decomposition of Acids

- $HCOOH + RCOOH \xrightarrow[300°\,C]{\text{Mn or Th oxide}} RCHO + H_2O$ (Aldehyde)
- $RCOOH + RCOOH \xrightarrow[300°\,C]{\text{Mn or Th oxide}} RCOR + H_2O$ (Ketone)

Hydration of Alkynes

- $CH\equiv CH + H_2O \xrightarrow[60\text{-}70°C]{1\%\ HgSO_4,\ 42\%\ H_2SO_4} CH_2=CH-OH \overset{\text{Tautomerism}}{\rightleftharpoons} CH_3CHO$ (Ethanal)

By Wacker's Process

- $CH_2=CH_2 + H_2O \xrightarrow[CuCl_2]{PdCl_2} CH_3CHO + 2HCl + Pd$
- $CH_3-CH=CH_2 + H_2O \xrightarrow[CuCl_2]{PdCl_2} CH_3-CO-CH_3 + 2HCl + Pd$

Cleavage of Glycol

- $R-C(R)(OH)-CH(OH)-R \xrightarrow{HIO_4} R-CO-R + R-CO-H + H_2O$ (Ketone, Aldehyde)

Ozonolysis of Alkene

- $H(R)C=C(R)R \xrightarrow[\text{(ii) } Zn/H_2O]{\text{(i) } O_3} R-CO-H + R-CO-R$ (Aldehyde, Ketone)
- $R_2C=CR_2 \xrightarrow[\text{(ii) } Zn/H_2O]{\text{(i) } O_3} 2R-CO-R$

Physical Properties

- **Boiling point order** Alcohols > Ketones > Aldehydes > Ethers > Hydrocarbons
- Solubility ∝ 1/Molecular mass
- Solubility in water is due to H-bonding between polar carbonyl group and water.
- Aromatic aldehydes and ketones are less soluble than corresponding aliphatic aldehydes and ketones.

POWER TIPS

Distinction Test

Test	Aldehydes	Ketones
Schiffs reagent	Pink colour	No colour
Fehling's solution	Red ppt.	No ppt.
Tollen's reagent	Silver mirror	No ppt.

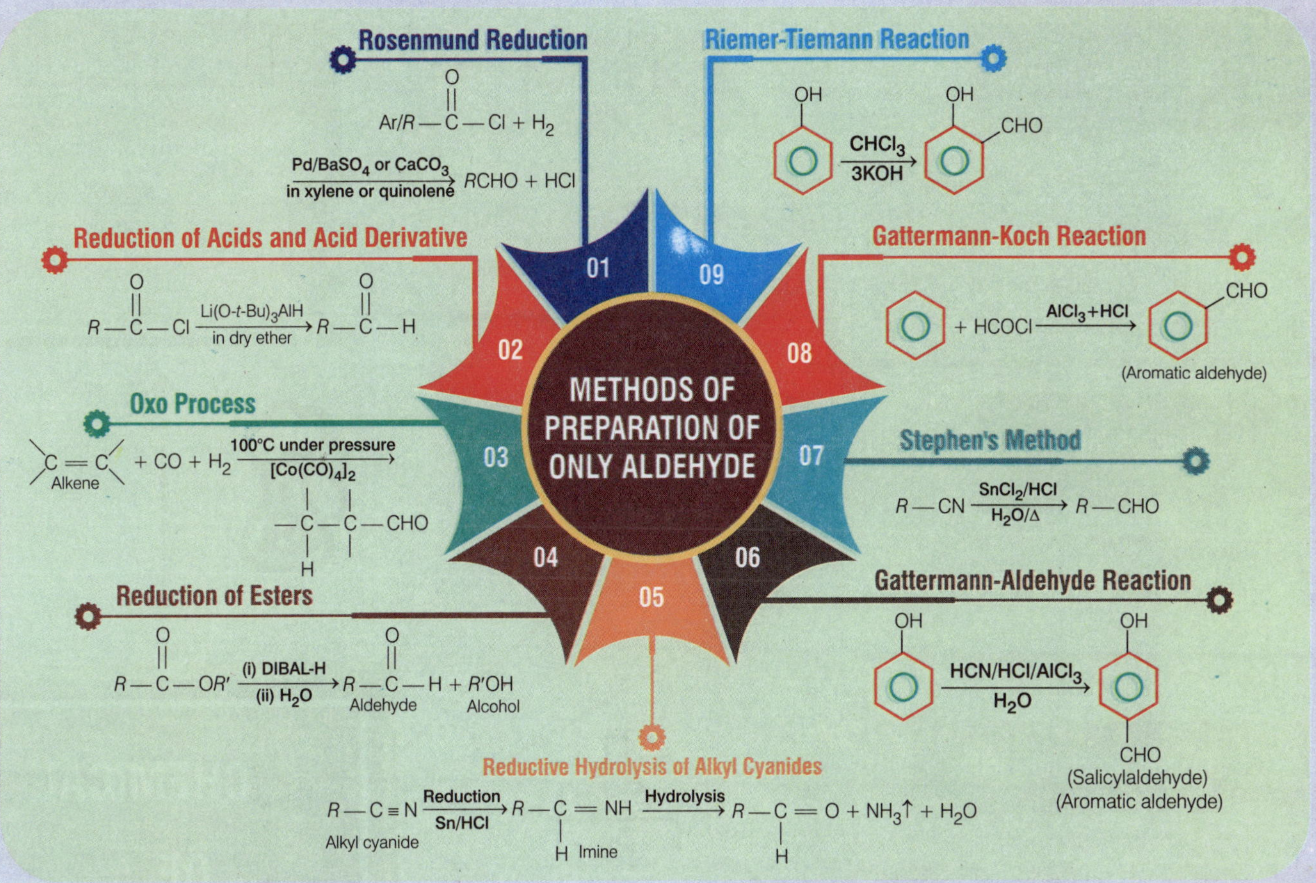
METHODS OF PREPARATION OF ONLY ALDEHYDE
01 Rosenmund Reduction
Pd/BaSO4 or CaCO3 in xylene or quinolene
RCHO + HCl
09 Riemer-Tiemann Reaction
CHCl3 3KOH
02 Reduction of Acids and Acid Derivative
Li(O-t-Bu)3AlH in dry ether
08 Gattermann-Koch Reaction
+ HCOCl AlCl3+HCl
(Aromatic aldehyde)
03 Oxo Process
Alkene
+ CO + H2 100°C under pressure [Co(CO)4]2
07 Stephen's Method
R—CN SnCl2/HCl H2O/Δ R—CHO
04 Reduction of Esters
(i) DIBAL-H (ii) H2O
Aldehyde
+ R'OH Alcohol
06 Gattermann-Aldehyde Reaction
HCN/HCl/AlCl3 H2O
(Salicylaldehyde)
(Aromatic aldehyde)
05 Reductive Hydrolysis of Alkyl Cyanides
Alkyl cyanide
Reduction Sn/HCl
Imine
Hydrolysis
+ NH3↑ + H2O

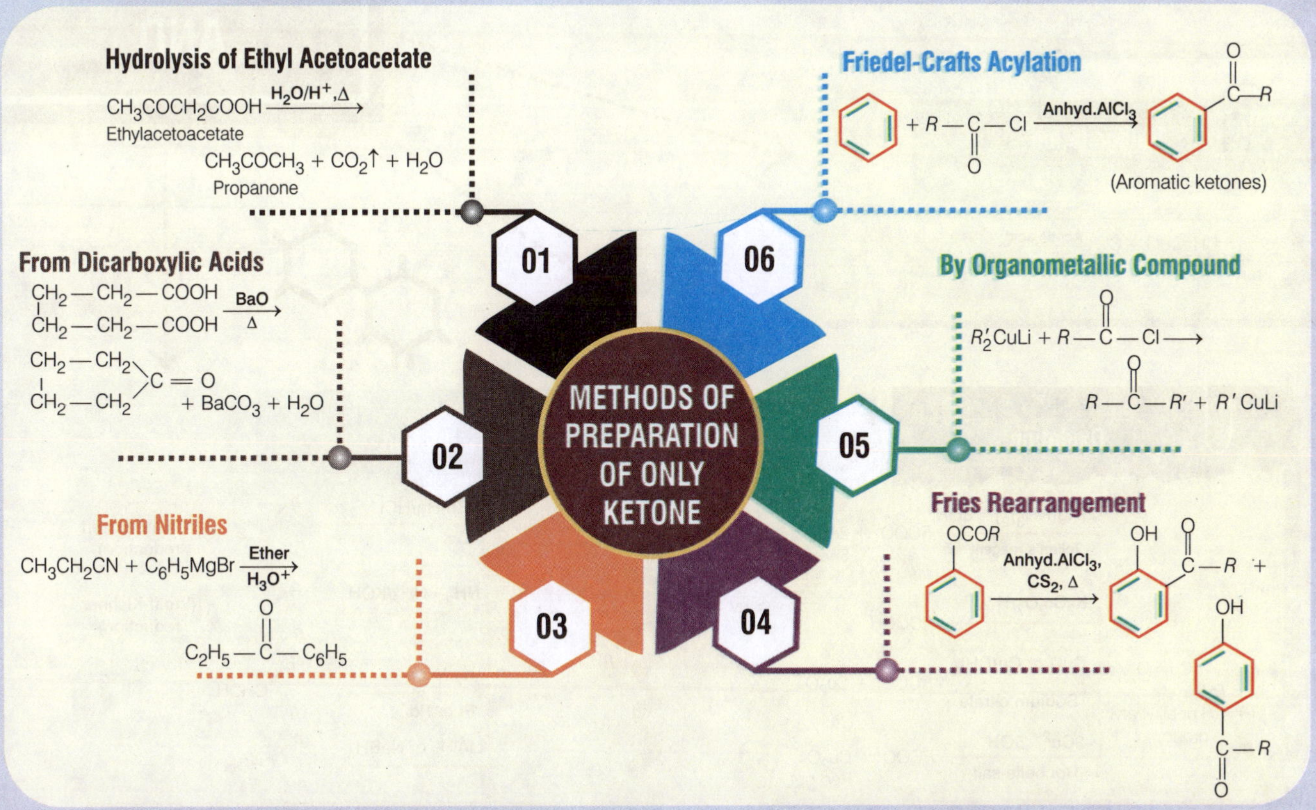
METHODS OF PREPARATION OF ONLY KETONE
01 Hydrolysis of Ethyl Acetoacetate
CH3COCH2COOH H2O/H+,Δ
Ethylacetoacetate
CH3COCH3 + CO2↑ + H2O
Propanone
06 Friedel-Crafts Acylation
Anhyd.AlCl3
(Aromatic ketones)
02 From Dicarboxylic Acids
BaO Δ
+ BaCO3 + H2O
05 By Organometallic Compound
R'2CuLi + R—C—Cl
R—C—R' + R'CuLi
03 From Nitriles
CH3CH2CN + C6H5MgBr Ether H3O+
C2H5—C—C6H5
04 Fries Rearrangement
OCOR
Anhyd.AlCl3, CS2, Δ

CHEMICAL OF AND

Reformatsky Reaction

$$R_2C{=}O + Br{-}\overset{\alpha}{C}H_2COOC_2H_5 \xrightarrow[\text{reflux}]{\text{Zn/ether}} R_2C(OZnBr){-}CH_2{-}\underset{\|}{C}(O){-}OC_2H_5 \xrightarrow{H_2O} R_2C(OH){-}CH_2{-}C(=O){-}OC_2H_5$$

Haloform Reaction

$$RCOCH_3 + 3X_2 + NaOH \longrightarrow \underset{\text{Haloform}}{CHX_3} + RCOONa$$

Benzil-Benzilic Acid Rearrangement

$$Ar{-}C(=O){-}C(=O){-}Ar \xrightarrow{NaOH/H^+} Ar_2C(OH){-}C(=O){-}H + H_2O$$

Willgerodt Reaction

$$C_6H_5COCH_3 \xrightarrow{(NH_4)_2S_x} C_6H_5CH_2CONH_2 + C_6H_5CH_2COONH_4$$

Claisen-Schmidt Reaction

$$C_6H_5{-}C(CH_3){=}O + CH_3COC_6H_5 \xrightarrow[\text{Al(Ot-Bu)}_3]{OH^-} C_6H_5{-}C(CH_3){=}CHCOC_6H_5$$

Halogenation

$$CH_3CHO + Cl_2 \xrightarrow{\text{Acetic acid}} ClCH_2CHO + HCl$$

Oxidation

$RR'C{=}O$ (R' = H or alkyl/aryl group)

- $\xrightarrow[\text{Tollen's reagent}]{2[Ag(NH_3)_2]^+,\ 3OH^-} RCOO^- + 2Ag\downarrow$ (Silver mirror test)
- $\xrightarrow{K_2Cr_2O_7/H^+} RCOOH$
- $\xrightarrow[\text{Sodium citrate}]{CuO \text{ or } Cu(OH)_2} RCOO^- + Cu_2O\downarrow$
- $\xrightarrow[\text{Rochelle salt}]{2Cu^{2+},5OH^-} RCOO^- + Cu_2O\downarrow$ (Red ppt.)

Reduction

$RR'C{=}O$

- $\xrightarrow{\text{Zn-Hg/HCl}} RR'CH_2$ (Clemmensen reduction)
- $\xrightarrow{NH_2{-}NH_2/KOH} RR'CH_2$ (Wolff-Kishner reduction)
- $\xrightarrow[\text{Pt or Pd}]{H_2/Ni \text{ or}} RR'CHOH$
- $\xrightarrow{LiAlH_4 \text{ or } NaBH_4} RR'CHOH$

PROPERTIES ALDEHYDES KETONES

Cannizzaro Reaction

$$\underset{\text{Formaldehyde}}{HCHO + HCHO} \xrightarrow{\text{Conc. KOH}} \underset{\text{Methanol}}{CH_3OH} + \underset{\text{Potassium formate}}{HCOOK}$$

Crossed Cannizzaro Reaction

$$\underset{\text{Formaldehyde}}{2HCHO} \xrightarrow{\text{Conc. NaOH}} \underset{\text{Methanol}}{CH_3OH} + \underset{\text{Sodium methanoate}}{HCOOK}$$

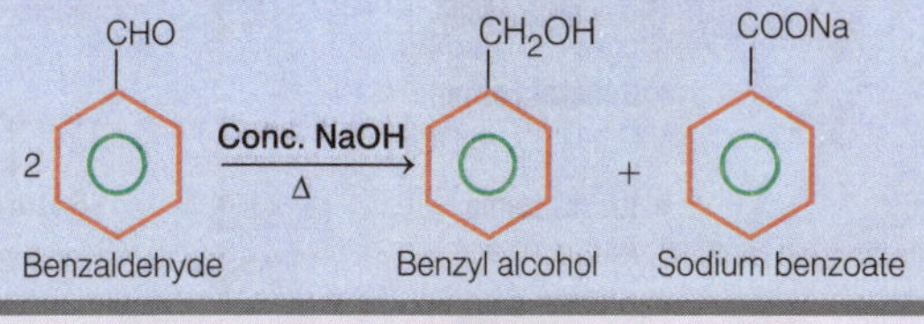

Benzoin Condensation

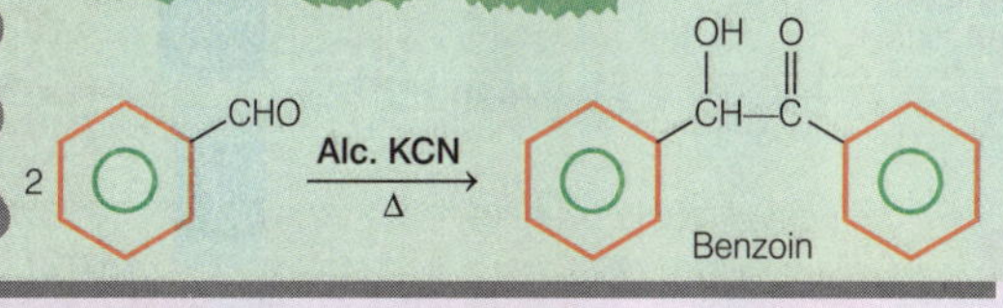

Perkin Condensation

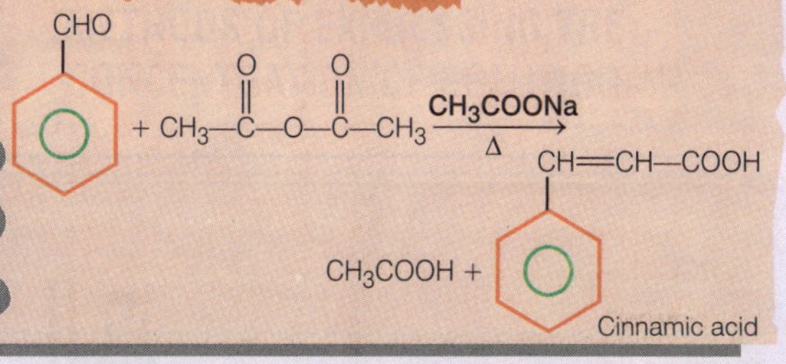

Knoevenagel Reaction

$$>C=O + H_2C\begin{smallmatrix}X\\Y\end{smallmatrix} \xrightarrow[\text{base (B)}]{\text{Amine}} >C=C\begin{smallmatrix}X\\Y\end{smallmatrix} + H_2O$$

Crossed Aldol Condensation

$$\begin{matrix}CH_3CHO\\+\\CH_3CH_2CHO\end{matrix} \xrightarrow[\Delta]{\text{NaOH}}$$

Self aldol product:
- $CH_3—CH=CH—CHO$
- $CH_3CH_2CH=C(CH_3)—CHO$

Crossed aldol product:
- $CH_3CH=C(CH_3)—CHO$
- $CH_3CH_2—CH=CH—CHO$

Aldol Condensation

$$2R—CH_2—\overset{O}{\overset{\|}{C}}—H \underset{}{\overset{\text{Dil. NaOH}}{\rightleftharpoons}} \underset{\text{Aldol}}{R—CH_2—\overset{OH}{\overset{|}{CH}}—\overset{R}{\overset{|}{CH}}—\overset{O}{\overset{\|}{C}}—H}$$

$$\downarrow \Delta, -H_2O$$

$$\underset{\alpha\text{-}\beta\text{-unsaturated aldehyde}}{R—CH_2—CH=\overset{R}{\overset{|}{C}}—\overset{O}{\overset{\|}{C}}—H}$$

CARBOXYLIC ACIDS

These are the organic compounds that contains carboxylic group (—C(=O)—OH).

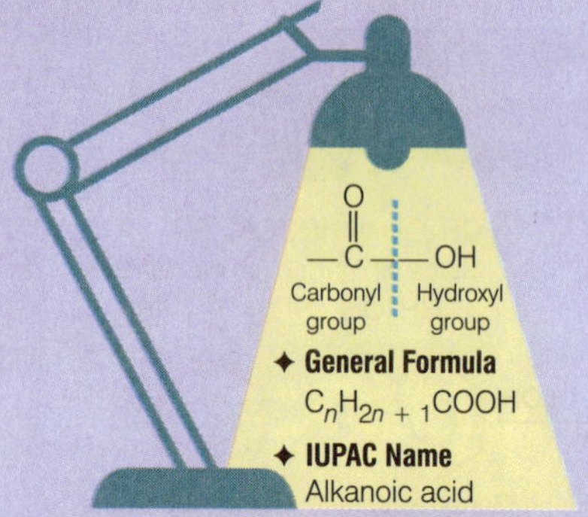

- **General Formula** $C_nH_{2n+1}COOH$
- **IUPAC Name** Alkanoic acid

- Monocarboxylic acids CH_3COOH (Monobasic)
  - **Saturated** CH_3CH_2COOH
  - **Unsaturated** $CH_2{=}CHCOOH$
- Polycarboxylic acids
  - **Dibasic** CH_2COOH–CH_2COOH
  - **Tribasic** CH_2COOH–$CHCOOH$–CH_2COOH

METHODS OF PREPARATION

RCOOH from:

- $RCH_2OH \xrightarrow[K_2Cr_2O_7, H^+]{[O]}$
- $RCOCH_3 \xrightarrow[H_2O]{X_2/NaOH}$
- $RCN \xrightarrow{H_2O, H^+, \Delta}$
- $RCX_3 \xrightarrow{NaOH}$
- $RMgX \xrightarrow[H_2O, H^+]{CO_2}$
- $RCOOR \xrightarrow{H_2O, H^+}$
- $RCONH_2 \xrightarrow{H_2O, H^+}$
- $RCH{=}CHR \xrightarrow{[O]}$
- $RCH{=}CH_2 \xrightarrow[H_3PO_4]{CO + H_2O}$

Benzoic acid from:

- $ArCH_3 \xrightarrow[KMnO_4, OH^-]{\Delta/[O]}$
- $ArCCl_3 \xrightarrow[\text{Fe catalyst}, H_2O]{Ca(OH)_2}$
- $ArH + COCl_2$
- $ArMgBr \xrightarrow[H^+/H_2O]{CO_2}$

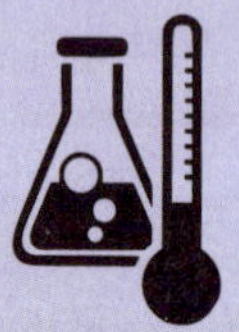

01 Reaction Involving Cleavage of —OH Bond

$R—C(=O)—O—H$

- $\xrightarrow{Na} 2RCOONa + H_2$
- $\xrightarrow{NaOH} RCOONa + H_2O$
- $\xrightarrow{Na_2CO_3} 2RCOONa + CO_2 + H_2O$

02 Reaction Involving Cleavage of C—O Bond

$R—C(=O)—OH$

- $\xrightarrow[P_2O_5, \Delta]{+RCOOH/H^+, \Delta} (RCO)_2O$ Anhydride
- $\xrightarrow[-H_2O]{R'OH/H^+} RCOOR$ Ester
- $\xrightarrow[\text{or } SOCl_2 \text{ in Pyridine}]{PCl_3 \text{ or } PCl_5} RCOCl$ Acid chloride
- $\xrightarrow[-H_2O]{NH_3, \Delta} RCONH_2$ Amide

03 Reaction Involving >C=O Group

$$R—C(=O)—OH \xrightarrow[H_3O^+ \text{ (Reduction)}]{LiAlH_4/\text{Ether or } B_2H_6/\text{Ether}} RCH_2OH$$

Chemical Properties

- Carboxyl carbon is less electrophilic than carbonyl carbon.
- A group attached to an acids is more acidic than hydroxyl group of alcohols and phenols.
- EWG increases the acidity while EDG decreases it.

04 Ring Substitution in Aromatic Acids

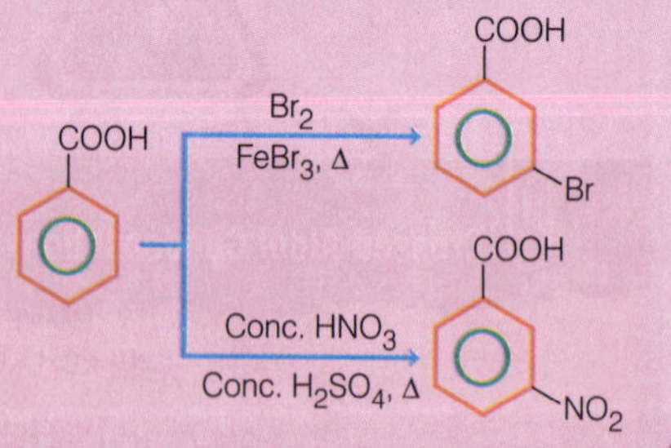

05 Reaction Involving —COOH Group

$$R—C(=O)—OH \xrightarrow[\Delta \text{ (Decarboxylation)}]{NaOH \text{ and } CaO} RH + Na_2CO_3$$

06 Reaction Involving —R Group

$$RCH_2—C(=O)—OH \xrightarrow[H_2O]{X_2/\text{Red P}} R—CH(X)—COOH$$

α-halocarboxylic acid

Physical Properties

- **Boiling point order** Carboxylic acids > Alcohols > Aldehydes > Ketones > Hydrocarbons
- Solubility $\propto \dfrac{1}{\text{No. of carbon atoms}}$
- Solubility in water is due to H-bonding.

CARBOXYLIC ACID DERIVATIVES

Obtained by replacement of —OH group of carboxylic acids by —*X*, —NH_2, —*OR* or OCO*R*.

ACID HALIDES

General Formula $R-\overset{\overset{O}{\|}}{C}-X$

ACID CHLORIDES

Preparation

By the Distillation of Acid Salts

- Distilling Na salts with PCl_3: $RCOCl + Na_3PO_3$ are produced.
- Distilling Na salts with $POCl_3$: $RCOCl + NaCl + NaPO_3$ are produced.

From Carboxylic Acids

- By reaction with $SOCl_2$
- By reaction with PCl_5
- By reaction with PCl_3

Chemical Properties

Acid Chloride *R*COCl

- Hydrolysis → $RCOOH + HCl$
- Ammonolysis with (NH_3) → $RCONH_2 + HCl$
- with $NH_2—NH_2$ → $R-\overset{\overset{O}{\|}}{C}-NH-NH_2$
- with amines
  - 1° → $RCON(H)-R' + HCl$
  - 2° → $RCON(R')-R' + HCl$
- Reduction
  - H_2/Lindlar's catalyst → $RCHO + HCl$
  - $LiAlH_4$ → RCH_2OH

ESTERS

General Formula *R*COO*R*′

Preparation

- From carboxylic acid.
- Reacting carboxylic salt with *RX*.
- Reacting alkene with an acid in presence of BF_3.
- By Tischenko reaction.

Chemical Properties

Ester, *R*COO*R*′

- Hydrolysis/H^+ → $RCOOH + R'OH$
- Ammonolysis (with NH_3) → $RCONH_2 + R'OH$
- With PCl_5 → $RCOCl + POCl_5 + R'Cl$
- $NaOR' + H_3O^+$ (Claisen condensation) → $RCH_2COCHRCOOR + R'OH$
- Br_2+Red P ($R = CH_3$, $R' = C_2H_5$) (Halogenation) → $CH_2-\overset{\overset{Br}{|}}{C}O + C_2H_5O^-$

ACID ANHYDRIDES

General Formula

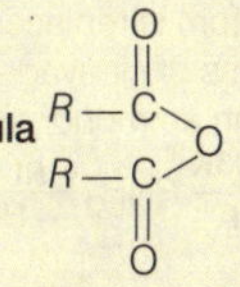

Preparation

- From carboxylic acids by reacting them with *R*COCl.
- By reacting acid halides with salts of fatty acids.
- By dehydration of anhydrous acid with P_2O_5.

Chemical Properties

Acid Anhydride

- Hydrolysis → $2RCOOH$
- Ammonolysis → $RCONH_2 + RCOOH$
- With amines
  - 1° → $RCONHR' + RCOOH$
  - 2° → $RCON(R)-R' + RCOOH$
- Reduction ($LiAlH_4$) → RCH_2OH
- With PCl_5 → $2RCOCl + POCl_3$

Chapter 09 Amines

AMINES

These are obtained by replacing one or more H–atoms of hydrocarbons with $-NH_2$ group.

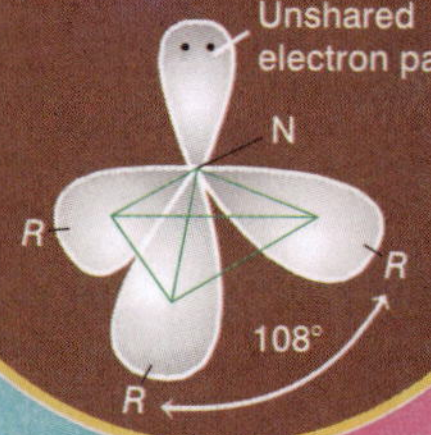

Aliphatic Amines

- These are alkyl derivatives of ammonia. e.g. CH_3NH_2

Nomenclature

Common name

- Aliphatic amine is named by prefixing alkyl group to amine, i.e. alkyl amine.
  e.g. Methyl amine (CH_3NH_2)

IUPAC name

- Derived by the replacement of 'e' of alkane by the word amines.
  e.g. CH_3NH_2 (methanamine)

Classification

Primary (1°)

- $R-\underset{}{\overset{H}{\overset{|}{N}}}-H$
- 2-hydrogen atoms are attached to N.

Secondary (2°)

- R_2NH
- 1 hydrogen atom is attached to N.

Tertiary (3°)

- R_3N
- Zero hydrogen atom is attached to N.

Quaternary Ammonium Salts ($R_4N^+X^-$)

- Formed by replacement of all the hydrogen atoms from ammonium ions (NH_4^+) with either alkyl or aryl group.
- X is halogen atom or hydroxyl group.

METHODS OF PREPARATION FOR MIXTURE OF AMINES

Hoffmann Ammonolysis Method

- Alkyl halide reacts with ethanolic solution of ammonia.
- Undergoes nucleophilic substitution reaction.
- Halogen atom is replaced by an amino group.
- This process of cleavage of $C-X$ bond by ammonia is Hoffmann ammonolysis.

$$RI^- \xrightarrow[-HI]{NH_3/393K} \underset{(1°)}{R\ddot{N}H_2} \xrightarrow[-HI]{RI} \underset{(2°)}{R_2\ddot{N}H} \xrightarrow[-HI]{RI} \underset{(3°)}{R_3\ddot{N}}$$

$$\xrightarrow[RI]{-HI} [R_4\overset{+}{N}]I^-$$

Quaternary ammonium salt

Reaction of Alcohol with Ammonia

$$R-OH + NH_3 \xrightarrow[620K]{Al_2O_3} RNH_2 + H_2O$$

$$ROH + RNH_2 \longrightarrow R_2NH + H_2O$$

$$ROH + R_2NH \longrightarrow R_3N + H_2O$$

$$ROH + R_3N \longrightarrow R_4\overset{+}{N}OH^-$$

Leuckart Reaction

- Ketones on reductive amination with $HCOONH_4$ or DMF gives amines.
- $$\underset{\text{Ketone}}{R-\overset{O}{\overset{||}{C}}-Me} + HCOONH_4 \xrightarrow[180\text{–}200°C]{\Delta} \underset{\text{Amine}}{R-\underset{NH_2}{\underset{|}{CH}}-Me} + H_2O + CO_2\uparrow$$

Preparation of 3° AMINES

Reaction of RX with NH_3

$$\underset{\text{Alkyl halide}}{3RX} + \text{Alc. } NH_3 \xrightarrow{\Delta} R_3N^+X^- \xrightarrow{NaOH} \underset{\text{3° amine}}{R_3N} + NaX$$

Reduction of N, N-disubstituted Amides

$$RCONR' \xrightarrow[Ether]{LiAlH_4} RCH_2-N\begin{matrix}R'\\R'\end{matrix}$$

Decomposition of Tetraalkyl Ammonium Hydroxide

$$R_4N^+OH^- \xrightarrow{\Delta} R_3N + H_2O + \underset{\text{Ethene}}{CH_2=CH_2}$$

Preparation of 2° AMINES

Reaction of RX with 1° Amines

- $$R-NH_2 + RX \xrightarrow{\Delta} R_2NH_2^+X^- \xrightarrow{NaOH} \underset{\text{2° amine}}{R_2NH} + NaX + H_2O$$

Reduction

- $$\underset{\text{alkyl isocyanide}}{RN \rightleftarrows C} + 2H_2 \xrightarrow{\text{Ni or Pt}} \underset{\text{2° amine}}{RNHCH_3}$$
- $$\underset{\text{Amides}}{R-\overset{O}{\overset{||}{C}}-\underset{H}{\underset{|}{N}}-R'} \xrightarrow[Ether]{LiAlH_4} \underset{\text{2° amine}}{RCH_2-\underset{H}{\underset{|}{N}}-R'}$$

Reductive Amination of Carbonyl Compound

- $$R-\overset{O}{\overset{||}{C}}-H \xrightarrow[-H_2O]{R'NH_2} \text{Imine} \longrightarrow R-CH_2-NH-R'$$

Physical Properties

- B.P. is higher than non-polar compound of same molecular mass.
- Miscible with water due to intermolecular H-bonding with H_2O molecules also.
- Lower amines are gases or low-boiling liquids.
- Have characteristic ammonia like smell.

Preparation of 1° AMINES

Reduction

- $R-C\equiv N \xrightarrow[LiAlH_4]{Reduction} RCH_2NH_2$ (Alkyl nitirile → Alkyl amine)
- $RNO_2 + 3H_2 \xrightarrow[H_2/Pt]{Ni/250°\text{ or }LiAlH_4} RNH_2 + 2H_2O$ (Nitroalkane → Amine)
- $RCONH_2 \xrightarrow{LiAlH_4} RCH_2NH_2 + H_2O$ (Amide → Amine)

Reductive Amination of Carbonyl Compounds

$R-CH_2-H \xrightarrow[-H_2O]{NH_3} R-CH=NH \xrightarrow[Ni]{H_2} RCH_2NH_2$

Schmidt Rearrangement

$R-\overset{O}{\overset{\|}{C}}-OH + N_3H \xrightarrow[\Delta]{Conc.\ H_2SO_4} RNH_2 + CO_2\uparrow + N_2\uparrow$

Carboxylic acid → 1° amine

Hoffmann Bromamide Degradation Reaction

$RCONH_2 + Br_2 + Aq\cdot 4NaOH \xrightarrow{\Delta} RNH_2 + 2NaBr + Na_2CO_3 + 2H_2O$

Amide → 1° amine

Lossen Rearrangement

$R-\overset{O}{\overset{\|}{C}}-NH-OH \xrightarrow[(ii)\ H_2O]{(i)\ \bar{O}H} RNH_2 + CO_2\uparrow$

Hydroxamic acid → 1° amine

Ritter Reaction

$Me_3C-OH + HCN + H_2SO_4 \longrightarrow Me_3C-NH_2$

3° alcohol → 1° amine

Curtius Method

$R-\overset{O}{\overset{\|}{C}}-Cl \xrightarrow{NaN_3} R-\overset{O}{\overset{\|}{C}}-N_3 \xrightarrow[\text{Intramolecular alkyl shift}]{-N_2} R-N=C=O \xrightarrow[\Delta]{2NaOH} R-NH_2 + Na_2CO_3$

Amine

Gabriel Pthalimide Synthesis

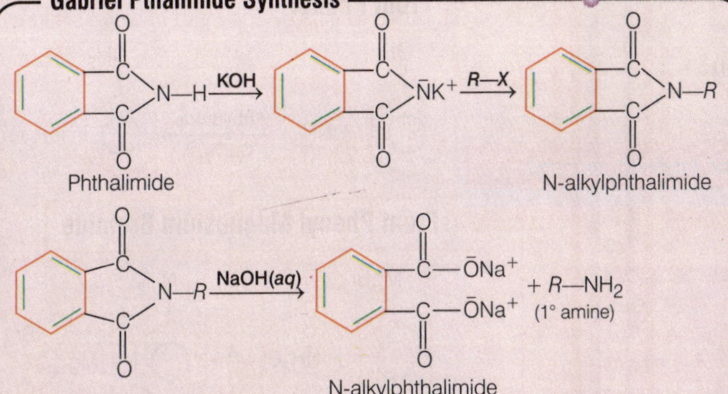

Basic Character of Amines

- They react with acids to form salts.
- Behaves as Lewis base due to presence of unshared pair of electrons in them.
- $K_b \propto \frac{1}{pK_b} \propto$ Basicity
- Order of basicity $3° > 2° > 1° > NH_3$.

CHEMICAL PROPERTIES

Nature of Aqueous Solution

- $RNH_2 + HOH \longrightarrow \overset{+}{R}NH_3OH^- \longrightarrow [RNH_3]^+ + OH^-$ (1° amine)
- $R_2NH + HOH \longrightarrow \overset{+}{R_2}NH_2OH^- \longrightarrow [R_2NH_2]^+ + OH^-$ (2° amine)
- $R_3N + HOH \longrightarrow \overset{+}{R_3}NHOH \longrightarrow [R_3NH]^+ + OH^-$ (3° amine)

With Mineral Acids

$RNH_2 + HCl \longrightarrow R\overset{+}{N}H_3Cl^-$

Amine (Base) + Hydrochloric acid → Salt

Reaction with Grignard Reagent

- $CH_3-NH-H + C_2H_5Mg-Br \longrightarrow CH_3-NH-MgBr + C_2H_6$
- $CH_3-N(CH_3)-H + C_2H_5Mg-Br \longrightarrow CH_3-N(CH_3)-Mg-Br + C_2H_6$

Acylation

$R-\overset{O}{\overset{\|}{C}}-Cl + H-NH-R' \xrightarrow{-HCl} R-\overset{O}{\overset{\|}{C}}-NH-R'$

N-substituted amide

Oxidation

- $RCH_2-NH_2 \xrightarrow{KMnO_4} RCH=NH \xrightarrow{H_3O^+} RCHO$
- $RCH_2-NH_2 \xrightarrow[{[O]}]{H_2SO_5} RCH_2NHOH + RCH=NOH + R-\overset{OH}{C}=NOH$ (N-alkyl hydroxyl-amine, Aldoxime, Hydroxamic acid)
- $R_2NH \xrightarrow[{[O]}]{KMnO_4} R_2N-NR_2$
- $R_2NH \xrightarrow[{[O]}]{H_2SO_5} R_2NOH$
- $R_3N \xrightarrow[{[O]}]{KMnO_4}$ No effect
- $R_3N \xrightarrow[{[O]}]{H_2SO_5} R_3NO$

AROMATIC AMINES

These are aryl derivatives of ammonia in which one or more H-atoms of ammonia is replaced by aryl group.

Common Name

When $-NH_2$ group is directly attached to benzene ring, the compound formed in called arylamine. Aniline is the simplest aryl amine.

IUPAC Name

- Suffix 'e' of arene is replaced by 'amine' e.g. $Ph-NH_2$ is benzenamine.

Methods of Preparation

Reduction of Nitro Compounds

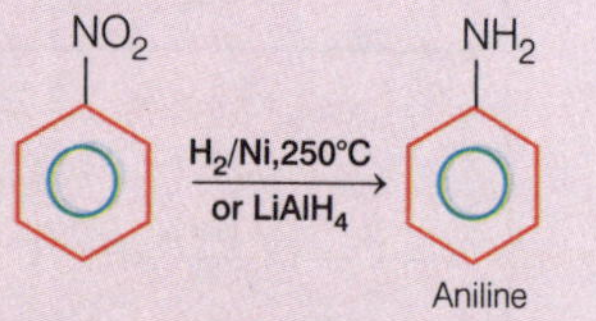

Ammonolysis of Aryl Chloride

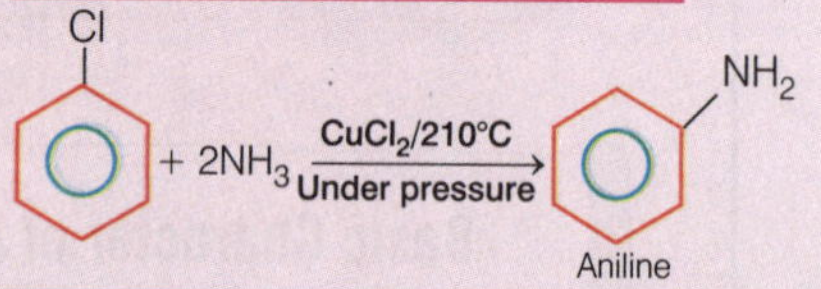

Hoffmann's Bromamide Degradation

$$Ar-\overset{O}{\overset{\|}{C}}-NH_2 \xrightarrow[(Br_2 + NaOH)]{NaOBr} \underset{Amine}{Ar-NH_2} + Na_2CO_3 + 2NaBr + 2H_2O$$

Reduction of Azo Compounds

$$Ar-N=N-Ar \xrightarrow[Ni,\ \Delta]{H_2} Ar-\underset{H}{N}-\underset{H}{N}-Ar \xrightarrow[Ni,\ \Delta]{H_2} 2ArNH_2$$

Schmidt Reaction

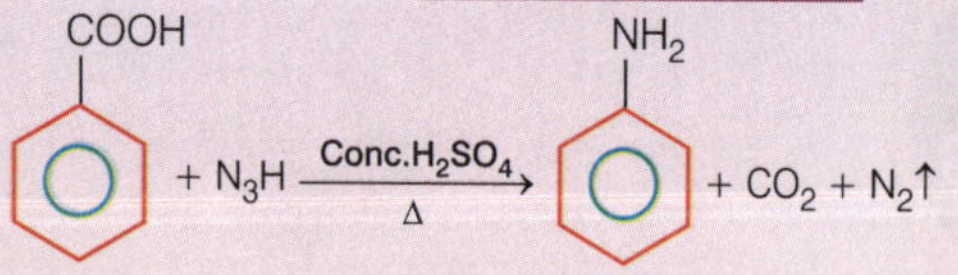

From Chlorobenzene

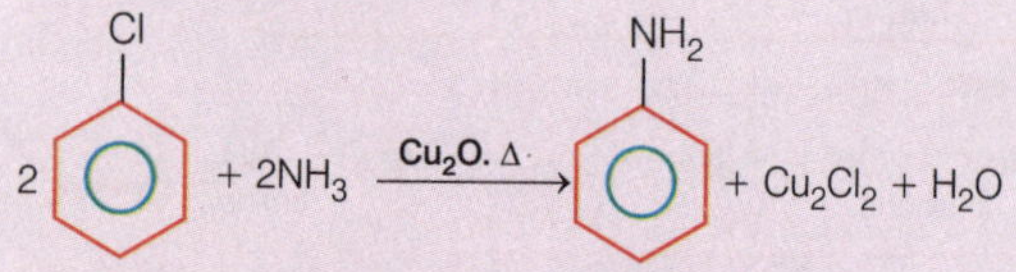

From Phenol

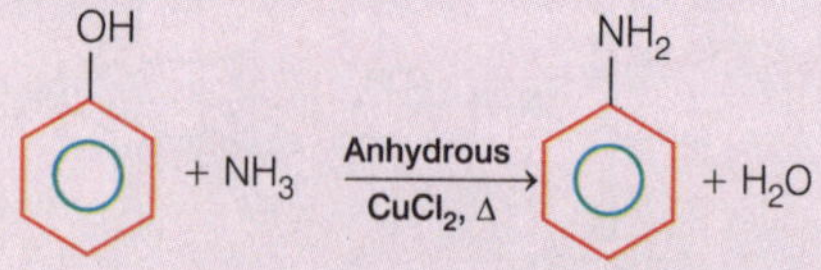

From Phenyl Magnesium Bromide

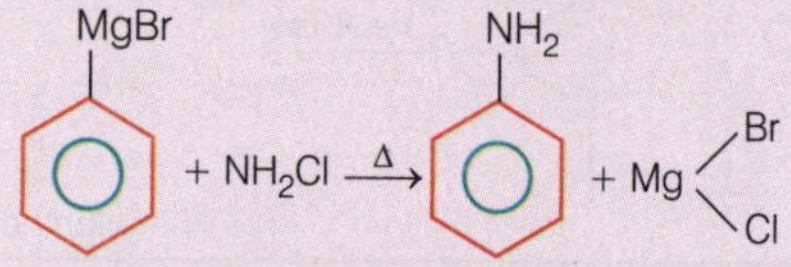

By the Hydrolysis of Isocyanide

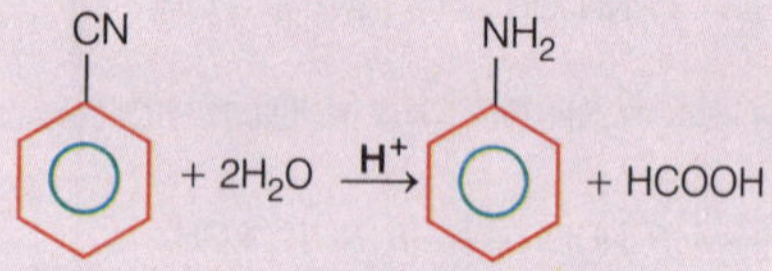

From Benzene Sulphonic Acid

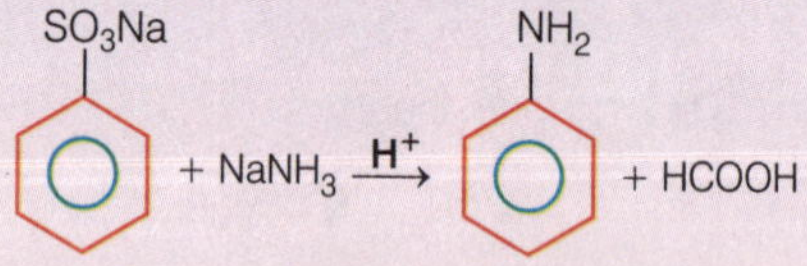

Electrophilic Substitution

Bromination

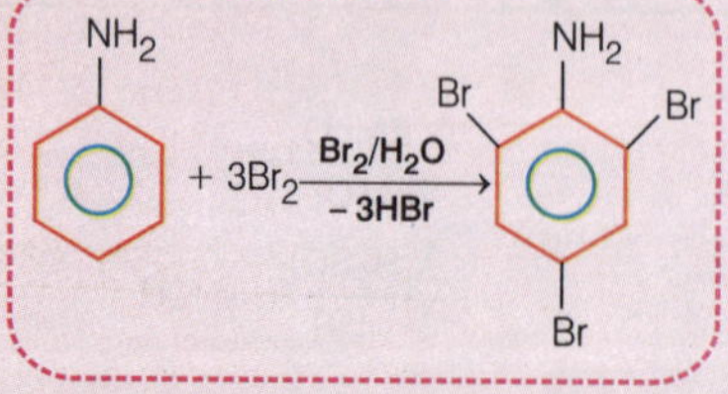

Sulphonation

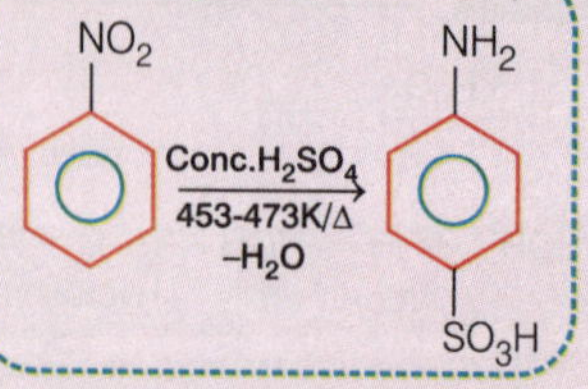

Nitration

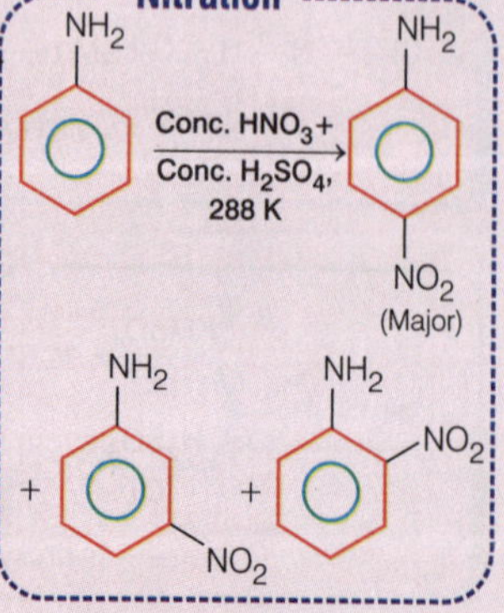

Physical Properties

- They are colourless liquids, or solids having characteristics odour.
- Turn brown in air due to oxidation. Have high boiling point due to intermolecular H-bonding.
- Sparingly soluble in water.

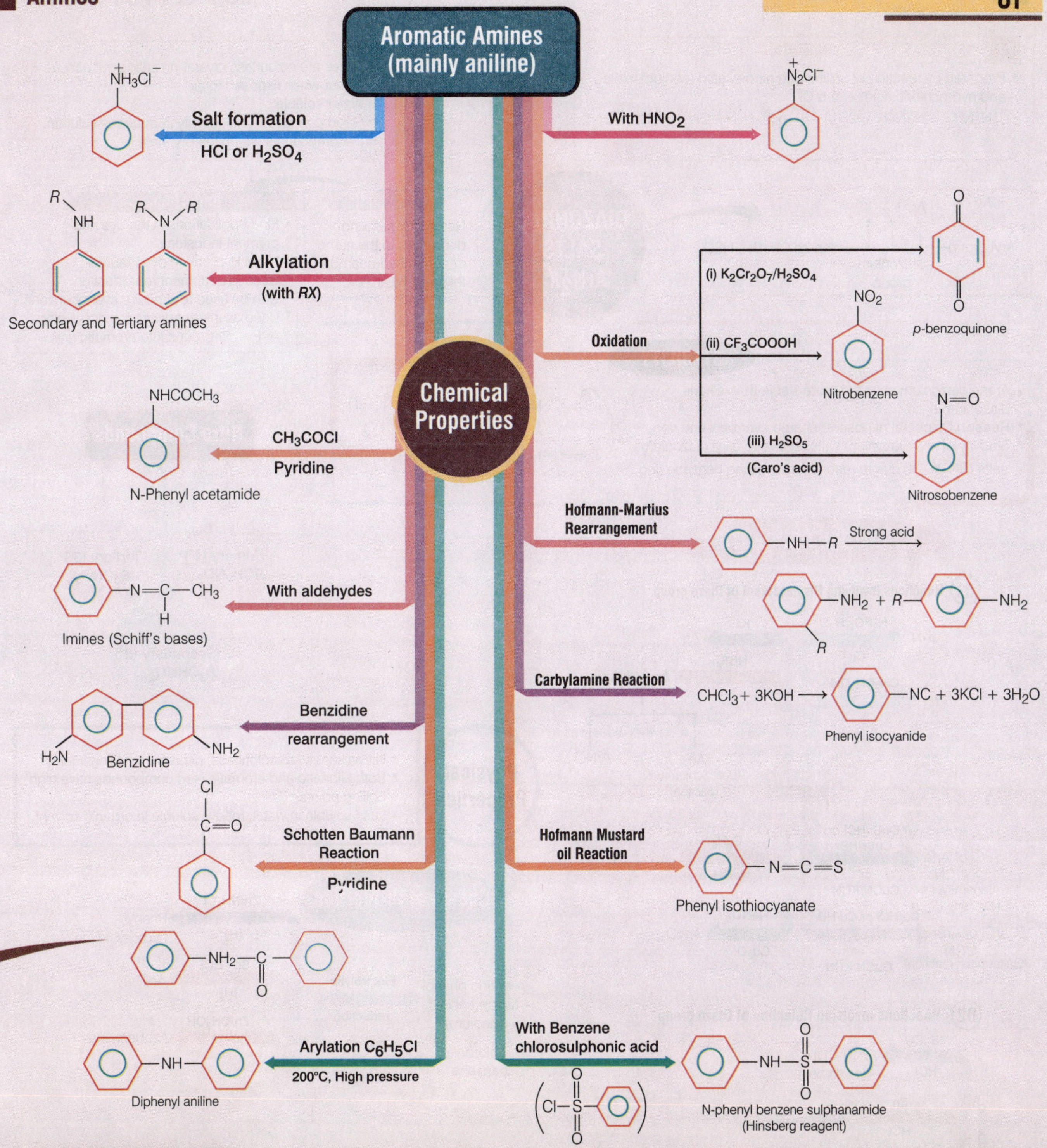

POWER TIPS

➤ Aniline fails to give Friedel Crafts Reaction as aniline acts as a Lewis base. So $AlCl_3$ being an electrophile forms salt with it that is, $C_6H_5NHAlCl_3$

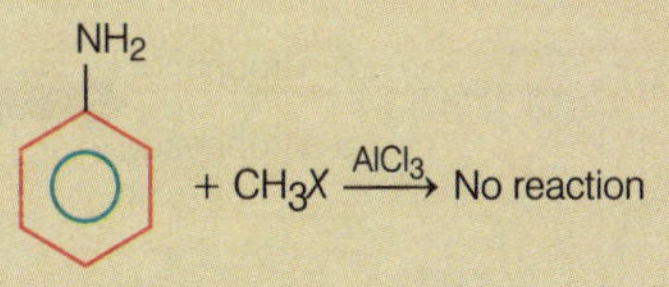

Preparation

- Prepared by reaction of aniline with nitrous acid (sodium nitrite and hydrochloric acid) at 0-5°C.
- $C_6H_5NH_2 + NaNO_2 + 2HCl \xrightarrow{0\text{-}5°C} C_6H_5N_2^+ Cl^- + NaCl + 2H_2O$

Physical Properties

- These are colourless crystalline solids but acquire colour when exposed to air.
- Water soluble.
- Good conductor of electricity in aqueous solution.
- Decomposes easily in the dry state.

DIAZONIUM SALTS $ArN_2^+X^-$

Ar N_2^+ X^-

Aryl group — Ar; Diazonium group — N_2^+; X^- can be Cl^-, Br^-, HSO_4^-

Nomenclature

- Named by suffixing diazonium to the name of parent hydrocarbon followed by anion.

Importance

- Find applications in the dye and pigment industries.
- Used to produce dyes fabrics.
- Used in document reproduction.
- Can be used to produce cyanobenzene.
- Used as intermediates for introducing —F,— Br groups into aromatic ring.

STABILITY

- Arene diazonium salts are more stable than alkane diazonium salts.
- **Reason** Dispersal of positive charge over benzene ring.
- Stability of aryl diazonium salts relative to alkyl diazonium salts ($RN_2^+X^-$) is due to resonance involving benzene ring.

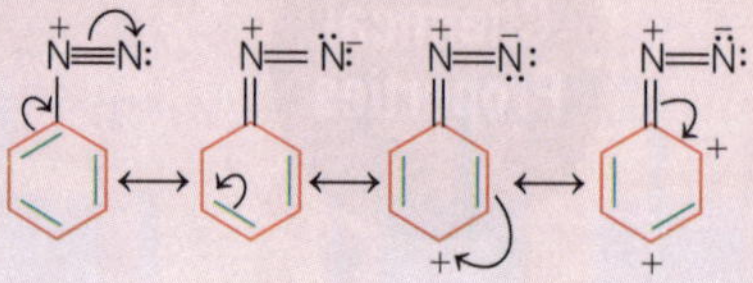

Nitro Compounds

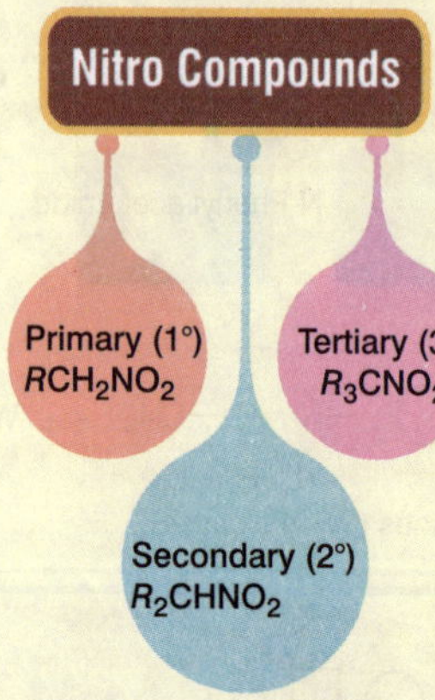

CHEMICAL PROPERTIES

01 Reactions Involving Displacement of Diazo group

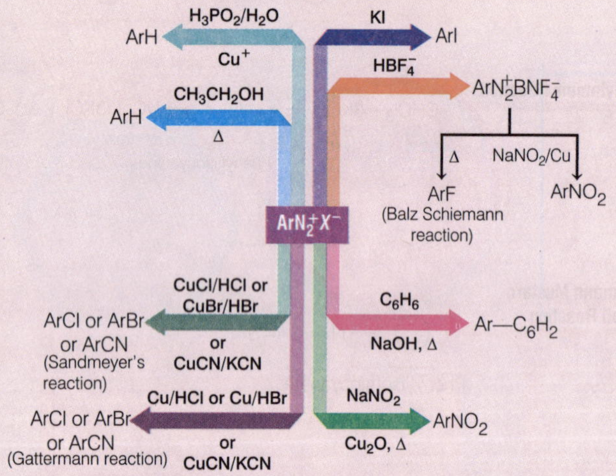

Physical Properties

- Nitroalkanes are colourless, pleasant smelling liquids.
- Both aliphatic and aromatic nitro compounds have high boiling points.
- Less soluble in water, readily soluble in organic solvent.

Chemical Properties

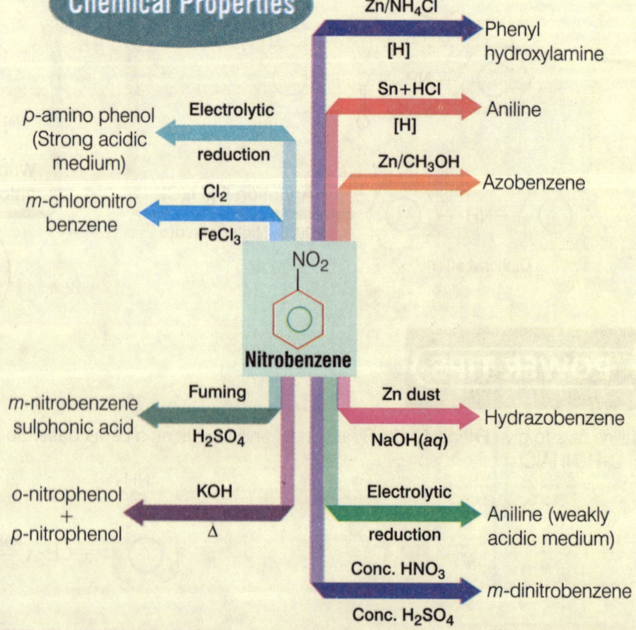

02 Reactions Involving Retention of Diazo group

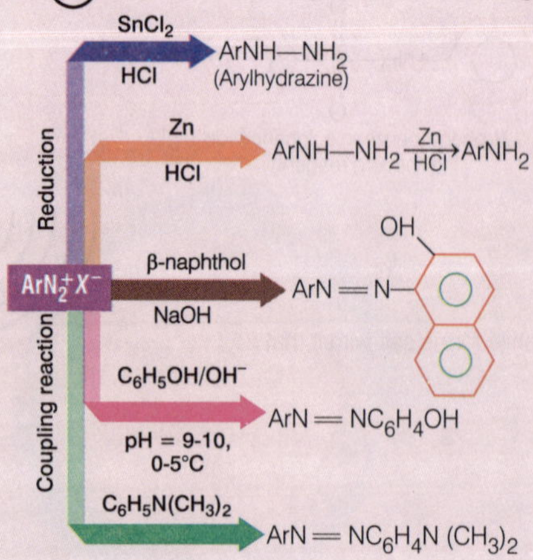

CYANIDES AND ISOCYANIDES

- These are isomeric compounds and also are derivatives of hydrogen cyanide that exist in two tautomeric forms.
  $H-C\equiv N \quad H-N\rightleftarrows C$
- On replacing hydrogen atom of cyanide by an alkyl or aryl group we get corresponding cyanide.
  $R-C\equiv N$ (Alkyl cyanide) $\quad Ar-C\equiv N$ (Aryl cyanide)
- On replacing hydrogen atom of isocyanide by an alkyl or aryl group, we get corresponding isocyanide.
  $R-N\rightleftarrows C$ or $Ar-N\rightleftarrows C$
  Alkyl isocyanide, Aryl isocyanide

Nomenclature

01 Cyanide

- In IUPAC system, alkyl cyanide is named as alkane nitrile.
- e.g. CH_3-CN
  Ethanentirite

02 Isocyanide

- In IUPAC system, the word isocyanide is added after the alkyl or aryl.
- e.g. $CH_3\equiv NC$
  Methyl isocyanide

Structures

01

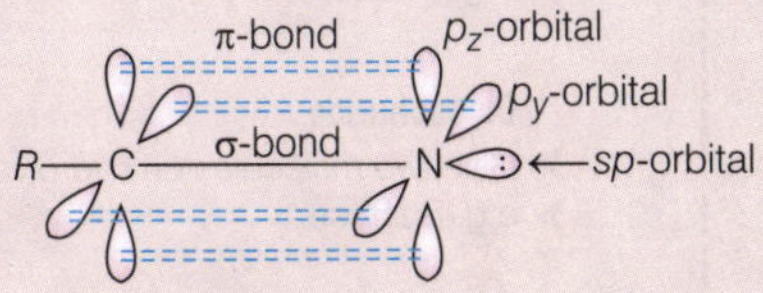

Orbital structure of alkyl cyanides

02

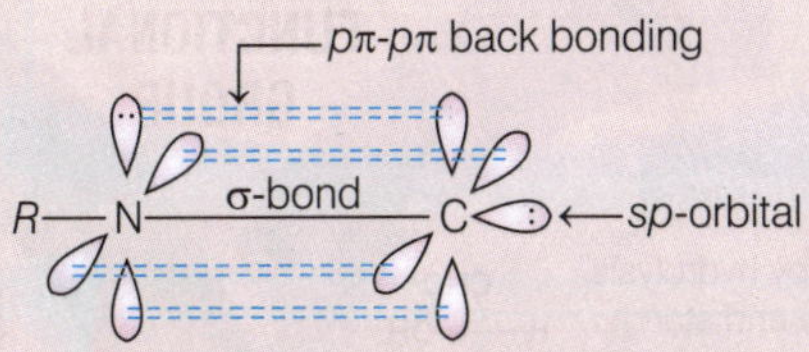

Orbital structure of alkyl isocyanides

CHEMICAL PROPERTIES

R — CN

- $\xrightarrow{H_2O/HCl}$ $R-COOH + NH_4Cl$ (Carboxylic acid)
- $\xrightarrow{R'-OH/H_2SO_4}$ $R-COOR'$ (Ester)
- $\xrightarrow{Na/C_2H_5OH}$ $R-CH_2-NH_2$ (1° amine)
- $\xrightarrow{SnCl_2/HCl}$ $RCH=\overset{+}{N}H + HCl \xrightarrow{H_2O} RCHO + NH_4Cl$

R — N ≡ C

- $\xrightarrow{Cl_2}$ $R-N=CCl_2$
- $\xrightarrow{Na/C_2H_5OH}$ (Reduction) $R-NH-CH_3$
- $\xrightarrow{H_2O/H^+}$ RNH_2 (1°) $+ HCOOH$ (Formic acid)
- $\xrightarrow{O_3}$ $R-N=C=O + O_2$

Physical Properties

Cyanides

- Alkyl cyanides are neutral substance.
- Pleasant odour.
- Soluble in water.
- Poisonous but less than HCN.

Isocyanides

- They are colourless.
- Unpleasant smelling liquid.
- Soluble in organic solvent but insoluble in water.
- More poisonous than isomeric cyanide.

Chapter 10 Biomolecules

BIOMOLECULES
Complex organic molecules that form the basis of life and are required for their growth and maintenance.

- Carbohydrates
- Proteins
- Lipids
- Vitamins
- Enzymes
- Nucleic Acids

CARBOHYDRATES

Optically active polyhydroxy aldehydes or ketones or the compounds that produces such units on hydrolysis.

ON THE BASIS OF FUNCTIONAL GROUP

Aldoses
- Contains aldehyde group (—CHO)
- e.g. Aldotriose (Glyceraldehyde) Aldohexose (Glucose, Galactose, Mannose)

Ketoses
- Contains keto group >C=O
- e.g. Ketotriose (dihydroxyacetone) Ketopentose (Ribulose).

D-(+)-Glucose
- Prepared by hydrolysis of sucrose and starch.
- α-glucose and β-glucose undergoes mutarotation. Differs in configuration at chiral C*.

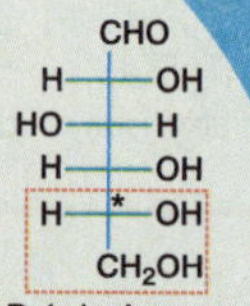

D-(+)-glucose

D-(–)-Fructose
- C_2 is chiral.
- Two isomers are α-D-fructopyranose and β-D-fructopyranose.

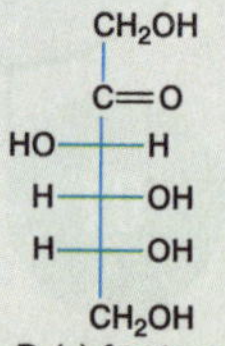

D-(–)-fructose

Monosaccharides
- They cannot be broken into smaller molecules on hydrolysis.
- General formula $C_nH_{2n}O_n$, n = 3 to 7
- e.g. Glucose, fructose, galactose

Oligosaccharides
- Yields 2-10 monosaccharides units on hydrolysis.
- e.g. Lactose

Disaccharide
- Give two molecules on hydrolysis.
- e.g. Sucrose.

Trisaccharides
- Give three molecules on hydrolysis.
- e.g. Raffinose.

Tetrasaccharides
- Give four molecules on hydrolysis
- e.g. Stachyose

Polysaccharides
- Upon hydrolysis yields more than ten monosaccharides.
- e.g. Cellulose, starch, glycogen

03 Starch
- Composed of amylose and amylopectin.
- Amylose—water soluble, unbranched.
- Amylopectin—water insoluble, branched chain.

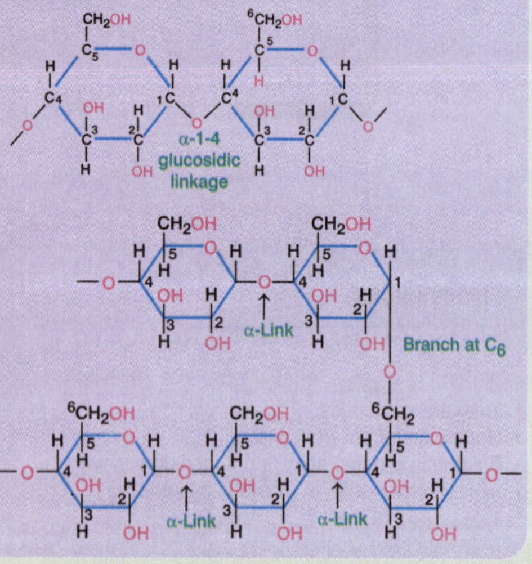

02 Glycogen
- More branched than starch.
- Present in animal brain, liver etc.

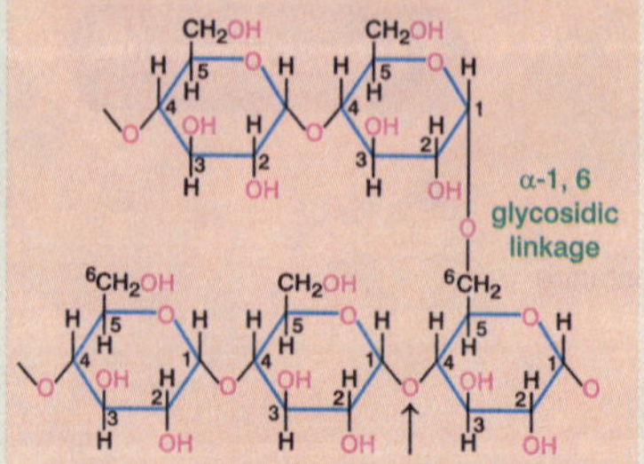

01 Cellulose
- Composed of β-D-Glucose units joined by glycosidic linkage between C_1 of one glucose unit and C_4 of another glucose unit. Present in plant cell.

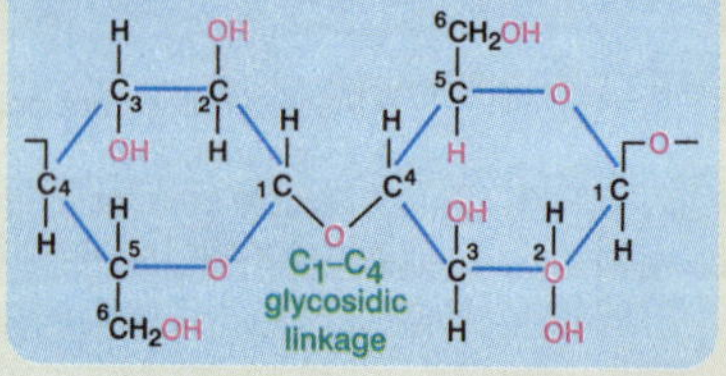

Types of Disaccharides

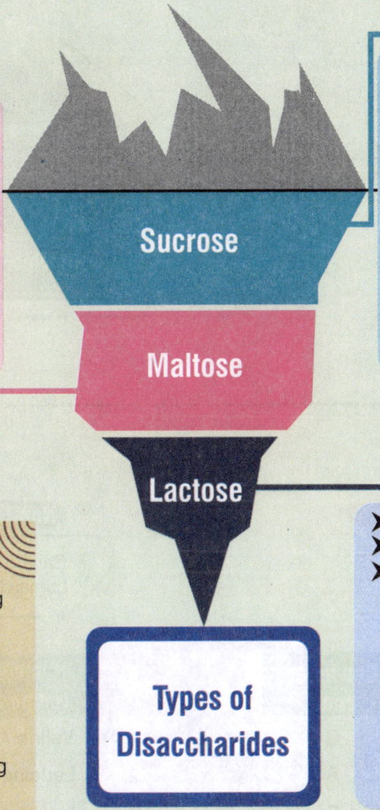

Maltose

- Reducing sugar.
- Monomers are two α-D-Glucose units.

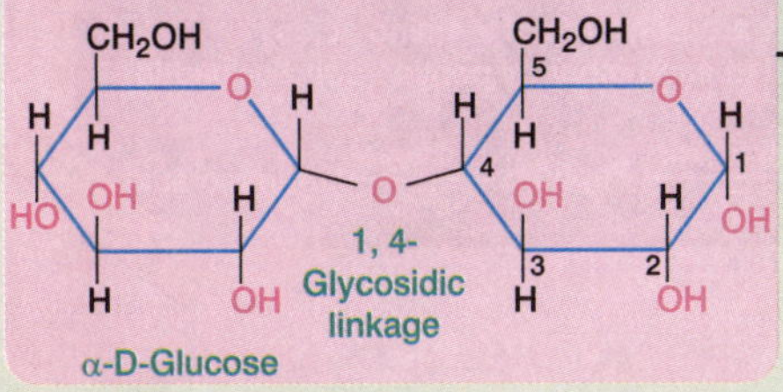

Sucrose

- Non-reducing sugar.
- Monomers are D-(+)-glucose and D-(–)-fructose.
- Glycosidic linkage is present.
- Also called as **invert sugar**.

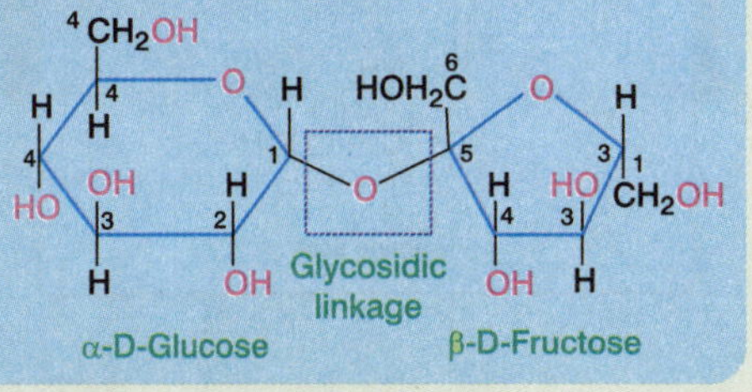

Lactose

- Reducing sugar
- Also called as milk sugar
- Monomers are β-D-Galactose and β-D-Glucose

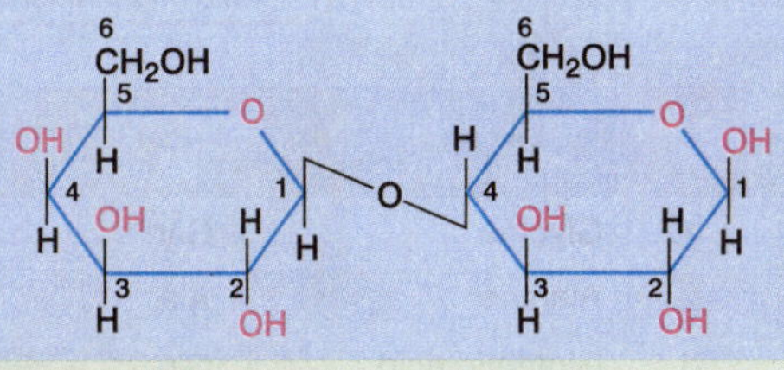

POWER TIPS

- **Reducing sugar** Carbohydrates who containing free aldehyde and ketonic group and reducing Fehling's solution and Tollen reagent.
- **Non-reducing sugar** Carbohydrates that does not have a free aldehyde and ketone group and does not reduce Fehling's solution and Tollen reagent.
- Glucose, fructose, lactose, maltose are reducing sugar and sucrose, starch, cellulose, glycogen are non-reducing sugar.

CHEMICAL REACTIONS OF GLUCOSE

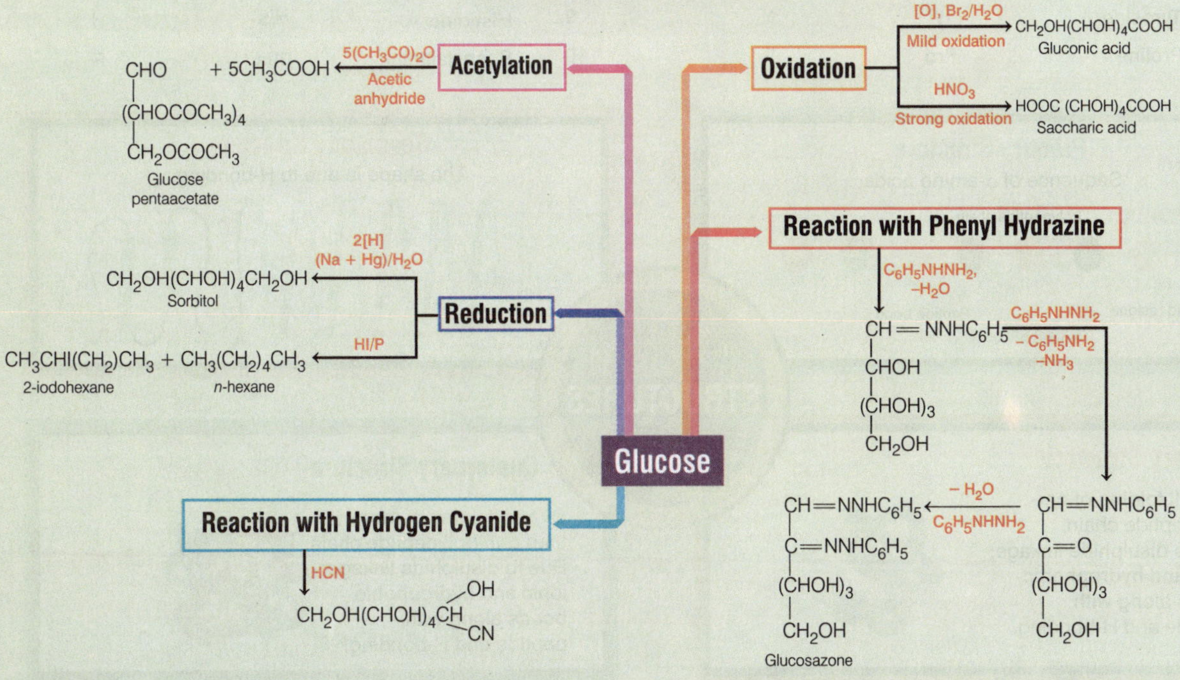

AMINO ACID

- Bifunctional molecule with both acidic carboxylic group (—COOH) and basic amino group (—NH_2).

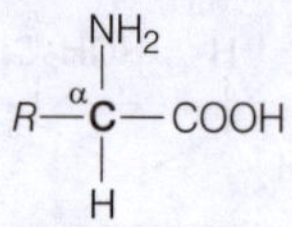

α-amino acid

PROTEINS

- Polymers in which the monomeric units are α-amino acids.
- All proteins are polymers of α-amino acids. Connected to each other by peptide bond or peptide linkage

$$\text{Proteins} \xrightarrow{\text{Hydrolysis}} \text{Peptides} \xrightarrow{\text{Hydrolysis}} \alpha\text{-amino acid}$$

Essential Amino Acid

Cannot be synthesised in the body and must be obtained through diet.

S.No.	Name of the amino acids	Three letter symbol	One letter code
1.	Glycine	Gly	G
2.	Alanine	Ala	A
3.	Glutamic acid	Glu	E
4.	Aspartic acid	Asp	D
5.	Glutamine	Gln	Q
6.	Asparagine	Asn	N
7.	Cysteine	Cys	C
8.	Serine	Ser	S
9.	Tyrosine	Tyr	Y
10.	Proline	Pro	P

Non-Essential Amino Acid

Can be synthesised in the human body.

S.No.	Name of the amino acids	Three letter symbol	One letter code
1.	Valine	Val	V
2.	Leucine	Leu	L
3.	Isoleucine	Ile	I
4.	Arginine	Arg	R
5.	Lysine	Lys	K
6.	Threonine	Thr	T
7.	Methionine	Met	M
8.	Tryptophan	Trp	W
9.	Histidine	His	H
10.	Phenylalanine	Phe	F

STRUCTURES

Primary Structure

Sequence of α-amino acids.

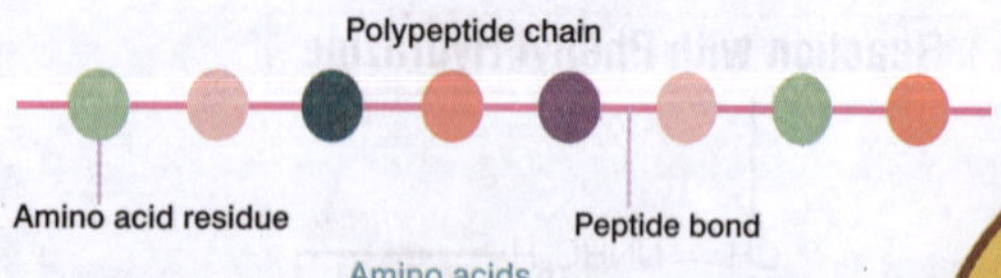

Secondary Structure

The shape is due to H-bonding.

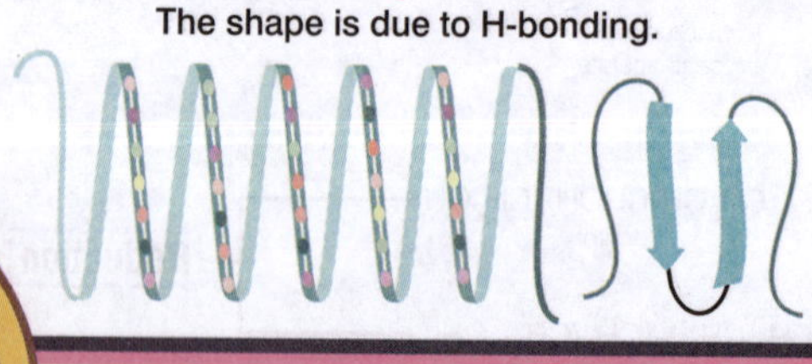

Tertiary Structure

Overall folding of one polypeptide chain. Due to disulphide linkage, ionic and hydrophobic bonds along with peptide and H-bonding.

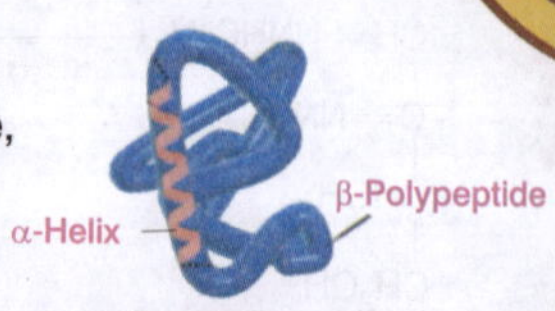

Quaternary Structure

Overall folding of more than one polypeptide chain. Due to disulphide linkage, ionic and hydrophobic bonds along with peptide and H-bonding.

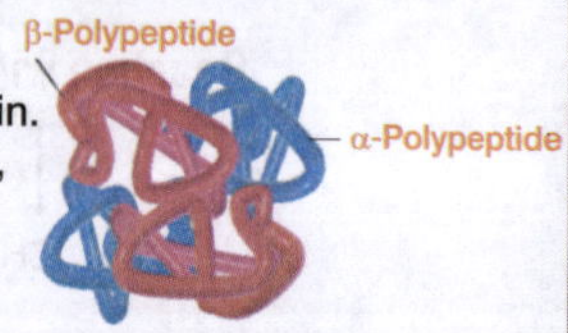

Tests for Detection of Amino Acids

- **Ninhydrin Test**
  Used to detect α-amino acids.
- **Sanger's or DNP method**
  For determination of N-terminal amino acid residues.

POWER TIPS

- Protein cofactor complex is called holoenzyme while the inactive protein part is apoenzyme.

Holoenzyme ⇌ Apoenzyme + Cofactor

Classification

Fibrous proteins

- Have thread like structure.
- e.g. Keratin, collagen, myosin etc.

Globular protein

- Have spheroidal shape.
- e.g. Enzymes, hormones.

α-Helix

- Formed due to intramolecular H-bonds between the C ═ O of one amino acid residue and the N—H of 4th amino acid residue.
- e.g. α-keratin in hair, myosin in muscles.

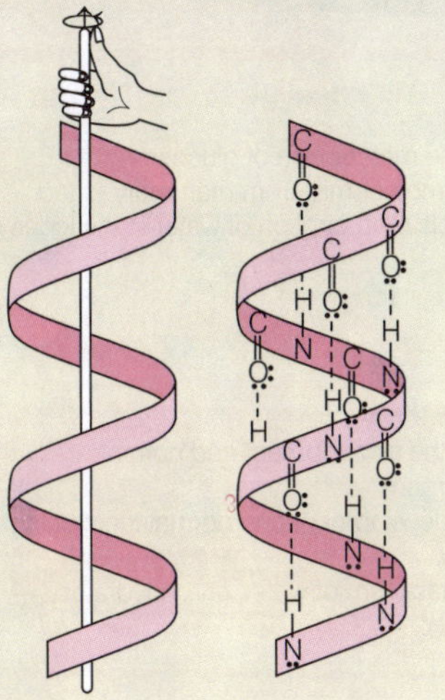

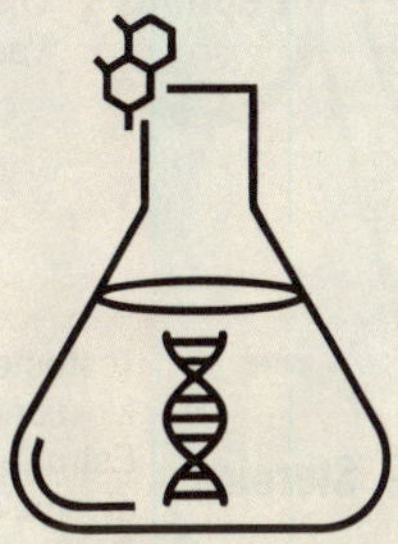

Denaturation

- Due to coagulation, native shape of the protein is destroyed and biological activity is lost.
- 2° and 3° structures are destroyed, 1° remains intact.

β-Pleated Sheet

- Formed due to intermolecular H-bonds between two neighbouring polypeptide chain in a *zig-zag* manner.
- e.g. Silk protein fibroin.

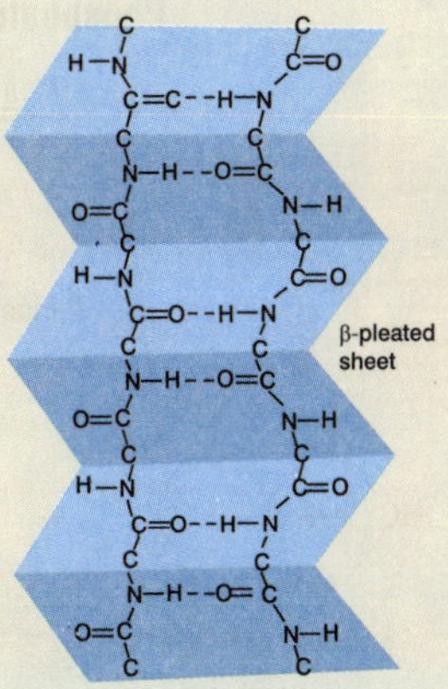

Enzymes

These are biological catalysts and are globular protein.

↓

Properties

- Highly specific.
- Highly efficient.
- Requires optimum temperature and pH for maximum efficiency.
- Almost all enzymes are globular protein.

↓

MECHANISM

STEP 01

Bonding of enzyme to the substrate to form complex.

$$\underset{\text{Enzyme}}{E} + \underset{\text{Substrate}}{S} \longrightarrow \underset{\text{Enzyme-substrate complex}}{[ES]}$$

STEP 02

Product formation in the complex.

$$\underset{\text{Enzyme-product association}}{EP} \longrightarrow \underset{\text{Enzyme}}{E} + \underset{\text{Product}}{P}$$

HORMONES

Act as intercellular messengers. Produced by endocrine gland and poured directly in the blood stream.

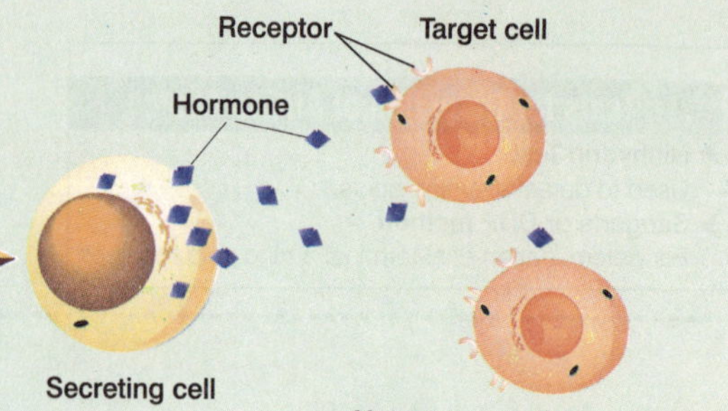

CLASSIFICATION

Amines

Thyroxine Controls the metabolism of protein, carbohydrates and lipids. Produced in thyroid gland.
Adrenaline Releases glucose from glycogen and fatty acids from fats.

Peptides

Insulin Regulates the metabolism of glucose.
Oxytocin Releases mother milk from mammary gland.
Vasopressin Controls reabsorption of water in the kidney.

Steroids

Testosterone Regulates the development and normal functioning of male sex organ.
Estrogen Regulates the development and normal functioning of female sex organ.
Cortisone Regulates metabolism of water, carbohydrates, fats and mineral salts.

Nucleic acid = Pentose sugar + Base + Phosphoric acid

Nucleic acids

Pentose Sugar

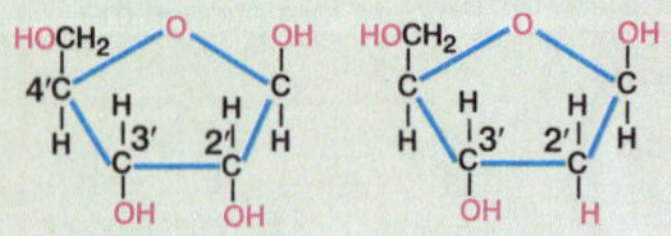

Ribose   Deoxyribose

Nitrogenous Base

Pyrimidine

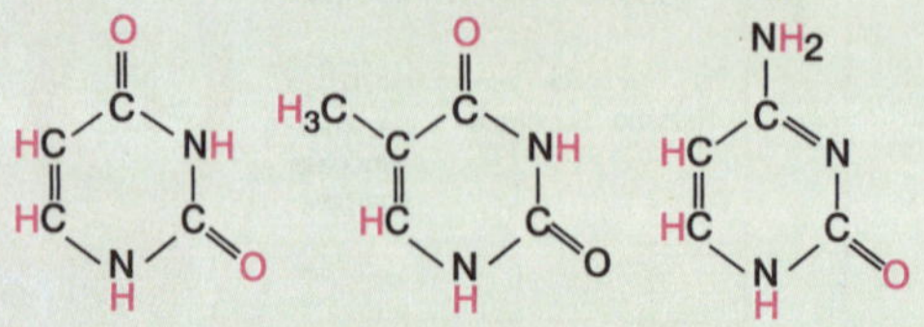

Uracil (U)   Thymine (T)   Cytosine (C)

Purine

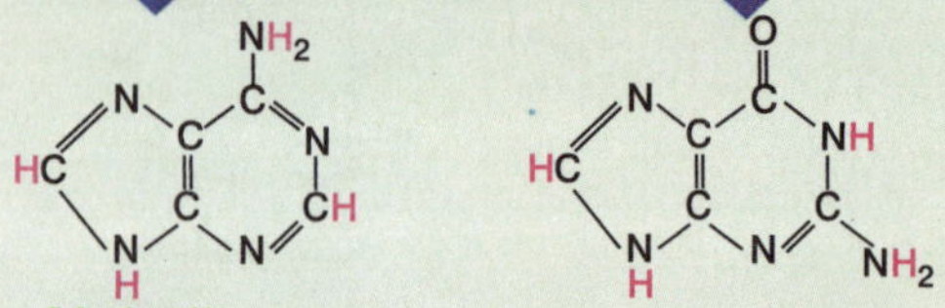

Adenine (A)   Guanine (G)

Phosphate Group

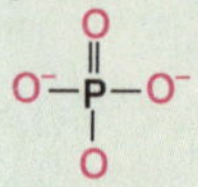

Organs Secreting Hormone

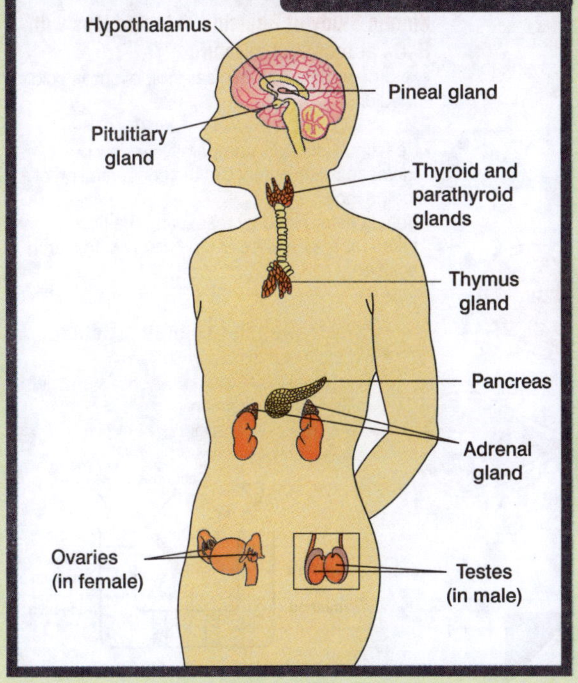

Vitamins

Organic compounds that are required in small amounts in our diet. Their deficiency causes specific diseases.

Vitamin	Deficiency Disease
Vitamin A, (Retinol)	Xeropthalmia
Vitamin B_1, (Thiamine)	Beri-Beri
Vitamin B_2, (Riboflavin)	Cheilosis
Vitamin B_6, (Pyridoxine)	Convulsions
Vitamin B_{12}, (Cyanocobalamin)	Pernicious aneamia
Vitamin C, (Ascorbic acid)	Scurvy
Vitamin D, (Cholecalciferol)	Rickets
Vitamin E, (Tocopherol)	Increased fragility of RBC
Vitamin K, (Phylloquinone)	Increased blood clotting time

Water Soluble Vitamins

- Must be supplied regularly in diet
- Regularly excreted in urine (except vitamin B_{12}) e.g. Vitamin B and Vitamin C.

Fat Soluble Vitamins

- Soluble in fat and oils.
- Stored in liver and adipose tissues. e.g. Vitamin A, D, E and K.

DNA

- Sugar is β-D-2-deoxyribose.
- Nitrogen bases are
  - **Purine** Adenine (A) and Guanine (G)
  - **Pyrimidine** Cytosine (C) and Thymine (T)

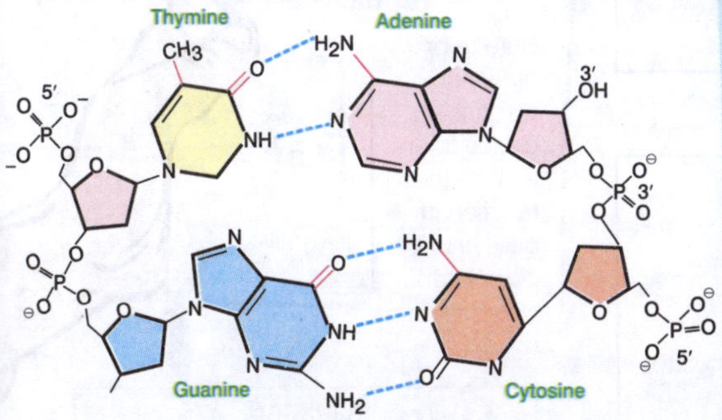

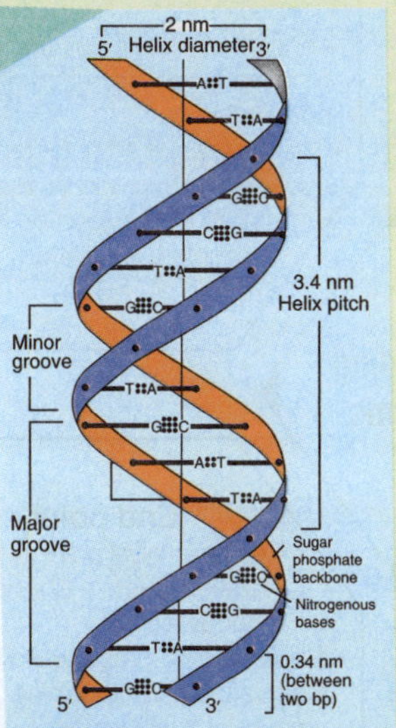

Double helical model of DNA

RNA

- Sugar is β-D-ribose.
- Nitrogen bases are
  - **Purine** Adenine (A) and Guanine (G)
  - **Pyrimidine** Cytosine (C) and Uracil (U)

CHARGAFF'S RULE

Total amount of purine = Pyrimidine

$(A + G) = (C + T)$

- **Double Helical Structure** Pairing takes place between C and G ($C \equiv G$) and A and T ($A = T$)

POWER TIPS

- Pentose sugar + Base = Nucleoside
  Nucleoside + Phosphoric acid = Nucleotide
- Dinucleotides are formed by a phosphodiester linkage between 5′ and 3′ carbon atoms of the pentose sugar.

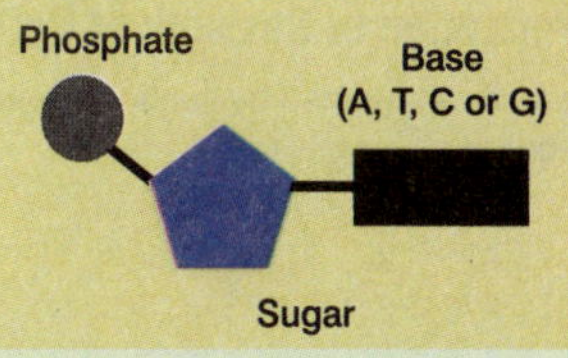

Chapter **11**

Principles Related to Practical Chemistry

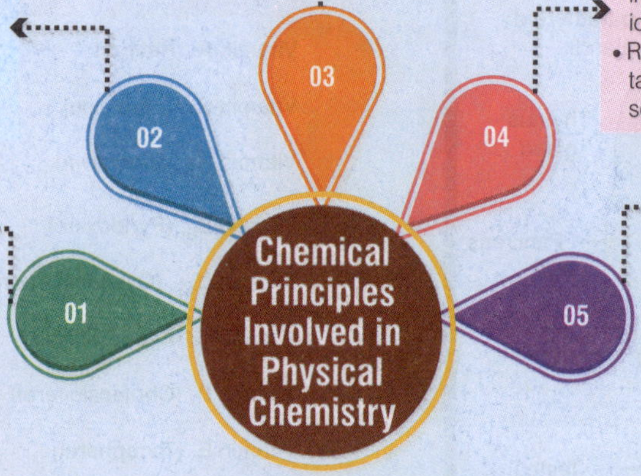

Enthalpy of Neutralisation

- It is the amount of heat absorbed or evolved on dissolving one mole of it in excess of the solvent at a given temperature and pressure.
- When heat is absorbed, it is positive.
- When heat is evolved, it is negative.

Enthalpy of solution of $CuSO_4$

- The heat evolved when one mole of H^+ ions is completely neutralised by a base.
- Neutralisation reaction in case of HCl and NaOH is according to Arrhenius theory.

Preparation of Lyophilic Colloid

- These colloids are prepared directly by mining the substance with the dispersion medium.

Kinetic Study of Reaction of Iodide ions with H_2O_2 at room temperature

- Hydrogen peroxide oxidises iodide ions in acidic medium.
- $2I^- + H_2O_2 + 2H^+ \longrightarrow I_2 + 2H_2O$
- Reaction velocity is comparatively slow but increases with increase in the concentration of iodide ions.
- Rate is determined by measuring the time taken for appearance of blue colour with starch solution.

Preparation of Lyophobic Colloid

- Mechanical disintegration
- Electrical disintegration/Bredig's arc method
- Ultrasonic dispersion
- By condensing vapours
- Exchange of solvent

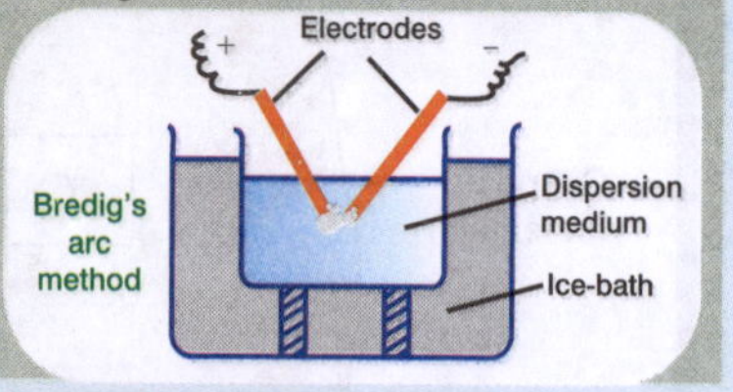

Defining Terms

Standard solution

- A reagent of a known concentration used in the titrimetric analysis.
- Used for various volumetric procedures, such as determining the concentration of solutions with an unknown concentration in titrations.

Titration

- It is a quantitative technique used to determine the unknown concentration of a solution by reacting it with a solution of known concentration.
- The process of adding standard solution from a burette to an analyte until a reaction is complete is **titration.**

Equivalence point

- The point in titration process when the amount of titrant is chemically equivalent to the amount of analyte in a sample.
- It can be identified using indicators (color change), pH meters, or conductivity measurements depending on the type of titration.

End point

- A observable point in the titration where a physical change occurs.
- It is used as a practical way to stop the titration and determine the amount of titrant required.

Acid-Base Titration

This method is used to determine the strength of an acid or alkali.
Based on Neutralisation Reaction

$$\underset{\text{Acid}}{AH} + \underset{\text{Base}}{BOH} \longrightarrow \underset{\text{(Salt)}}{AB} + H_2O$$

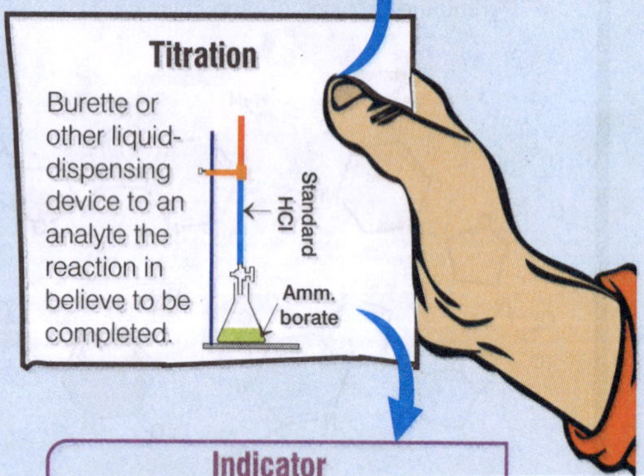

Indicator

- Chemical substance that undergoes a colour change at the end point.
- End point is determined by using acid-base indicator.
- Acid-base indicators posses two different colour in acidic and basic medium.

POWER TIPS

➤ Determination of Strength of NaOH

- It can be determined by titrating it against standard solution of oxalic acid.
- **Indicator**-phenolphthalein

$$\begin{array}{c}COOH\\|\\COOH\end{array} + 2NaOH \longrightarrow \begin{array}{c}COONa\\|\\COONa\end{array} + 2H_2O$$

➤ Determination of Strength of HCl

- It can be determined by titrating it against Na_2CO_3 solution.
- **Indicator**—Methyl orange
- $Na_2CO_3 + 2HCl \longrightarrow 2NaCl + H_2O + CO_2\uparrow$

Types of Titration

01 Direct Titration

The analyte is directly titrated with a standard solution (titrant) e.g. Titrating HCl with NaOH to determine the conc. of HCl.

02 Indirect Titration

Multi-step process.
Analyte reacts with a reagent then titrated.
e.g. Anions that form ppt. with metal cations and do not react with EDTA can be analysed.

03 Back Titration

This titration is followed when direct titration is not possible. Used for those substance which are not water soluble, or which are weak acids or bases by nature.
e.g. Determining the quantity of a sample of metal or metal carbonate.

04 Conductometric Titrations

The titration in which end point is determined by measuring changes in conductance of solution upon addition of reagent.

(a) Strong acid against strong base

$HCl + NaOH \longrightarrow NaCl + H_2O$

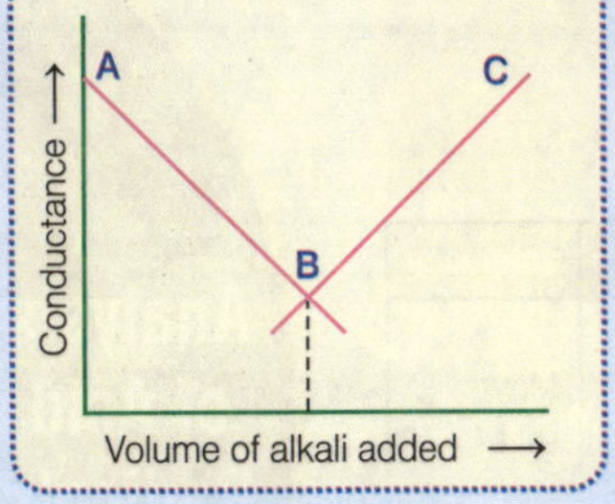

(b) Strong acid against weak base

$HCl + NH_4OH \longrightarrow NH_4Cl + H_2O$

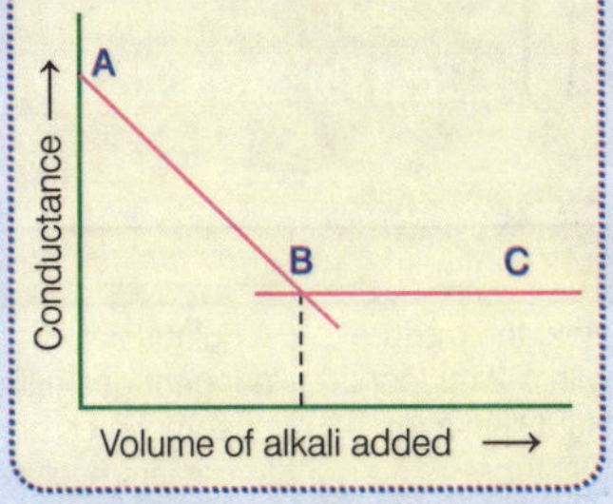

(c) Weak acid against strong base

$CH_3COOH + NaOH \longrightarrow CH_3COONa + H_2O$

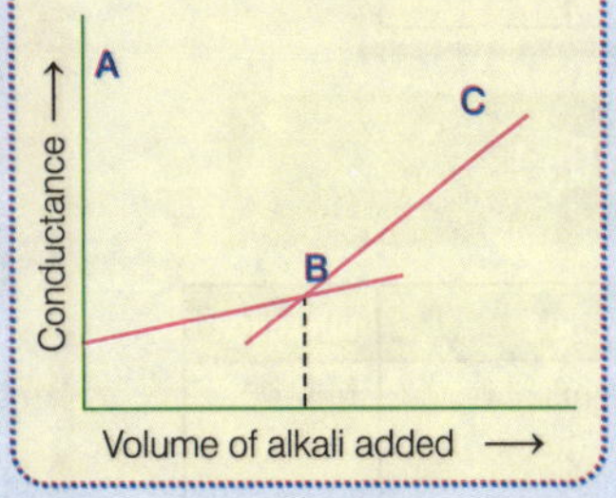

(d) Weak acid against weak base

$CH_3COOH + NH_4OH \longrightarrow CH_3COONH_4 + H_2O$

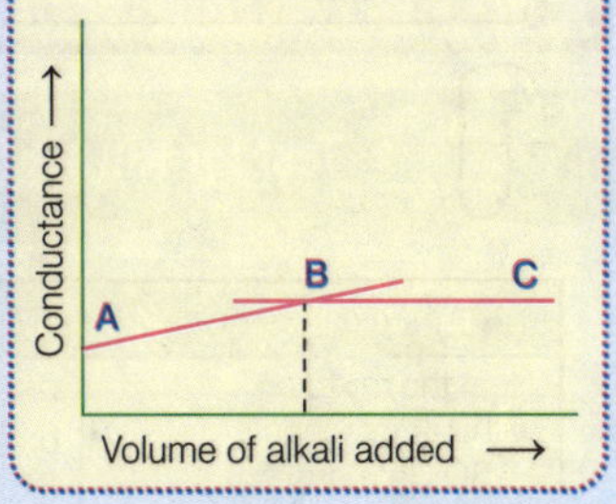

pH CURVE FOR CHOOSING SUITABLE INDICATOR

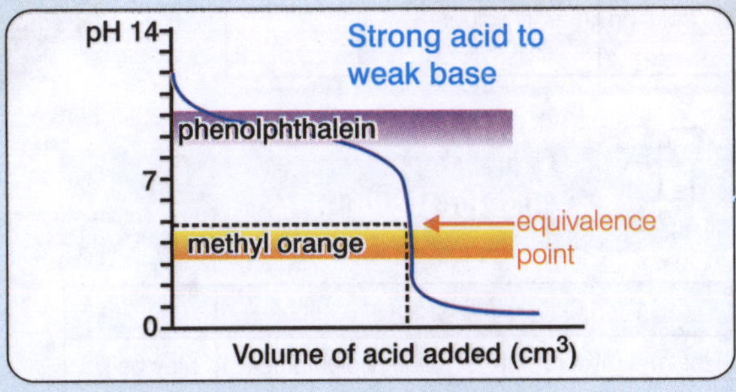

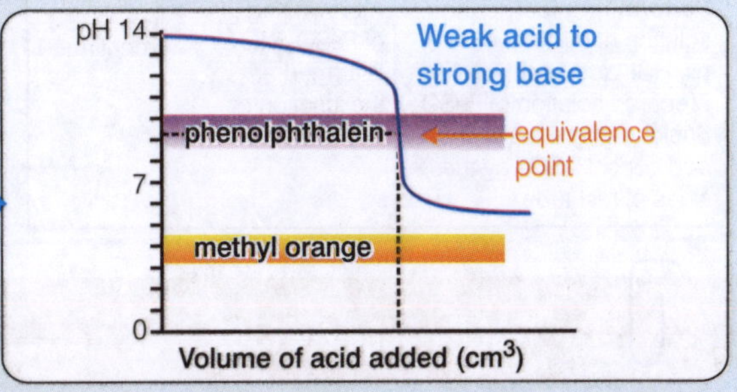

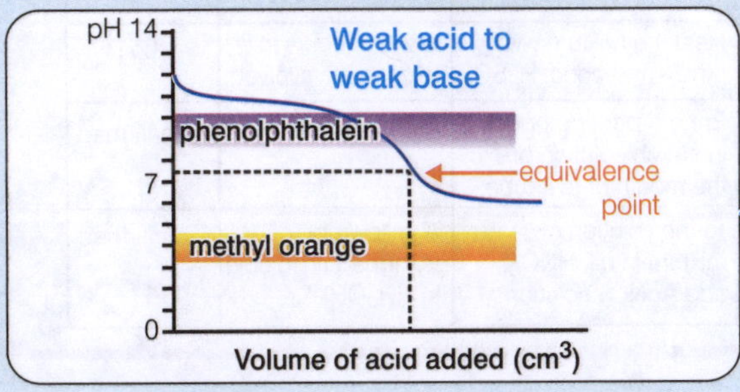

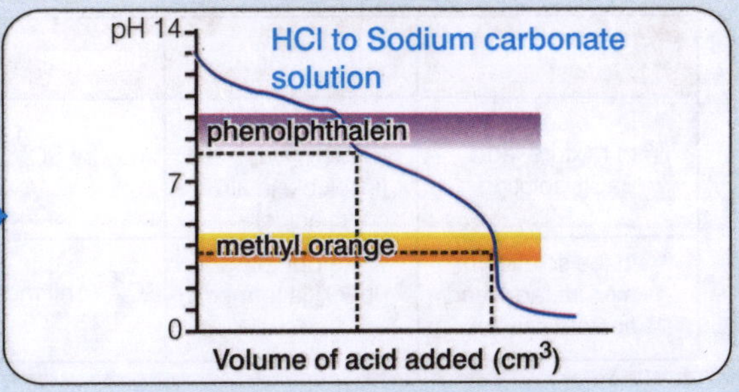

SALT ANALYSIS

Process that determines the composition and concentration of salts in a sample.

Wet Tests

Confirmatory test to determine the possible radicals predicted by dry test.

Dry Test

- Physical observation
- Effect of heating
- Smell of compound
- Solubility of salts
- Charcoal cavity test
- Borax Bead test
- Cobalt nitrate test
- Microcosmic salt bead test

Analysis of Acid Radicals

Test for $(CO_3)^{2-}$

Experiment	Observation	Inference
Take mixture in a dry test tube and add dil. HCl or H_2SO_4 and Warm	Brisk effervescence with the evolution of colourless and odourless gas (CO_2)	may be (CO_3^{2-})
Pass the evolved gas into lime water [$Ca(OH)_2$]	Lime water turns milky	(CO_3^{2-}) confirmed
Pass excess lime water to the evolved gas	Milkiness disappears	(CO_3^{2-}) confirmed

Test for S^{2-}

Experiment	Observation	Inference
Take mixture in a dry test tube and add dil. HCl or H_2SO_4 and warm gently	A colourless gas (H_2S) with smell of rotten eggs evolved	may be S^{2-}
Bring filter paper dipped in lead acetate over the mouth of test tube	Filter paper turns black due to formation of PbS	S^{2-} confirmed

Test for Sulphate (NO_2^-)

Experiment	Observation	Inference
Take mixture in a dry test tube and add dil. HCl. Warm gently	Brown fumes (NO_2) with pungent odour are evolved	may be NO_2^-
Add 2-3 drops of KI and starch solution in the test tube	Deep blue or violet colour appears	NO_2^- confirmed

Test for Nitrate (NO_3^-)

Experiment	Observation	Inference
Heat the mixture with 1-2 mL conc. H_2SO_4 in a dry test tube.	Pungent light brown gas (NO_2) is evolved.	May be NO_3^-
Heat the mixture with copper turnings and conc. H_2SO_4.	Deep brown fumes (NO_2) in excess are evolved.	May be NO_3^-
Perform ring test To the solution of mixture in dil. HCl, add freshly prepared solution of $FeSO_4$. Shake well gradually and add conc. H_2SO_4 by the sides of test tube.	A brown ring of $FeSO_4{\cdot}NO$ is formed at the junction of two liquids.	NO_3^- confirmed

Test for Bromide (Br^-)

Experiment	Observation	Inference
Heat the mixture with 1-2 mL conc. H_2SO_4 in a dry test tube.	A colourless, pungent gas (HBr) or sometimes brown fumes are evolved.	May be Br^-
Heat the mixture with MnO_2 and conc. H_2SO_4.	Red brown vapour of Br_2 evolved.	Br^- confirmed
To the solution of mixture in dil. HNO_3 add $AgNO_3$ solution.	A pale yellow ppt. of AgBr is formed (hardly soluble in NH_4OH).	Br^- confirmed

Test for Sulphate (SO_4^{2-})

Experiment	Observation	Inference
In the solution of mixture, add $BaCl_2$ solution.	A curdy white ppt. ($BaSO_4$) is formed (insoluble in all conc. acids).	May be SO_4^{2-}
In the solution of mixture, add lead acetate solution.	White ppt. of $PbSO_4$ is formed.	SO_4^{2-} confirmed

Test for Iodide (I^-)

Experiment	Observation	Inference
Heat the mixture with 1-3 mL conc. H_2SO_4.	Dark violet fumes (I_2) are evolved.	May be I^-
Heat the mixture with MnO_2 and conc. H_2SO_4	Violet vapours in excess are evolved.	May be I^-
Bring a paper dipped in starch solution on the mouth of test tube.	Paper turns blue.	I^- confirmed
To the solution of mixture in dil. HNO_3, add $AgNO_3$ solution.	A yellow ppt. of AgI is formed (insoluble in NH_4OH)	I^- confirmed

Preparations

Mohr's Salt [$FeSO_4 \cdot (NH_4)_2SO_4 \cdot 6H_2O$]

- A double salt also called as **ferrous ammonium sulphate**.
- Prepared by mixing the solution of ferrous sulphate and ammonium sulphate.
- Then evaporate and cool it to obtain the green crystals of Mohr salt.

Potash Alum $KAl(SO_4)_2 \cdot 12H_2O$

- Also known as double salt.
- Prepared by dissolving K_2SO_4 and $Al_2(SO_4)_3$ in equimolar ratio in small amount of water and drops of conc. H_2SO_4.
- On cooling colourless crystals of potash alum obtained.

Analysis of Basic Radicals

Test for Lead (Pb^{2+})

Experiment	Observation	Inference
Hot filtrate is taken and add K_2CrO_4.	Yellow ppt. of $PbCrO_4$ is obtained which is soluble in NaOH but insoluble in CH_3COOH.	Indicates the presence of Pb^{2+}
Hot filtrate is taken and add KI	Yellow ppt. of PbI_2 is formed.	Pb^{2+} confirmed
Dilute H_2SO_4 is added to hot filtrate and mixture is cooled	White precipitate of $PbSO_4$ is obtained which is soluble in CH_3COONH_4 solution.	Pb^{2+} confirmed

Test for Copper (Cu^{2+})

Experiment	Observation	Inference
Take black ppt.of CuS in the test tube and add HNO_3.	Blue coloured solution is obtained	It indicates the presence of Cu^{2+}
Divide blue solution obtained into three parts.		
Add CH_3COOH and $K_4[Fe(CN)_6]$ to first part.	Chocolate brown ppt. is formed	Cu^{2+} confirmed
Add aqueous NH_3 (excess) in second part of blue solution.	Deep blue solution is obtained	Cu^{2+} confirmed
Add KSCN is the third part of blue solution.	Black ppt. is obtained	Cu^{2+} confirmed

Test for Iron (Fe^{3+})

Experiment	Observation	Inference
Add dilute HCl in red brown ppt. divide into two parts.	Precipitate dissolves	Fe^{3+} confirmed
Add $K_4[Fe(CN)_6]$ in the first part of the above solution.	Dark blue colour is obtained	Fe^{3+} confirmed
Add KCNS in the second part of the solution.	Dark (Blood) red colour is obtained	Fe^{3+} confirmed

Test for Zinc (Zn^{2+})

Experiment	Observation	Inference
Dissolve white ppt. of ZnS in dil. HCl and divide it into two parts.	Soluble chloride is formed.	It indicates the presence of Zn^{2+}.
Add NaOH in the solution. White ppt. is obtained which is soluble in excess of NaOH.	White ppt. of ZnS reappears on passing H_2S into soluble sodium zincate solution	Zn^{2+} confirms
Solution is acidified with acetic acid and add $K_4[Fe(CN)_6]$	Bluish white is obtained	Zn^{2+} confirms

Tests for Calcium (Ca^{2+})

Experiment	Observation	Inference
Dissolve the ppt. in acetic acid ,add ammonium oxalate solution (excess) and heat.	White ppt. appears	Ca^{2+} confirmed
Acidified white ppt. obtained above by adding dilute CH_3COOH and add $KMnO_4$ solution drop wise and HCl	Pink colour of $KMnO_4$ disappears	Ca^{2+} confirmed

Tests for (Mg^{2+})

Experiment	Observation	Inference
Filtrate of group V is heated with NH_4OH and Na_2HPO_4.	A fine crystalline ppt. on scratching the side of the test tube.	Mg^{2+} confirmed

DETECTION OF FUNCTIONAL GROUPS

Detection of Unsaturation

	Test	Reaction	Confirmation
(i)	Baeyer's or $KMnO_4$ test	$2KMnO_4 + H_2O \longrightarrow 2KOH + 2MnO_2 + 3[O]$ $>C=C< + H_2O + [O] \longrightarrow >C(OH)-C(OH)<$	Disappearance of pink colour of $KMnO_4$
(ii)	Br_2-CCl_4 test	$>C=C< + \underset{\text{Red brown}}{Br_2} \xrightarrow{CCl_4} >C(Br)-C(Br)<$	Disappearance brown colour.

Detection of Phenolic Group

	Test	Reaction	Confirmation
(i)	$FeCl_3$ test	$FeCl_3 + 6C_6H_5OH \longrightarrow \underset{\text{Violet}}{[Fe(OC_6H_5)_6]^{3-}} + 3H^+ + 3HCl$	Appearance of violet colouration
(ii)	Azo dye test	$C_6H_5NH_2 + NaNO_2 + HCl \xrightarrow{0\text{-}5°C} C_6H_5N_2^+Cl^-$ $C_6H_5N_2^+Cl^- + C_6H_5OH \xrightarrow{pH\ 9\text{-}10} \underset{p\text{-Hydroxyazobenzene}}{HO-C_6H_4-N=N-C_6H_5}$	Formation of orange or red dye
(iii)	Liebermann nitroso test	$C_6H_5OH \xrightarrow[H_2SO_4]{NaNO_2} \underset{p\text{-nitrosophenol}}{HO-C_6H_4-N=O} \xrightleftharpoons{\text{Tautomerises}}$ 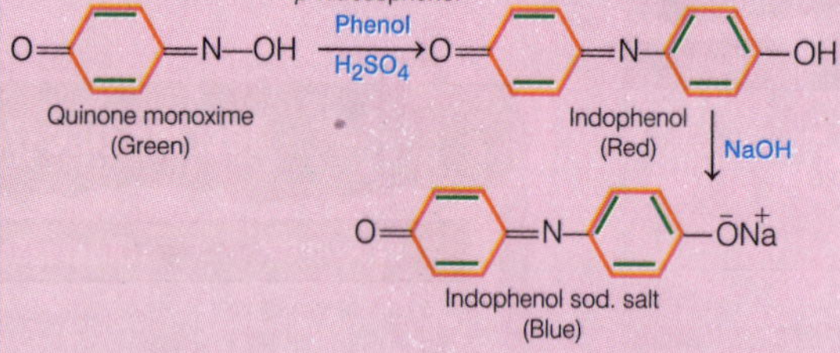	
		Appearance of deep blue or green colour which turns red on dilution and again blue on adding sodium hydroxide solution.	

Tests For Distinction

For Hydroxyl Group

Test	Phenol	Alcohol
$FeCl_3$ Test	Gives blue, violet or red colouration	×
Br_2-water Test	Given white precipitate	×
Azo-dye Test	Forms orange-red colour dye	×

For Carbonyl Group

Test	Aldehyde	Ketones
Tollen's test	Give shiny silver mirror	×
Fehling's solution test	Gives red ppt.	×
Schiff's reagent test	Gives pink colour	×
Reduction with $LiAlH_4$	Reduced to 1° alcohol	Reduced to 2° alcohol

Detection of Amino Group

Azo dye Test

Compound

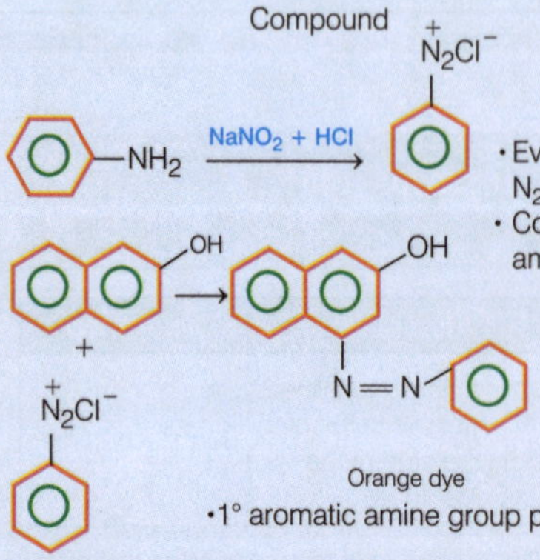

- 1° aromatic amine group present.

Nitrous acid test

Compound + HNO_2

- Evolution of N_2 gas
- Confirms 1° amine group

- Formation of yellow oily compound
- Confirms 2° amine group

- Formation of water soluble nitrite salts.
- Indicates 3° amine group

Isocyanide Test

Compound + $CHCl_3$ + KOH

- Offensive smell
- Confirms presence of 1° aliphatic or aromatic amines

Detection of Alcoholic Group

Test	Reaction	Confirmation
(i) Ester test	$RCOOH + R'OH \xrightarrow[\Delta]{\text{conc. } H_2SO_4} \underset{\text{Ester}}{RCOOR'} + H_2O$	Fruity smell of ester indicates —OH group
(ii) Ceric ammonium nitrate test	$2ROH + \underset{\text{Ceric ammonium nitrate}}{(NH_4)_2[Ce(NO_3)_6]} \longrightarrow \underset{\text{Pink or red}}{[(ROH)_2Ce(NO_3)_4]} + 2NH_4NO_3$	Appearance of red colour
(iii) Xanthate test	$ROH + KOH(s) \xrightarrow{\Delta} \underset{\text{Potassium alkoxide}}{RO^-K^+} + H_2O$; $RO^-K^+ + S{=}C{=}S \longrightarrow R{-}O{-}C({=}S)S^-K^+$ Potassium alkyl xanthate (Yellow ppt.)	Formation of yellow ppt.

Detection of Aldehydic Group

Test	Reaction	Confirmation
(i) Tollen's test	$RCHO + 2[Ag(NH_3)_2]OH \longrightarrow RCOONH_4 + 3NH_3 + H_2O + \underset{\text{Silver mirror}}{2Ag(s)}$	Formation of silver mirror along the sides of the test tube.
(ii) Fehling's test	$RCHO + 2Cu^{2+} + 5OH^- \longrightarrow \underset{\text{Red ppt.}}{Cu_2O\downarrow} + RCOO^- + 3H_2O$	A red ppt. is formed (only by aliphatic aldehydes).
(iii) Schiff's test	RCHO + *p*-rosaniline hydrochloride in saturated solution of SO_2 in water (colourless solution)	Appearance of pink colour.

Detection of Ketonic Group

Test	Reaction	Confirmation
(i) Iodoform test	$R{-}CO{-}CH_3 + 3I_2 + 4NaOH \rightarrow 3NaI + CHI_3\downarrow + RCOONa + 3H_2O$	Formation of yellow ppt. of CHI_3 (for methyl ketones only)
(ii) Sodium nitro-prusside test	$RCOCH_3$ + sodium nitroprusside solution + NaOH $\longrightarrow \underset{\text{(Red coloured)}}{[Fe(CN)_5 NO RCOCH_2]^{3-}}$	Appearance of wine-red colour (for methyl ketones only)

PREPARATION OF ORGANIC COMPOUNDS

Acetanilide

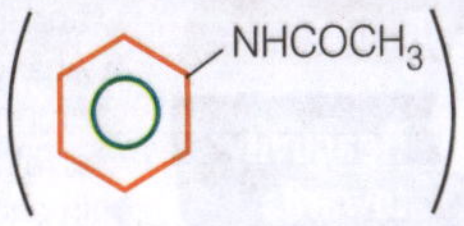

- Can be prepared by direct acetylation of aniline.

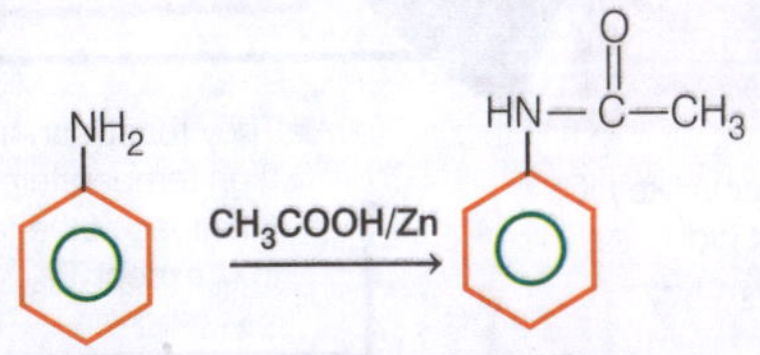

Aniline → Acetanilide

Aniline Yellow or *p*-Amino Azobenzene

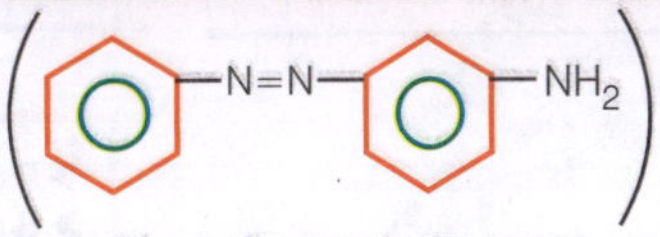

- Can be prepared from diazoaminobenzene.

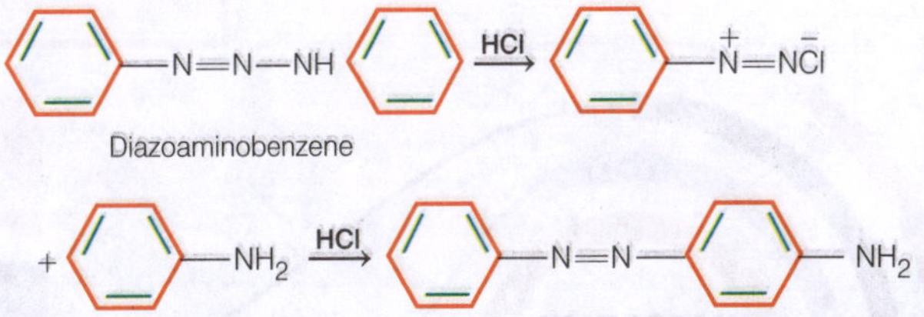

Diazoaminobenzene; Aniline; *p*-amino azobenzene

p-Nitroacetanilide

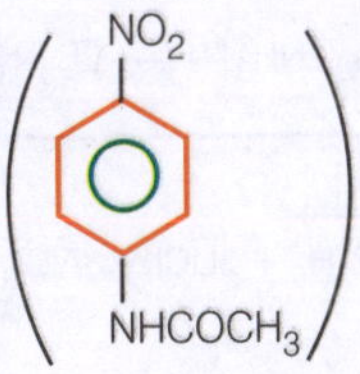

- Can be prepared by the nitration of acetanilide.

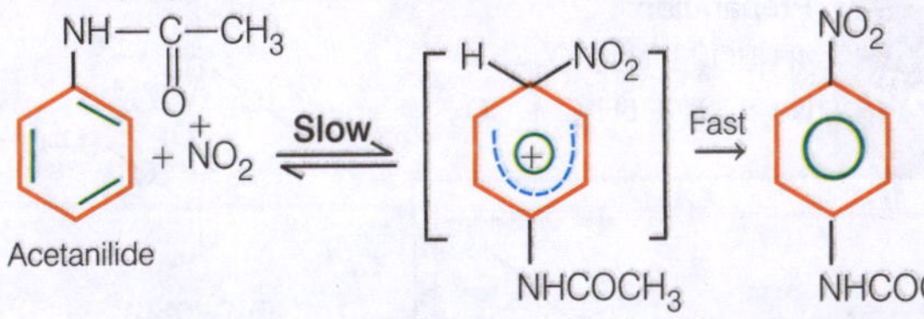

Acetanilide → *p*-nitroacetanilide

Iodoform (CHI_3)

- Can be prepared from acetone.

$$(H_3C)_2C{=}O + NaOI \longrightarrow (I_3C)(H_3C)C{=}O \xrightarrow{NaOH} CH_3\overset{-\ +}{COONa} + \underset{\text{Iodoform}}{CHI_3\downarrow}$$

- The compounds containing $CH_3{-}\overset{O}{\overset{\|}{C}}{-}$ and $CH_3{-}\underset{OH}{\underset{|}{CH}}{-}$ groups give iodoform test.

Chapter 12 p-Block Elements

GROUP 13 ELEMENTS

- Boron(B)
- Gallium (Ga)
- Aluminium (Al)
- Thallium (Tl)
- Nihonium(Nh)
- Indium(In)

Characteristics Feature of *p*-Block

- Elements in which last electron enters into any of the outermost *p*-orbitals are *p*-block elements.
- General electronic configuration ns^2np^{1-6} (except He).

Physical Properties

- **Atomic Radii**
  Increases from B to Al, (decrease from Al to Ga and then increases).
- **Melting and Boiling Point**
  M.P decreases sharply on moving down the group from B to Ga and then increase from Ga to Tl. B.P decreases from B to Tl.
- **Ionisation Enthalpy**
  B < Tl > Ga > Al > In
- **Oxidation State**
  B > Al > Ga > In > Tl (stability of+3 O.S)
- Al < Ga < In < Tl (stability of +1 O.S)

Electronic Configuration

[Noble gas] ns^2np^1

Abundance

Al is most abundant metal and third most abundant element by mass in Earth's crust.

Anomalous Behaviour of Boron

- Due to small size, high I.E and absence of *d*-orbitals.
- Exhibits allotropy.
- Forms only covalent compound.
- Forms monomeric halides.
- B does not form B^{3+} ions in solution.

Chemical Properties

Reactivity towards air

- They react with dioxygen at high temperatures to form trioxides of the formula M_2O_3.
- Except Ga, In, Tl other react with dinitrogen at high temperature to form nitrides of the formula MN.
- Basic character of their oxides and hydroxides increases down the group.

B_2O_3 or $B(OH)_3$ — Acidic

Al_2O_3 or $Al(OH)_3$, Ga_2O_3 or $Ga(OH)_3$ — Amphoteric

In_2O_3 or $In(OH)_3$, Tl_2O or $TlOH$ — Basic

Reactivity towards water

- B does not react with water or steam. Al reacts with water and forms protective layer of Al_2O_3.
- Ga and In do not react with cold or hot water.

Reactivity towards alkalies

- Above 773 K, B reacts with alkalies forming borates and liberating H_2 gas.
- Al and Ga being amphoteric react with alkalies, liberating H_2 gas.
- In and Tl do not react with alkalies.

Reactivity towards halogens

- They react with halogens at high temperature forming trihalides of the formula MX_3 except TlI_3.

Reactivity towards acids

- B does not react with non-oxidising acids like HCl.
- B reacts with strong oxidising acids at high temperature forming boric acid H_3BO_3.

IMPORTANT COMPOUNDS OF BORON

Boranes (B_nH_{n+4}/B_nH_{n+6})

- $B_2H_6 + 2NH_3 \xrightarrow{\text{low temp.}} B_2H_6 \cdot 2NH_3$
- $3B_2H_6 \cdot 2NH_3 \xrightarrow{473\ K} 2B_3N_3H_6 + 12H_2$

Diborane (B_2H_6)

Preparation

$4BCl_3 + 3LiAlH_4 \xrightarrow{\text{Ether}} 2B_2H_6 + 3LiCl + 3AlCl_3$

Four 2c-2e⁻ bonds.
Two 3c-2e⁻ bonds.

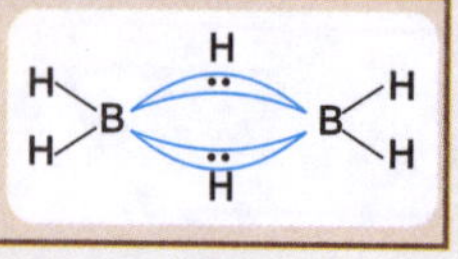

Borax ($Na_2B_4O_7 \cdot 10H_2O$)

Preparation

$4H_3BO_3 + Na_2CO_3 \longrightarrow Na_2B_4O_7 + 6H_2O + CO_2$

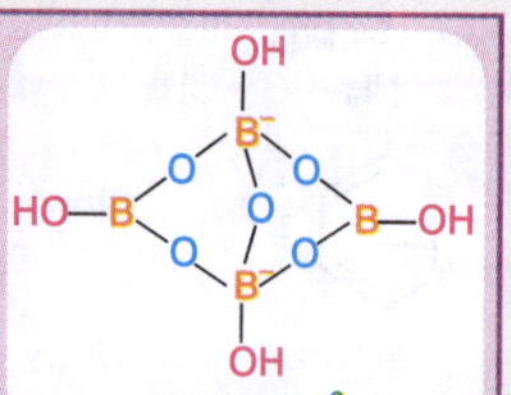

$[B_4O_5(OH)_4]^{2-}$

Orthoboric Acid (H_3BO_3)

Preparation

$Na_2B_4O_7 + 2HCl + 5H_2O \longrightarrow 4H_3BO_3 + 2NaCl$

Lewis acid

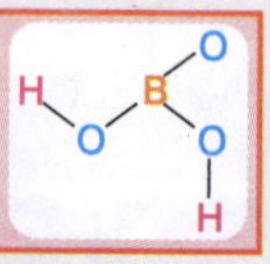

GROUP 14 ELEMENTS

- Carbon (C)
- Tin (Sn)
- Silicon (Si)
- Lead (Pb)
- Germanium(Ge)

Physical Properties

- **Atomic and Ionic Radii**
  I.E, M.P, B.P, stability of +4 oxidation state decreases down the group.
- I.E and M.P of Pb is higher than Sn.
- Catenation property decreases down the group.

Electronic Configuration

[noble gas] ns^2np^2

Abundance

Carbon is 17th most abundant element by an Earth's crust and Si is the second most by mass.

Metallic Character

C	Si, Ge	Sn, Pb
Non metal	Metalloids	Metals

Anomalous Behaviour of Carbon

- Due to small size, high I.E and absence of *d*-orbitals. Size of carbon is smallest.
- High electronegativity, high I.E., maximum tendency of catenation and multiple bonding. Also, shows allotropy.

Chemical Properties

Reactivity towards air

- They form oxides of the formula *MO* and MO_2 on heating with air.
- Acidic strength of their oxides decreases down the group.

CO_2, SiO_2	GeO_2	SnO_2, PbO_2
Acidic	Less acidic	Amphoteric
CO, SiO	GeO	SnO, PbO
Neutral	Acidic	Amphoteric

Reactivity towards water

- C, Si and Ge do not react with water, Sn decomposes stream liberating H_2 gas.
- Pb do not react with water due to protective layer of oxide.

Reactivity towards acids

- C and Si do not react with non-oxidising acids.
- Ge (metal) forms germanium chloroform ($GeHCl_3$) on heating with HCl.
- Sn reacts slowly with dil. HCl and readily with conc. HCl.
- Pb reacts with dil. HCl.

Reactivity towards alkalies

- C does not react with alkalies.
- Si reacts slowly with cold alkali and readily with hot alkali.
- Sn and Pb react slowly with cold alkali and readily with hot alkali.

Reactivity towards halogens

- They form halides of the formula MX_4 and MX_2
- Except C, all react directly with halogens.
- Except C and Si, all form dihalides.

IMPORTANT COMPOUNDS OF CARBON & SILICON

Silicones

Contain repeated R_2SiO units held by Si—O—Si linkages.

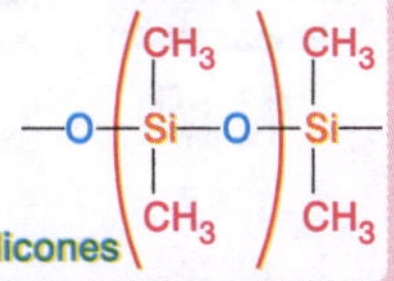

Silica (SiO_2)

Purest form of silica is quartz or rock crystal.

Oxides

- CO is poisonous and neutral oxide.
- CO_2 is greenhouse gas, non-combustible and acidic oxide that react withwater to form carbonic acid (H_2CO_3).
- Used in artificial respiration as 'Carbogen' (95% O_2+5% CO_2).
- This helps stimulate breathing by increasing respiratory drive.

Silicates

- Basic unit is SiO_4^{4-} .
- **3D-Silicates**: Zeolites ($Na_2AlSi_2O_8{\cdot}H_2O$).

GROUP 15 ELEMENTS

- Nitrogen (N)
- Phosphorus (P)
- Arsenic (As)
- Antimony (Sb)
- Bismuth (Bi)
- Moscovium (Ms)

Electronic Configuration

[Noble gas] ns^2np^3

Nature

N, P — Non-metals; As, Sb — Metalloids; Bi — Metal

Physical Properties

- **Atomic Volume and Radii** Increases on moving down the group. I.E is higher than group 14 elements.
- **Metallic Character** Increases on moving down the group
- **Electronegativity** Decreases down the group from N to Bi.
- All elements shows allotropy except Bi.
- **Oxidation State**
  N > P > As > Sb > Bi (Stability of +O.S)
  N < P < As < Sb < Bi (Stability of +O.S)

POWER TIPS

Anomalous Behaviour of Nitrogen

- Exists in atomic form. Forms trinegative ion N^{3-} while other members do not form.
- Chemically inert under ordinary conditions due to high bond dissociation energy.
- Do not show pentacovalency and do not form complex due to non-availability of *d*-orbitals.

Chemical Properties

Penta-halides

- PCl_5 has a trigonal bipyramidal structure.
- PCl_5 is molecular in gaseous phase
- Exist as $[PCl_4]^+$ $[PCl_6]^-$ in crystalline state.
- PBr_5 and PI_5 exist in ionic forms as $[PBr_4]^+$ $[Br^-]$and $[PI_4]^+[I^-]$ respectively in solid state.

Reactivity towards oxygen

- Trioxides of N, P and As are acidic.
- Sb_2O_5 is amphoteric.
- Bi_2O_3 is basic.
- Stability of pentaoxide.
  $P_2O_5 > As_2O_5 > Sb_2O_5 > N_2O_5 > Bi_2O_5$

Reactivity towards Halogen

- Form trihalides of AX_3 and pentahalides of AX_5 type.
- **Trihalides**
  Have pyramidal structure.
- **Acidic character**
  $NH_3 > PH_3 > AsH_3 > SbH_3$
- **Basic character**
  $NI_3 > NBr_3 > NCl_3 > NF_3$

Reactivity Towards Hydrogen

- $Mg_3N_2 + 6H_2O \longrightarrow 3Mg(OH)_2 + 2NH_3$
- $Ca_3P_2 + 6H_2O \longrightarrow 3Ca(OH)_2 + 2PH_3$
- $Zn_3As_2 + 6HCl \longrightarrow 3ZnCl_2 + 2AsH_3$

Other Halides

- Mixed halides of nitrogen are also known.
- These are unstable and difficult to isolate.
- As and Sb form mixed halides.

Oxides of Nitrogen

Except Bi all elements of this group form oxyacids.

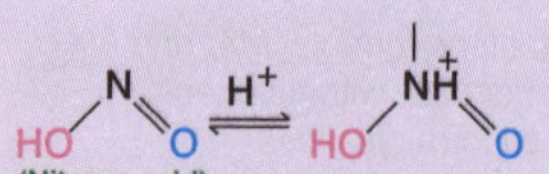

(Nitrous acid)

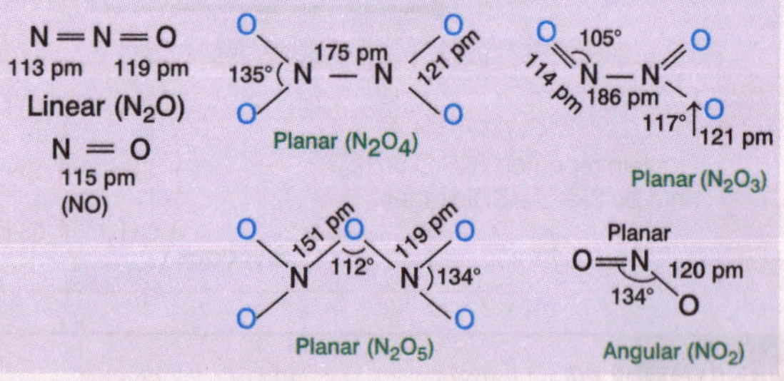

Oxoacids of Phosphorus

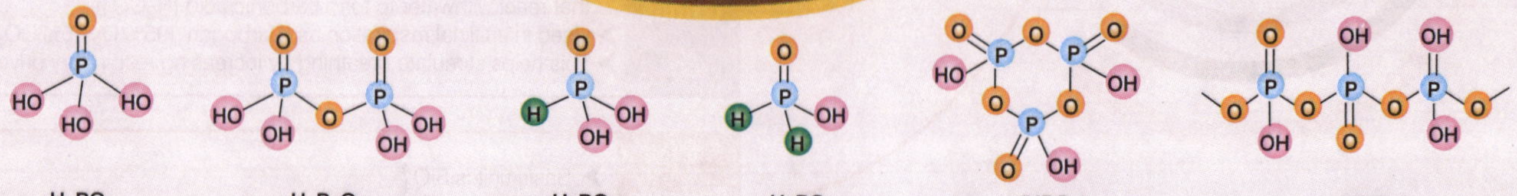

H_3PO_4 Orthophosphoric acid	$H_4P_2O_7$ Pyrophosphoric acid	H_3PO_3 Orthophosphorus acid	H_3PO_2 Hypophosphorus acid	$(HPO_3)_3$ Cyclotrimetaphosphoric acid	$(HPO_3)_n$ Polymetaphosphoric acid

GROUP 16 ELEMENTS

- Oxygen (O)
- Sulphur (S)
- Tellurium (Te)
- Polonium (Po)
- Selenium (Se)

Electronic Configuration

[Noble gas] ns^2np^4

Nature

- O, S — Non-metals
- Se, Te — Metalloids
- Po, Lv — Metals

Anomalous Behaviour of Oxygen

- Due to small size, high charge density and non-availability of *d*-orbitals.
- Oxygen is diatomic.
- Maximum covalency is 2.
- Only the hydride of oxygen is non-poisonous and is a liquid.
- It shows oxidation state of –2 .
- H_2O shows hydrogen bonding due to the presence of electronegative oxygen atom.

Physical Properties

- **Atomic Volume and Atomic Radii** Increases on moving down the group.
- **Physical State** Oxygen is gas, all other elements are solid.
- **Ionisation Energy** Decreases on moving down the group.
- **M.P and B.P** Increases, on moving down the group.
- From O to Te.

POWER TIPS

- Structure of H_2O_2 in gas phase.

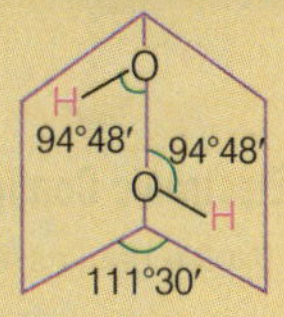

Compounds of Oxygen

Dioxygen (O_2)

Preparation

$$2HgO(s) \xrightarrow{\Delta} 2Hg(l) + O_2(g)$$

$$2Na_2O_2 + 2H_2O \longrightarrow O_2(g) + 4NaOH$$

Properties

It is colourless, odourless, tasteless and sparingly soluble in water.

Structure :Ö═Ö:

Ozone (O_3)

Preparation

$$3O_2 \xrightarrow[\text{discharge}]{\text{electrical}} 2O_3$$

Properties

Pale blue gas, dark blue liquid and violet black solid.

Structure

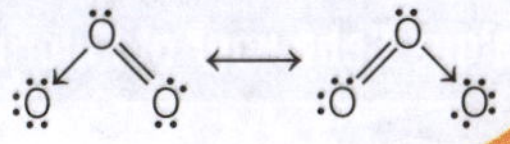

ALLOTROPES OF SULPHUR

01 Rhombic/ α-sulphur

- Stable at temperature below 369K.
- Its crystal structure contains cyclic S_8 rings.

02 Monoclinic/ β-sulphur

- It is formed by melting rhombic sulphur.
- It is stable above 369 K

03 γ-Sulphur

- Obtained by decomposing ethylene xanthate of copper (I) in pyridine.

Compounds of Sulphur

Preparation of H_2SO_4 (Contact process)

S $\xrightarrow{\text{Air}}$ Burner $\xrightarrow{SO_2}$ Dust Chamber → Cooling and Drying → Arsenic Purifier → Testing Box → Pre-Heater → Catalytic converter → Absorption Tower (SO_3, H_2SO_4) → $H_2S_2O_7$ (Oleum) $\xrightarrow{H_2O}$ $2H_2SO_4$

Oxoacids of Sulphur

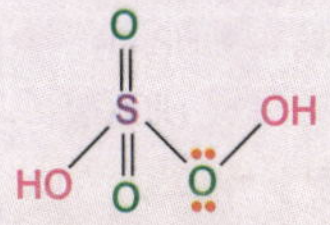

Peroxomono sulphurous acid (Caro's Acid) [H_2SO_5]

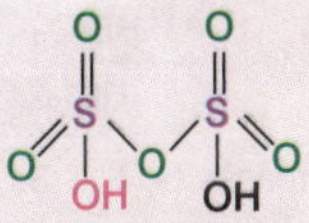

Pyrosulphuric acid (Oleum) [$H_2S_2O_7$]

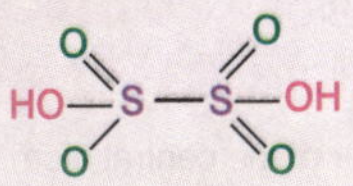

Dithionic acid [$H_2S_2O_6$]

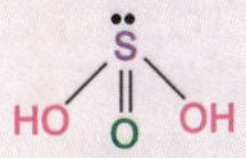

Sulphurous acid [H_2SO_3]

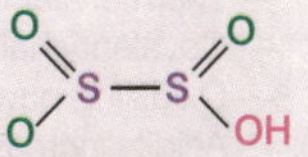

Dithionous [$H_2S_2O_4$]

GROUP 17 ELEMENTS

- Fluorine (F)
- Chlorine (Cl)
- Bromine (Br)
- Iodine (I)
- Astatine(At)
- Tennessine(Ts)

Electronic Configuration

[Noble gas] ns^2np^5

Physical Properties

- **Atomic and Ionic Radii** Increases down the group.
- I.E very high, decreases down the group.
- **Electronegativity** Decreases down the group.
- **Electron Gain Enthalpy** Decreases from F to Cl and increases from Cl to I.
- M.P. and B.P. increases down the group.

Reactions of Xenon

- Forms three binary fluorides XeF_2, XeF_4 and XeF_6

$Xe(g) + F_2(g) \xrightarrow{673\ K,\ 1\ bar} XeF_2(s)$
(Excess)

$Xe(g) + 2F_2(g) \xrightarrow{873\ K,\ 7\ bar} XeF_4(s)$
(1:5 ratio)

$Xe(g) + 3F_2(g) \xrightarrow{573\ K,\ 60\text{-}70\ bar} XeF_6(s)$
(1:20 ratio)

Xenon-Oxygen Compounds

- $XeF_6 + 3H_2O \longrightarrow XeO_3 + 6HF$
- $XeF_6 + H_2O \longrightarrow XeOF_4 + 2HF$
- $XeF_6 + 2H_2O \longrightarrow XeO_2F_2 + 4HF$

Chemical Properties

- Reactivity : $F_2 > Cl_2 > Br_2 > I_2$
- Ionic character: $M\text{—}F > M\text{—}Cl > M\text{—}Br > M\text{—}I$
- Reaction with metals : form different halides
- **Oxyacids**
  Hypohalous acid HXO_3 Halous acid HXO_2, Halic acid, HXO_3, Perhalic acid $HClO_4$.

Compounds of Halogen

Preparation

$NaCl + H_2SO_4 \xrightarrow{420\ K} NaHSO_4 + HCl$

$NaHSO_4 + NaCl \xrightarrow{823\ K} Na_2SO_4 + HCl$

Properties

- Colourless pungent smelling gas.
- Easily liquified, extremely soluble in water.

Oxide

(i) Dichloro oxide
$[Cl_2O]$

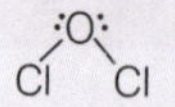

(ii) Chlorine dioxide
$[ClO_2]$

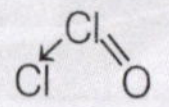

Interhalogen Compounds

- Compounds containing two or more halogen atom in their molecule.
- Types
  - AX (ClF, BrCl)
  - AX_3 (ClF_3, ICl_3)
  - AX_5 (BrF_5, IF_5)
  - AX_7 (IF_7)
- **Uses of Interchalogen Compounds.**
  (i) ClF_3 and BrF_3 are used as fluorinating agents.
  (ii) It is used for the preparation of polyhalide.

Anomalous Behaviour of Fluorine

- Most reactive due to low dissociation energy of F—F bond.
- Exhibits only –1 oxidation state.
- Shows covalency of one only due to absence of *d*-orbital.
- Has highest tendency for ionic compound formation due to high electronegativity.

POLYHALIDE IONS

These are the cations and anions that contains more than two halogen atoms.

PSEUDO HALIDE ION

CN^- (cyanide) OCN^- (cyanate)
SCN^- (Thiocyanate) N_3^- (Azide)

Oxoacids of Halogens

Variation of the general properties of oxoacids of halogens.

Halogen	Hypohalous acids (O.S. of halogen = +1)	Halous acid (O.S. of halogen = +3)	Halic acids (O.S. of halogen = +5)	Perhalic acid (O.S. of halogen = +7)
F	HOF	–	–	–
Cl	HClO	$HClO_2$	$HClO_3$	$HClO_4$
Br	HBrO	–	$HBrO_3$	$HBrO_4$
I	HIO	–	HIO_3	HIO_4

Thermal stability ↓ Oxidising power ↓ Acidic strength ↓

- Oxidation number of the central atom increases (+ 1, + 3, + 5, + 7) ⟶
- Thermal stability increases ⟶
- Covalent character of *X*—O bond increases ⟶
- Oxidising power decreases ⟶
- Acidity increases ⟶
- Electronegativity of the central atoms remains the same ⟶

POWER TIPS

Important Minerals of Fluorine

- Fluorspar or Fluorite : CaF_2
- Cryolite : Na_3AlF_6
- Fluorapatite : $3Ca_3(PO_4)_2$
- Thermal stability of hydrides :
  HF > HCl > HBr > HI
- Thermal stability increase with increase in oxidation state of halogen.
  $HClO < HOClO < HOClO_2 < HOClO_3$
- Hydro halo acids:
  HF < HCl < HBr < HI

GROUP 18 ELEMENTS

- Helium (He)
- Neon (Ne)
- Argon (Ar)
- Krypton (Kr)
- Xenon(Xe)
- Radon(Rn)
- Oganesson (Og)

Electronic Configuration

[Noble gas] ns^2np^6

Occurence

Radon and oganesson a radioactive element. All noble gases occur in the elemental state in the atmosphere.

Physical Properties

- All noble gases are colourless, odourless, and tasteless.
- High I.E. decreases down the group.
- **Electron Gain Enthalpy** (E.G.E) E.G.E is positive.
- M.P Ne < Ar < Kr < Xe < Rn B.P are very low.
- **Atomic Radii** Increases down the group.
- **Solubility in Water** He<Ne<Ar<Kr<Xe<Rn
- **Liquification of Gases** It is difficult to liquify inert gases as their atoms are holded by weak van der Waal's forces.

POWER TIPS

- Helium-oxygen mixture is used for artificial respiration in deep seas diving and in treatment of astma.
- Helium forms no real chemical compounds. Among noble gases only xenon forms chemical compounds.

Chemical Properties

- Noble gases have very high ionisation energies.
- Electron affinity of noble gases are almost zero.
- They are highly inert.

Compound of Xenon

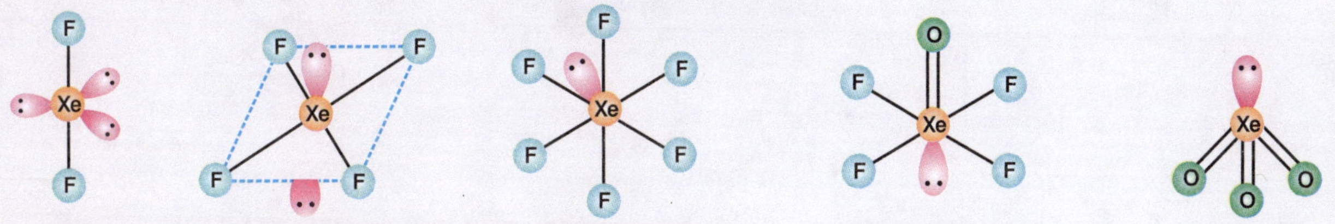

Linear | Square planar | Distorted octahedral | Square pyramidal | Pyramidal

USES

Helium
- Used in filling balloons for meterological observation.
- Liquid helium is used as cryogenic agent.
- It is used in gas cooled nuclear reactors.

Neon
- Used in discharge tubes and fluorescent bulbs.
- Neon bulbs are used in botanical gardens.
- Neon is used in TV tubes, advertisement signs and signal indicators, etc.

Argon
- Provide inert atmosphere.
- Used for filling electric bulbs.
- This gas is used in gas chromatogrpahy.

Krypton
- Used in light bulbs designed for special purpose.
- Used in high efficiency miner's cap lamps.
- Kr-85 is used to measure thickness of sheet of metals and plastic.

Xenon
- In electric flash bulbs for high speed photography.
- Used in lasers.
- It used to measure blood flow.

Radon
- Used in the treatment of cancer.
- Used in radiography.
- Used for detecting dislocations and defect in metals.